# THE KATHAKOCA

# THE KATHAKOCA;
## OR,
## TREASURY OF STORIES.

**Translated from Sanskrit Manuscripts**

**by**

**C. H. TAWNEY, M. A.**

GYAN

*Published by*

GYAN

Gyan Publishing House
5, Ansari Road
Daryaganj, New Delhi-110002
Phone: 011-47034999, 9811692060
E-mail: books@gyanbooks.com

*Distribution Network*
gyanbooks.com
India, USA, Canada, UK, Australia, France



ISBN : 978-81-212-2583-0 (PB)
First Published, 1895

2nd Impression 2021

*Printed at:* Gyan Press, Delhi.



**The Kathakoca**
Author: C. H. Tawney

*ORIENTAL TRANSLATION FUND.*

NEW SERIES.

II.

---

# THE KATHÁKOÇA;

OR,

# TREASURY OF STORIES.

**Translated from Sanskrit Manuscripts**

BY

C. H. TAWNEY, M.A.,

*Translator of the 'Kathá Sarit Ságara,' 'Uttararámacharita,' 'Málavikágnimitra,' and 'Two Centuries of Bhartṛihari.'*

**With Appendix, containing Notes,**

BY

PROFESSOR ERNST LEUMANN,

*Of the Strassburg University.*

*PRINTED AND PUBLISHED UNDER THE PATRONAGE OF THE ROYAL ASIATIC SOCIETY;*

AND SOLD AT

22, ALBEMARLE STREET, LONDON.

1895.

# CONTENTS.

# PREFACE.

THE stories contained in the Kathákoça are, in their present form, at any rate, intended to illustrate the tenets and practice of Jainism. In other words, though they are genuine fragments of Indian folk-lore, they have been edited by some Jain theologian for the purpose of the edification of the votaries of that religion. It seems, accordingly, desirable to give a short account of Jainism, in order to render these tales intelligible.

The religion of the Jains, called in Sanskrit Jainas, or Árhatas, the followers of the Jina or Arhat, *i.e.*, 'the conqueror of the world,' or 'the holy one,' arose in the same part of India, and about the same time, as Buddhism,* but it has not, like that religion, become extinct in India proper.† On the contrary, it still numbers among its adherents many wealthy and influential men. It ought to appeal to the sympathy of Europeans, as it claims to be, like Buddhism, a universal religion. As Hofrath Bühler points out, it opens its arms even to the despised foreigner or

* I may as well at once acknowledge my obligation to the following scholars: Hofrath Bühler, and Professors Cowell, Gough, Hoernle, Jacobi, Leumann, and Weber. I shall have, in the course of the following pages, frequently to refer to their works. Hofrath Bühler's Vortrag 'Ueber die Indische Secte der Jaina' contains an excellent summary of Jainism, to which I am largely indebted. I regret that it has not been translated into English. But Jainism does not seem to be popular in this country. At least, I have never heard of 'Esoteric Jainism.'

† There are, of course, Buddhists in the districts of Chittagong and Darjiling.

Mlechchha.* But it has not spread like Buddhism, possibly because its morality has been, in some respects, too rigid for ordinary human nature, and its doctors inferior in tact and knowledge of the world to their Buddhist rivals.†

The real founder of the sect was the Jina Vardhamána, usually known by the title of Mahávíra, or great hero, who was a contemporary of Gautama Buddha and of Gosála, the son of Mankhali, the founder of the sect of the Ájívikas mentioned in the edicts of Açoka.‡

It must be admitted that the Jains believe in twenty-four Jinas, but probably only the twenty-third, Párçva, and the twenty-fourth, Vardharmána, have any claim to be considered historical.§ It is possible that Vardhamána was a reformer rather than a founder, and only improved on the doctrines of Párçva. Vardhamána was the son of Siddhártha, who belonged to a noble warrior race, that of the Jnátṛi Kshatriyas. He was born in Kuṇḍagráma, a suburb of Vaiçálí. His mother was Triçalá, the sister of Cheṭaka, who is sometimes called King of Videha, though he was probably only *primus inter pares*, and in the Kathákoça is represented as being besieged by Koṇika in Vaiçálí.‖ He was also related to the ruling dynasty in Magadha, as Cheṭaka's daughter Chellaná was married to King Çreṇika or Bimbisára.¶ Shortly after the death of his parents,

* *I.e.*, Barbarian. The term includes Indian Muhammadans, as well as Europeans and other non-Indian *Gesindel*.

† In this connection I may refer to a remark of Horace Hayman Wilson in his translation of the 'Mudrá Rákshasa' ('Hindu Theatre,' vol. ii., p. 217). Professor Jacobi seems to think that the founder of the Jain religion was quite willing to use his family influence for the advancement of his tenets. That some Jains were not wanting in a due respect for princes and great men may be inferred from the attempt made in the 'Kathákoça' to whitewash the parricide Koṇika or Ajátaçatru (see p. 177 of the following translation).

‡ See Hoernle's 'Uvásaga Dasáo,' Appendix I. and II.

§ The names of all the twenty-four will be found in Jacobi's translation of the 'Kalpa Sútra,' and in Colebrooke's Essays, edited by Cowell, vol. ii., p. 187 and ff.

‖ See pp. 178-180 of the following translation.

¶ Bühler's Vortrag, p. 19; Jacobi's Introduction to the translation of the 'Ácháránga Sútra,' pp. xi., xii. and xiii. See also note 8 in Hoernle's translation of the 'Uvásaga Dasáo.' The Lichchavis, a class of nobles in Vaiçálí, are mentioned in connection with Buddha, as well as with Mahávíra.

which took place in his thirty-first year, he abandoned the world, and became a wandering ascetic. 'For twelve years he led a life of austerities, visiting even the wild tribe of the country called Rádhá. After the first year he went about almost naked.'* He then considered himself a perfected saint. The period of his activity as a religious teacher extended to over thirty years. The sphere of his operations was the kingdoms of Koçala, Videha, Magadha, and Anga, corresponding to the modern Oudh, and the provinces of Tirhut and Behar. He was frequently brought into connection, in the course of his life, with Bimbisára, called Çreṇika, and his sons Abhayakumára and Ajátaçatru, or Koṇika the parricide. He died in Pává or Pápá, the modern Padraona.† The date of his death is variously given as 545, 527, and 467 before Christ.‡ In the second century after Mahávíra's death the Jain community was torn by schism, and about the beginning of the first century before Christ it finally split up into the Çvetámbaras, or white-robed, and the Digambaras, or naked, Jains.§ These distinctions still subsist, though Hofrath Bühler assures us that the Digambaras, or 'sky-clothed,' have been compelled by the progress of civilization to relax in practice the rigour of their theory.

The object of the Jain religion, as of most Indian systems, is to escape from the bonds of metempsychosis, or the never-ending cycle of births and deaths. There is no mention, as far as I know, of metempsychosis in the Ṛig Veda. But after the joyous Vedic religion had lost its hold on the minds of men, the doctrine of the transmigration of souls began to oppress the philosophical

* Jacobi's Introduction to his translation of the 'Ácháránga Sútra, p. xv. See also pp. 79 and ff. of the translation. There his sufferings are most minutely related.

† Bühler's Vortrag, p. 20.

‡ *Ibid.*, note 15. 'The last date,' observes Bühler, 'is certainly wrong, if the view now generally adopted that Buddha died between 482 and 472 B.C. is right, as Buddhist tradition mentions that the Jain Tírthankara died in the lifetime of Buddha. The date generally accepted now is 527 B.C.'

§ Introduction to Hoernle's translation of the 'Uvásaga Dasáo,' p. ix.

thinkers of India with a weight of gloomy foreboding.* The operation of this doctrine has, in my opinion, never been better described than by Professor Gough. I quote from p. 21 of his 'Philosophy of the Upanishads,' a book which seems to me to set forth, in a way intelligible to Europeans, the main ideas which underlie the religions and philosophies of India:

'The doctrine of metempsychosis, a belief widely spread among the lower races of men, coming slowly and surely to lay hold of the Hindu mind, this penal retribution† came to be expected in a series of embodiments in vegetal, animal, human, and extra-human shapes. Each living soul was to pass from body to body, from grade to grade, from sphere to sphere of life in obedience to a retributive operation, by which suffering followed evil-doing with the blind and fatal movement of a natural law. As the life has been, such will the next embodiment be in the series of lives; the present and the future, with their pains and transitory pleasures, being the outcome of what the soul has done in its anterior embodiments. The series of lives has had no beginning, and shall have no end, save to the perfected sage finally resolved into the fontal essence of the universe. A life of such and such experiences follows from works of such and such a nature, good works sending the soul upwards in the scale of embodiments into a life human, superhuman, or divine, and evil works sending the soul downwards into bestial, insect, vegetal, penal embodiments in this world, or in a nether world of torture. In this world, above, below, there is no place of rest; paradises and purgatories are but stages in the endless journey. In

* The doctrine of metempsychosis, as applied by the Jains, accounts in a very simple way for the inequality of human conditions. It would appear, also, that it must have a very beneficial effect on the morality of the votaries of that religion. This will, I think, strike everyone who peruses the tales contained in the 'Kathákoça,' though sometimes the crimes of one birth seem to be selected for punishment in an arbitrary way. It is only in human births that any advance can be made on the road to liberation. This doctrine is clearly enunciated in the 'Kathákoça.'

† Professor Gough has been speaking of the doctrine of penal retribution as we find it in the later period of Vedic religion.

every state there is nothing to expect but vanity, vexation, and misery. *Omnis creatura ingemiscit.* There is nothing to look for but grief and pain, broken at best with pleasures themselves fleeting, empty and unsatisfying: nothing to look for but sickness, decay, the loss of loved ones, death, and the fatal recurrence of fresh birth, through an endless succession of embodiments. Each present suffering, intolerable as it is, is the precursor to another and another, through lives without end. The very merit that wins a sojourn in a paradise, or the rank of a divinity, must sooner or later be exhausted, for the bankrupt soul to descend to a lower sphere. The pleasures of the paradise themselves are tainted with the fear of their expiry, and with the inequalities of the inmates of the paradise.'

It is from such intolerable evils that the promulgators of philosophical and religious systems in India have always undertaken to deliver their followers, and the Jain prophet was no exception to the general rule. But it is clear, from a perusal of the tales contained in the 'Kathákoça' and the 'Uvásaga Dasáo,' as well as those edited by Professor Jacobi in his 'Erzählungen in Maháráshtrí,' that, though no religious Jain could possibly be satisfied with anything less than absolute salvation from the miseries of existence as his ultimate object, the blessings of wealth and sovereignty were not absolutely despised by the writers of these works, but regarded as the reward of virtue in a previous life. This is one of the concessions to human frailty found in the Jain system.

This salvation from the miseries of existence is called *moksha* or *nirváṇa*, 'the absolute release from all actions by the decay of the causes of bondage and existence.'* This release does not imply annihilation, for we read in the 'Sarva Darçana Sangraha' that some consider *moksha* to be 'the abiding in the highest regions, the soul being absorbed in bliss, with its knowledge unhindered, and itself

* 'Sarva Darçana Sangraha,' p. 58. It appears that the portion of this work dealing with the system of the Jains was translated by Professor Cowell.

untainted by any pain or impression thereof.'* Hofrath Bühler tells us that *moksha* can be 'attained even while the soul is still in the body. But when the body falls to pieces, the soul flits into the No-world (Aloka), the heaven of the liberated, lying outside the world. There it continues for ever in its original, that is to say, in its pure, intellectual essence. Its condition is that of perfect rest, disturbed by nothing.'† The attainment of *moksha* is usually preceded by the attainment of *kevalajnána*, or absolute, unimpeded knowledge. The possessor of this knowledge is called a *kevalin*.‡

The means by which *moksha* is to be attained are called, as in the case of Buddhism, the three jewels—right faith, right knowledge, and right conduct.§ Right faith is unswerving belief in the Jina, originally a man 'bound' like others, but who has attained, by his own exertions, emancipation and complete knowledge, and has preached the truth to suffering humanity.‖ Right knowledge is the knowledge of the system promulgated by the Jina. Its chief doctrines are as follows: ¶

The world, which includes not only the visible world, but the various fabulous heavens, hells, and continents of the Brahmanical cosmology, as improved on by the luxuriant

* 'Sarva Darçana Sangraha,' p. 59.

† Bühler's Vortrag, pp. 8 and 9.

‡ The other kinds of knowledge are (1) *Mati*; (2) *Çruta*; (3) *Avadhi*, and (4) *Manas-paryáya* ('Sarva Darçana Sangraha,' p. 46). *Avadhi* (or *Ohi*) occurs frequently in the 'Kathákoça.' I have translated it by 'limited knowledge.' It is limited to material or physical objects (Hoernle's 'Uvásaga Dasáo,' appendix iii., p. 44). *Manas-paryáya* is knowledge of the thoughts of another, 'produced by the abolition of all the obstructions of knowledge caused by the veil of envy.' *Mati* is right perception; *Çruta* is clear knowledge based on *Mati*.

§ Bühler's Vortrag, p. 5.

‖ The Jain prophet is usually, as I have already stated, called Jina or Arhat. But he is also called Sarvajna, or 'the All-knowing,' and Tírthankara or Tírthakara, which is variously interpreted as the 'Finder of the ford through the ocean of the Samsára,' and as 'the Prophet' or 'Founder.' He also shares with Gautama the title of Buddha 'the Enlightened,' Siddha and Tathágata, 'the Perfected.' (Bühler's Vortrag, p. 6). See also Jacobi's 'Ácháránga Sútra,' Introduction, pp. xix. and xx.

¶ Here I follow Bühler's Vortrag very closely. See p. 8.

imagination of the Jains, is uncreated.* It subsists without a governor, and is eternal. Its component parts are six substances: Souls, *Dharma*, or moral merit, *Adharma*, or sin, space, time, and the atoms of matter. By the combination of these atoms are produced the four elements, earth, fire, water and air, and human bodies, as well as the phenomena of the world of sense, and the heavenly worlds. The Jains are as extravagant with regard to time as with regard to space. They consider that human bodies and human lives increase during the Utsarpiní and diminish during the Avasarpiní, periods of incredible length.† 'Souls are independent, real entities, the basis of which is pure intelligence, and which possess an impulse towards action.'‡ The doctrine of the bondage of souls, as held by the Jains, is practically identical with the view held by Indian thinkers generally. But the Jains stand alone, as far as I know, in maintaining that, to borrow Hofrath Bühler's words, souls are to be found 'in apparently lifeless masses, in stone, in clods of earth, in drops of water, in fire and in wind.'

The third jewel is right conduct. It divides itself into two branches, according as it is incumbent on the Jain monk or the Jain layman. The Jain monk, on entering the order, takes five vows; he promises to do no injury to living beings, not to indulge in lying speech, not to take things not given, to observe chastity, and to practise renunciation of the most complete kind in respect of worldly goods. In fact, he is forbidden to call anything his own. Not only is he to abstain from these sins himself in thought, word and deed, but he is not to cause others to be guilty of them, or to connive at their being guilty of them.§ These rules are carried out in the life of the ascetic with a minuteness that seems to the Western mind almost childish. For

* See the 'Sarva Darçana Sangraha,' p. 45.

† For further details see Wilson's 'Essays on the Religion of the Hindus,' vol. i., pp. 308 and 309.

‡ Bühler's Vortrag, p. 8.

§ See Bühler's Vortrag, p. 11; Hoernle's 'Uvásaga Dasáo,' note 21, and Jacobi's Introduction to his translation of the 'Ácháránga Sútra,' p. xxiii.

instance, the first precept, not to do injury to living beings (*ahiṃsá*), involves the utmost circumspection in eating, drinking, and walking, so as to avoid injury to any living creatures. Consequently Jain ascetics have to wear a mouth-protector, to prevent insects from entering their mouths, and to carry a broom and a straining-cloth. The broom is used by them for sweeping the road, and the place where they walk or sit down, in order to remove insects. The straining-cloth is, of course, used for straining water.* For the same reason, they are not allowed to travel during the four months of the rainy season, when insect life is most abundant.† The Jain monk must also be careful not to injure eggs, seeds and sprouts. He must, if he is young and strong, wear only one robe; in any case, not more than three. He has to submit to the tonsure, or apparently, according to the strict letter of the law, to tear out his hair. He has to subsist by begging, and is forbidden to remain for more than one night in the same village, except during the rainy season.‡ He has to observe the most strict fasts, to stand motionless in unnatural positions, and eventually he is expected to starve himself to death by abstaining from sixty meals.§

The rules binding on laymen are less strict. The layman is expected to abstain from gross (*sthúla*) violation of the five precepts. Fidelity to the marriage vow takes the place of absolute chastity, and a promise not to increase one's wealth by unfair means, that of absolute renunciation of property. Nevertheless, it must be remarked that the

* Jacobi's Introduction to his translation of the 'Ácháránga Sútra,' p. xxviii.

† 'Bühler's Vortrag, p. 13.

‡ Jacobi and Bühler have shown that most of these rules are copied from those laid down for Bráhman ascetics. It would appear from the 'Aupapátika Sútra' (ed. Leumann), § 29, that an ascetic may remain five nights in a town.

§ According to Hofrath Bühler, this is considered by the strict Digambaras indispensable for all ascetics. Even the Çvetámbaras consider it a sure road to Nirváṇa. He adds that even now the heads of the Digambara sect end their lives in this way.

Jain laymen, whose careers are narrated in the 'Uvásaga Dasáo,'* are represented as men of enormous wealth. Perhaps this is intended to increase the merit of their self-denial. There can be no doubt that, at the present day, many Jain laymen owe their influence to their riches. Even laymen are recommended to starve themselves to death, though this mode of leaving the world is not absolutely necessary in their case.† They are, of course, forbidden to indulge in flesh and spirituous drinks, and in other kinds of food, such as honey and fresh butter, which involve injury to animal life. Agriculture is forbidden, as an injury to the 'earth-body.' ‡ Even the ordering another man to plough a field is stigmatized as a sin.§ The result of all this teaching has been, as Hofrath Bühler points out, to make Jain laymen serious, well-conducted and humane men, ready to endure great sacrifices for their religion, and especially for the welfare of animals. Advantage has been taken of this under British rule to enlist their sympathies in favour of veterinary science.‖

Hofrath Bühler considers it as a concession to the lay mind, that the originally atheistic Jain system is fitted out with an elaborate cult. It will be evident, from a perusal of the 'Kathákoça,' that the Jains do actually worship gods many and lords many. The Jinas are adored with flowers and incense and candles; hymns of praise are sung in their honour, and pilgrimages are made to places hallowed by their memories. The reception of lay disciples brought about, according to the same authority, another effect. The necessity of instructing the laity turned the wandering

* This is the text-book containing precepts for Jaina laymen. It has been edited and translated by Dr. Hoernle in the 'Bibliotheca Indica.' The 'Áchángha Sútra,' which contains the corresponding precepts for monks, has been edited by Professor Jacobi in the series of the Pali Text Society, and translated by him in vol. xxii. of the 'Sacred Books of the East.'

† For this 'last mortal emaceration,' see Hoernle's 'Uvásaga Dasáo,' p. 54.

‡ Bühler's Vortrag, p. 14.

§ In Hoernle's 'Uvásaga Dasáo,' pp. 27-30, will be found a list of forbidden foods and occupations.

‖ One such instance is known to the writer.

ascetic into the 'keeper of a cell,' in a monastery. From this resulted the establishment of a monkish hierarchy, which is a characteristic feature of the Jain religion. The leisure which these stationary teachers enjoyed gave a stimulus to literary production. The earliest Jain treatises are written in a peculiar form of Prákrit, but the Jains soon found it necessary to employ Sanskrit in their controversies with Bráhmans. 'But they did not rest satisfied with merely setting forth in Sanskrit the doctrines of their own religion. They threw themselves into the secular learning of the Bráhmans. They have achieved such success in grammar, in astronomy, and even in belles-lettres, as to win for them the admiration of their opponents. Some of their works are even now of importance for European science.'*

In the 'Kathákoça' there is occasional mention made of nunneries and of the honour paid to holy women. Hofrath Bühler tells us that nuns are only admitted by the Çvetámbaras, and that the Digambaras will have nothing to do with them.† They even go so far as to deny salvation to women. The author of the 'Sarva Darçana Sangraha' concludes the section on the Jains with the following words: 'A woman attains not the highest knowledge, she enters not Mukti, so say the Digambaras, but there is a great division on this point between them and the Çvetámbaras.'

In the notes to my translation I have pointed out many close resemblances of detail between the Jain stories contained in the 'Kathákoça' and European tales.‡ It is in my opinion highly probable that the European stories in which these resemblances appear were borrowed from India. It has been shown by Professors Max Müller,

* Bühler's Vortrag, pp. 17 and 18.

† Jain nuns are principally recruited from child-widows (Bühler's Vortrag, note 5).

‡ Instances will be found on pp. 61, 87, 89, 91, 92, 106, 121, 127, 133, 134, 135, 151, 165, 167, 171, 172, 185, 187, 219, 226. In some cases I have merely referred to notes in my translation of the 'Kathá Sarit Ságara.'

Benfey and Rhys Davids, that Indian Buddhist stories actually travelled through Persia to Europe. Indeed, it is no longer denied that numerous mediæval stories came to Europe from India, though it may reasonably be doubted whether these stories originated in India. Mr. Andrew Lang, who has discussed this question very exhaustively, is of opinion that 'the borrowing theory is excellent if it is sufficiently limited. Mährchen certainly did set out from mediæval India, and reached mediæval Europe and Asia in abundance. Not to speak of oral communications in the great movements, missions and migrations, Tartar, crusading, commercial and Buddhistic, in all of which there must have been "swopping of stories," it is certain that Western literature was actually invaded by the *contes*, which had won a way into the literature of India.'* This statement is, I think, as great a concession as any rational advocate of the 'borrowing theory' ought to expect.†

But it may reasonably be asked how these Jain stories came to be carried to far distant countries, in view of the fact that Jainism has been almost entirely limited to India. The true explanation probably is that these stories were carried abroad, not by the Jains, but by the Buddhists, for both Jains and Buddhists used the folklore of Eastern India for the purpose of religious edification. An instance will perhaps make my meaning clear, and furnish support to my theory, or, rather, the theory which I have adopted.

Professor Jacobi, in his introduction to the 'Pariçishṭa Parvan,' a well-known Jain work, relates the following incident with regard to a queen who had deserted in succession two husbands:

* 'Myth, Ritual and Religion,' vol. ii., p. 313. 'The Migration of Symbols,' treated of by Sir George Birdwood and Count Goblet d'Alviella, is, of course, free from the linguistic difficulty to which the 'borrowing theory' is exposed in the case of tales.

† It seems probable that the Indians borrowed some fables from the Greeks, as they were admittedly their pupils in numismatics and astronomy, and possibly, also, to a certain extent in sculpture, architecture, and the dramatic art. The resemblance between Greek and Indian novels has been pointed out by me in the notes to my translation of the 'Kathá Sarit Ságara.'

'The queen and her new lover had set out on their journey, and reached a swollen river. The robber proposed to bring over first the queen's clothes and jewels, and then herself. But when he had crossed the river with everything the queen had on her body, he thought it safer to part company with so dangerous a woman, and left her naked like a new-born babe on the opposite bank. In this plight she was discovered by the Vyantara god, the late elephant-driver,* who had resolved on saving her soul. He therefore took the form of a jackal, who had a piece of flesh in his mouth. But seeing a fish, who had jumped out of the water and tumbled on the dry ground, he let go the flesh and rushed on the fish; the fish, however, jerked itself again into the water, while a bird, coming suddenly down, seized the piece of flesh. The queen, seeing this, laughed at the jackal, who had lost his flesh and missed the fish, whereupon the transformed god rejoined that she had lost her first and her second lovers. He exhorted her to repent of her sins and take refuge with the Jinas. The queen followed his advice, and became a nun.'

Curious to say, this story is found in China, in the so-called 'Avadánas,' translated from the Chinese by Stanislas Julien. It is called 'The Woman and the Fox.' The following is a translation from the French:

'Once on a time there was a woman rich in gold and silver who loved a man. She took with her, in order to follow him, her gold, her silver and her clothes; then they set off together, and arrived on the brink of a rapid river. Her lover said to her, "Give me your riches, in order that I may carry them over first; I will subsequently come back for you."

'The man, having carried over all these precious articles, took to his heels, and never came back again. The woman remained on the bank of the river, and gave herself up for lost, as no one came to her help. She saw a fox (*renard sauvage*) which had caught a hawk, and, having seen a fish

* One of her husbands.

in the river, had let go the hawk in the hope of catching the fish. But the fox did not succeed in catching the fish, and lost its first prize (the hawk). The woman said to the fox: "You must be very stupid; in your eagerness to get two things you have lost both." "I confess," said the fox, "that I have been stupid, but your stupidity far exceeds mine." '*

This story is said by the translator to be extracted from a purely Buddhist encyclopedia, entitled 'Fa-youen-tchou-lin.' It is well known that the Chinese borrowed from the Northern Buddhists, but this story is also found in the 'Pali Játakas,' edited by Fausböll.† There we find a story called the 'Chulladhanuggaha Játaka.' The Chulladhanuggaha, who is the hero of this story, after killing with his arrows an elephant and forty-nine robbers, is, owing to his wife's treachery, killed by the chief of the robbers. The chief of the robbers deserts her. Then Sakka (Indra) assumes the form of a jackal with a piece of flesh, while Mátali, by his order, assumes the form of a fish, and Panchasikha that of a hawk. Precisely the same drama is enacted as in the Jaina form of the story, with the result that the woman becomes ashamed and repents.

Whatever theory may eventually prevail, I trust that folklorists will welcome, as a contribution to their science, these Jain tales, which are, as far as I can see, absolutely free from any suspicion of European influence. This appears to be not always the case with tales collected by missionaries and travellers among savage tribes. It is, of course, far from my intention to attempt to disparage the labours of painstaking collectors. It is only by careful industry that abiding results are won in any science, and it is not likely that the 'science of fairy-tales' will prove an exception to the general rule. Collections like that of Somadeva‡ are no doubt liable to falsification by literary embellishment. I think that little of that corruption will be found in the

* 'Les Avadánas,' traduits par Stanislas Julien, vol. ii., p. 11.
† Vol. iii., p. 222.
‡ The compiler of the 'Kathá Sarit Ságara.'

present volume. I have already stated my belief that the tales have been slightly improved with a view to religious edification.

On p. 69 will be found a description of a spiritualistic séance. The medium is apparently inspired by the god Hanumán, the leader of the monkeys, who assisted Ráma in the war that he waged against the ten-headed Rávana, who carried off Sítá, the wife of Ráma. During this war Hanumán distinguished himself by flying to the Himálaya to fetch medicinal herbs for the benefit of the wounded. On p. 75 there is an instance of a sneeze being regarded as a good omen, as it was apparently among the ancient Greeks. I do not remember any similar instance in Sanskrit literature. It is possible that here we have an instance of the preservation of an old Aryan superstition. It is not surprising that such a notion should be found in a Jain work, as the literature of the Jains has never been Brahmanized, to use Mr. Talboys Wheeler's forcible expression.* On pp. 72 and 75 there are instances of belief in the prophetic import of a φήμη. One feels that something extraordinary was required to encourage the two friends to undertake their daring enterprise. Students of folklore will, no doubt, discover in these tales many interesting points which have escaped my notice.

The account of the war between Koṇika (or Kúṇika), called Ajátaçatru by the Buddhists, and his uncle Cheṭaka (or Cheḍaga), which begins on p. 175, is no doubt historical. It would appear that Koṇika's behaviour to his father Bimbisára, though decidedly unfilial, is represented by the author of this work in a more favourable light than it usually is, or, perhaps, ought to be. The statement in the 'Kathákoça' with regard to the behaviour of the head-queen agrees closely with that found in the 'Amitáyur Dhyána Sútra,' translated from the Chinese by Mr. J. Takakusu.† 'The chief consort of the king, Vaidehí by name,' mentioned in that work, is no doubt identical with

* I believe I owe this remark to a suggestion of Hofrath Bühler.

† 'Sacred Books of the East,' vol. xlix., p. 161.

Chellaná, or Chillaná, the daughter of Cheṭaka, who is sometimes called King of Videha. Ajátaçatru, or Koṇika, is generally supposed to have murdered his father. His remorse for that crime seems to have disposed him favourably towards Buddhism.*

Perhaps some readers will find the last story of the book the most interesting. It is a Jain version of the story of Nala and Damayantí. The tale, as told in the 'Mahábhárata,' is well known in England, having been edited by Sir Monier Williams, and translated by Dean Milman. The story as told in the 'Kathákoça' furnishes an admirable instance of the way in which Jain teachers improved popular tales with a view to edification. The change of the name Damayantí into Davadantí is perhaps intended to render the borrowing less obvious. The etymological explanation seems a little forced.

I proceed to give a short account of the MSS. of the 'Kathákoça' which I have used,† and of the philological peculiarities of the work.

My translation is made from a text based on the following MSS.:

1. A MS. in the Sanskrit College, kindly lent to me while I was in India by the principal, Mahámahopádhyáya Maheça Chandra Nyáyaratna, C.I.E. Professor Bendall, to whom I showed it, seemed to think that it was at least two hundred years old. This I call A. It seemed to me to be very correctly written. It is in places so rubbed as to be absolutely illegible.

2. A copy kindly procured for me by Pandit Ráma Miçra Çástrí, of Benares. This I call B.

3. A copy which Atmárám Muni kindly had made for me at the request of Dr. Hoernle. This I call C.

4. A copy which Professor Bendall had made of a MS. at Benares. He was good enough to send this to me

* Bühler's Vortrag, p. 21.

† I am well aware that my resources in the way of MSS. have been deficient. I heard from Hofrath Bühler, when my translation was nearly printed, that there are some good MSS. in the Bombay Presidency.

at my request. This I call D. I have not collated it carefully, but it seems to agree with B. Both B and D are incomplete. They end with the termination of the story of Kanakaratha.

The other two MSS. contain two more stories, viz., the story of Báhubali, and the story of Nala and Davadantí.

The 'Kathákoça' is written in Sanskrit, interspersed with Prákṛit *gáthás*. The Sanskrit is of the type called 'mixed,' as it contains many ungrammatical constructions and many Prákṛit words. As in the 'Tantrákhyána,' of which Professor Bendall gave an account in the *Journal* of the Asiatic Society of Great Britain and Ireland, vol. xx., part iv., the passive participle in *ta* is used in an active sense. The following words appear to deserve notice, as being found in the Sanskrit portion of the work. I give references to the leaves of the Sanskrit College MS.

*Mutkalápya* is used in the sense of 'having taken leave of,' and *mutkalita* in the sense of 'sent, impelled.' The former word is found on folio 3 B, 5 A, 6 B, and 45 A, and the latter on folios 4 A and 16 A.

*Sáhita* is twice found in the sense of 'seized,' viz., on folios 3 B and 4 A. I find that Mr. Bendall remarks, in his paper above referred to (p. 468), that *kút* is used in the 'Tantrákhyána' in the sense of 'strike.' I have found *kuṭ* (with a short *u*) used twice in this sense in the 'Kathákoça.' On folio 45 A, I read *yashṭimushṭyádibhiḥ kuṭyamánáṃ*, where the participle agrees with *yoginím*, and evidently means 'being struck.' On 42 A I find *kuṭyate mahisháṇaṃ*, which I translate 'oxen are smitten.' On folio 11 B the participle *chhibita* is used. This is the Prákṛit *chhivai*, which Hemachandra, in his 'Deçínámamálá,' explains as *spriçati*. Another curious participial form is *chhikkita*, in the phrase *kenápi chhikkitaṃ*, 'somebody sneezed' (folio 29 B). I see that Sir Monier Williams has the nouns *chhikkana* and *chhikká* in the sense of sneezing. In Hindustání there is a word *chhínkná*, 'to sneeze.' The word *chatati* is frequently used, apparently in the sense of the Hindustání *chaṛhná*. Ordinary Prákṛit words are *talárika,** watchman (5 B); *nírangí*, veil (30 A); *dugunchá* = *jugupsá* (22 A); *mayagala*, elephant (88 B).

The following words appear to be Hindi: *Guphá*, cave (3 B); *chiṭhí*, letter (11 B), which is obviously the modern *chiṭṭhí*. The following words must, I think, be explained from Marathí: *Meṇa*, wax (51 A); and *darraḍaka*, vessel. The latter word is found spelt in various ways on folios 51 A and 53 A. I believe it to be the modern Marathí *davaḍá*. On folio 18 A the locative *angesale* is found. It must mean 'in the nest.'

I think I have said enough to show the 'mixed' character of the Sanskrit part of the book. The words that may be called pure Sanskrit frequently appear in forms inadmissible in classical Sanskrit, and the syntax is extremely loose and irregular.

At the end of the volume will be found some valuable notes, for which I am indebted to Professor Leumann, whose wide acquaintance with Jain literature is well known. He has cleared up many points on which my translation fails to throw light, and has corrected many errors into which I have fallen. My best thanks are also due to Mr. F. F. Arbuthnot for compiling the index.

* *Taláraka* is also found. *Talára* is noted by Dr. Schmidt as occurring in the *Çukasaptati*. The word *daṇḍapáçika*, also noted by Dr. Schmidt, is found on folio 42 B.

# THE KATHÁKOÇA;

OR,

## *TREASURY OF STORIES.*

---

OM ! Honour to him who is free from passion !

Hateful calamities flee afar,
Successes suddenly establish themselves,
Glories adorn dwellings
Through worship paid to the spiritual father of the world.

First a story concerning the worship of him who is free from passion.

STORY CONCERNING THE WORSHIP OF THE JINA.

Once on a time,* in the city of Çankhapura there was a king named Çríçankha; in that city dwelt a merchant named Dhanada. He was very rich and had four sons. One day that merchant, reflecting that fortune is fickle, caused to be made a temple in honour of him who is free from passion, and established there an image with great rejoicing. Subsequently, owing to impeding works in a former birth, he lost all his property. Through excessive poverty he abandoned that town, and took up his abode in a village near it, and spent some time living on what his sons gained by going backwards and forwards between the city and the village. Then, a great occasion having arrived, on a day of the moon's change coming once in four months,† Dhanada

* Instead of 'once on a time,' C. has 'In this Jambúdvípa in Bharatakshetra.'

† Atmárám Muni informs me that these days are the day of the full moon of the white fortnight in Phálguna, Ashádha, and Kártika.

went to Çankhapura with his sons, who were going there; and as he ascended the steps of his own temple, he was presented by the woman who looked after his own garden with flowers* and four other things. With these he worshipped the mighty Jina. And at night, when he was exclaiming against his poverty in the presence of the spiritual preceptor, he was presented by him with a charm for propitiating the Yaksha Kapardin. Once, on a night in the middle of the black fortnight, when he was worshipping this charm, the Yaksha Kapardin† manifested himself to him, and said: 'Dhanada, give me the benefit of the worship that thou didst pay with flowers and four other things to the venerable one who is free from passion on the four-monthly festival.' Dhanada replied: 'I cannot give the benefit of even one flower offered in worship to anyone but the all-knowing one.' On this account the Yaksha Kapardin, seeing that Dhanada was of the same creed as himself, deposited in the four corners of his house four jars filled with gold, and then disappeared. Dhanada in the morning returned to his house, and when his sons began to run down his religion, he made over to them that treasure. His sons asked him most respectfully how he came to acquire that wealth. Then, in order to manifest in their hearts the power of true religion, he informed them that all that wealth had been bestowed by the Yaksha Kapardin, who had been conciliated by the power of worship of the Jina. They, having acquired opulence, returned to their own native city, and devoting themselves to building Jaina religious edifices and to preaching the Jaina doctrine, established the true faith in the minds

---

On these days the Jainas, after fasting, perform pious works, such as almsgiving, penance, meditation, confession, worship, honouring of spiritual superiors, etc. He also remarks that the word *parvan*, which is used here, is a term for any day specially suited for religious observance.

* Probably flowers, dresses, perfumes, garlands, and ornaments. See Dr. Hoernle's 'Uvásaga Dasáo,' p. 43, note 120.

† He is mentioned in Weber's 'Çatrunjaya Máhátmyam,' p. 44, as having 100,000 Yakshas under his orders.

of even men of alien creeds. Here ends the story of Dhanada concerning the worship of him who is free from passion.

Even one act of worship paid to the Jina produces for men all blessings, as rain showered down by a cloud produces in the appointed time great blessings in the form of crops.

STORY OF DEVAPÁLA.

In this very land of Bharata there is a town of the name of Vasantapura. In it lived a merchant, whose name, Jinadása,* well expressed his character. He had a servant of the name of Devapála, who was very well conducted, self-restrained, discriminating, appreciative of the good points of others, and devoted to his master. This servant's business was to take the cows to graze. Now, once on a time, the rainy season arrived.

The clouds rumbled, the tribes of long-tailed peacocks danced for joy;
There were drops of rain and lightnings in the heaven,
The torrents flowed with turbid stream,
The great water-receptacles† poured down rain.

At that time, as the servant, named Devapála, having led his cows to graze, was returning home, it happened that a river which flowed across his path, having been swelled by the rain, had become difficult to ford. While Devapála was looking at the river in flood, he saw in the water a stone image of the Jina, and reflected : 'Oh my good luck! Oh the accumulation of my merits ! Oh the totality of my actions in my past lives ! In which of them can my works have been deficient ?' At last there came a great downpour. He took that image of the Jina, and set it up in that very spot under a *pípal* tree, and made a vow that he would not touch food until he had worshipped it, and so returned home. The cloud‡ went on raining, and Devapála was prevented from performing his worship by the fact that the river was in flood. Accordingly he would not take

* Slave of the Jina.
† The rain-clouds.
‡ A Jaina is strictly forbidden to say 'The god rains.' See Jacobi's translation of the 'Ácháránga Sútra,' p. 152.

food, and refused to break his fast, even though Jinadása expostulated with him. At the end of seven days the cloud ceased to rain, so Devapála had seven days of fasting. At the end of the seven days of fasting he went to the bank of the river to worship the god.

By goodness the cloud rains, by goodness the gods prosper,
By goodness the earth is upheld, in goodness all is established.

The god, being pleased with the goodness of Devapála, gave him on the seventh day the sovereignty of that city. On the seventh day the king of that city died of cholera, and left no male issue. As there was no son to succeed him, the ministers appointed an elephant, and fastened to its temples a pitcher full of water, and let it go. It found the servant named Devapála asleep on the seventh day, under the *pípal* tree, and emptied the pitcher on his head.* They bestowed on him the kingdom. He put on magnificent garments, leaving his old clothes on the spot where he was found, and made his entry into the city with great public rejoicings, and became lord of it. One day that merchant took his old clothes and fastened them up at the gate of the palace avenue. All the king's retinue, when they saw them, were disgusted with him. King Devapála, seeing that everybody was disaffected, again went to the Jina and praised the lord. A demon in attendance on the lord said to him: 'The royal dignity has been given to thee, and no one can annul that decree. But go to thy palace and have an elephant made of clay; then take thy seat on that elephant, and propitiate it with

* In the 'Kathá Sarit Ságara' we read of an elephant let loose with a similar object. The man that it took up with its trunk and placed on its head was anointed king. In Jacobi's 'Erzählungen aus der Mahárashtrí' there is more than one allusion to this practice. At p. 62 five ordeals (*divváni*) are mentioned: 'On seeing him the elephant trumpeted, the horse neighed; he was sprinkled by the pitcher, and fanned by the chowries, and the umbrella stood over him.' See also the story of Amaradatta and Mitránanda in this work. The neighing of the horse reminds one of the story of Darius, the son of Hystaspes. In the 'Darímukhajátaka' (Fausböll, vol. iii., p. 238) an empty chariot is sent out. In the story of Karakandu, p. 37 of Jacobi's 'Erzählungen,' a horse is let loose. See also Jacobi's Introduction to his edition of the 'Pariçishta Parvan,' p. 46.

whole grain, calling to mind at the same time the spell containing the name of him who is free from passion. This having been done, the elephant will move like a real elephant, and all men, beholding thy marvellous power, will show thee reverence.' Devapála received with due attention this speech of the attendant demon, and went to his palace. There he had a clay elephant made, he mounted it, and uttering the name of the Jina, propitiated it with whole grain, whereupon it became alive. Then all the people looked upon the king with admiration, and respected him, so that he enjoyed unopposed sovereignty. Then one day it happened that the king with his retinue went to the house of that merchant named Jinadása. Thereupon the merchant presented him with a golden vessel full of jewels:

> Everyone is ready to confer a benefit on him who merits benefits;
> But seldom does a mother give birth to one who does good to the undeserving.

The king was pleased, and made the merchant keeper of the great seal. He then continued to govern his realm without anxiety. At length the king had erected in the middle of the city a gigantic temple of the Jina, towering aloft like a mountain. In it he had set up that very image of the Jina, and the king with his wives went day and night to the temple and worshipped him who is free from passion with sweet-smelling things, such as aloes, camphor, sandalwood, and fragrant flowers. One day, as the king with his wives was approaching the temple of the Jina, they were met by a *kápálika* carrying a bundle of wood on his head. The queen, as soon as she saw that *kápálika* thus employed, fainted. She remembered her former birth, and, being thereby deprived of her senses, she repeated over and over again the following verse:

> The water went to the river from the forest, but you were not converted;
> Alas! you became a *kápálika*, so that even now such is your state.

Then the queen's trance was dispelled. The king said:

'Queen, why was it that you fainted when you saw this *kápálika?*' She answered:* 'I remembered my former life. In a former birth I was a Pulindí, and he was my husband. One day a holy man arrived where we lived, and appointed a vow for the worship of the god. I took upon myself that vow, but my husband did not take it. I worshipped the Jina three times a day, in the forenoon, at noon, and in the afternoon; and owing to the merit of that piety I have now become your chief queen, while my husband is enduring this miserable condition.' When they heard this, all worshipped the god. Here ends the story of Devapála having reference to the worship of the god.

Now follows the subject of wrath.

> Rain, cloud, for fifteen days on the city of Kuṇálá,
> With raindrops as large as clubs, as by day, so also by night.

STORY OF THE TWO HERMITS THAT BROUGHT DOWN A DELUGE ON THE CITY OF KUṆÁLÁ.

In the city of Kuṇálá two hermits were remaining with restrained breath in the statuesque posture † during the rainy season. The cloud was raining everywhere. Some herdsmen blamed the holy men, saying: 'These hermits will prevent the cloud from raining.' The hermits flew into a passion, and the first said: 'Rain, cloud, on Kuṇálá.' The second said: 'For full fifteen days.' The first said: 'With raindrops as large as clubs.' The second said: 'As by day, so also by night.' Owing to this curse of the two hermits, the cloud rained for fifteen days, and the city was flooded. The hermits also perished and went to hell. Therefore wrath should not be indulged in.

STORY OF THE HERMIT AND THE CARTER.

On a lofty mountain a hermit named Saṃvara was in a statuesque posture. The goddess that fulfils the command of the Jina was pleased with him, and said to him: 'Great-souled one, if calamity should come

* I have inserted some words which the sense seems to require.

† See Dr. Hoernle's 'Uvásaga Dasáo,' appendix iii., p. 41. I have borrowed this term from him.

upon you, you should call me to mind.' One day the hermit went to a village to break his fast. As he was going along, a cart met him in the road. The hermit would not get out of the way. The driver of the cart spoke to him repeatedly, but he still declined to budge. Thereupon the carter, being angry, got down from his cart and beat the hermit with his cart-whip.* The hermit in wrath struck him back with his staff, and a combat ensued between the two men.†

STORY OF AÇOKADATTA AND HIS SON ÇRÍPATI.

In Southern Mathurá there lived a merchant named Açokadatta, who was lord of a crore. In Northern Mathurá a merchant named Samṛiddhidatta went on a trading journey with five hundred carts. He struck up a friendship with Açokadatta, and there was great affection on both sides. Samṛiddhidatta returned to his own city. One day a son was born in the house of Açokadatta. His name was called Çripati. Açokadatta announced to his friend when the ceremony of cutting the umbilical cord‡ would take place. A daughter was born in the house of Samṛiddhidatta, and he announced the ceremony to his friend in the same manner. The two friends agreed together that they must celebrate the joyful marriage of their two children. The betrothal took place; the auspicious moment was fixed. One day the merchant Açokadatta was suddenly seized with a terrible fever and died. Çrípati was appointed in his place, and carried on the weighty business of the house. One day Çrípati was sitting down to take his bath, when a golden bowl was spirited away; when he had finished his

* A conjectural translation of *piráṇakena.*

† It appears that this story is not completed. It resembles the 332nd Játaka. See Fausböll, vol. iii., p. 104. The MSS. here insert a passage which is found again before the twenty-sixth story, to which it forms a suitable introduction. It is out of place here. Two of the MSS. also insert: 'Here follows the story of Açokadatta, having reference to cheating.'

‡ *Vardhápanam.* But the word seems to mean in other passages 'good news.' That may be the meaning here.

ablutions, his bathing-seat also disappeared. He went to worship the god at the appointed time, but lo! the instruments used in the worship of the god disappeared, and at this moment he heard the news of the sinking of his ships. He sat down to take his food, when a plate disappeared; thirty-two golden cups for distributing vegetables and thirty-two spoons also were gone. A plate began to shake. He seized the plate with his hand as it was going off, and it went off leaving a piece behind.* Subsequently a man came to borrow money. He said: 'I must have a lakh; give it me.' When he went to look at his hoards, behold all his wealth had become dust. Seized with despondency, he took leave of his mother, and set out for a foreign country, taking with him the fragment of the plate. He ascended a mountain, and preparing to commit suicide, he was engaged in reciting his wishes for the next life, when a hermit in a cave, who was in the statuesque posture, saw him, and exclaimed: 'Çrípati, do not act rashly; by such a death you will attain the condition of a demon; do not die an evil death, for—

> In taking the halter, and in swallowing poison, in fire, and in entering the water,
> Wearied by hunger and thirst, they slay themselves, and become demons.

'Therefore do not inflict death on yourself.' Çrípati drew near and bowed before the saint. The saint said: 'Why are you intent on death?' Çrípati said: 'Hermit, the burning up of my wealth afflicts me.' The hermit said: 'Çrípati, wealth is unsubstantial, filthy, the cause of enmity; of this I will give you an instance:

STORY OF DEVADHARMA AND DEVAÇARMAN.

'Once on a time, in this very land of Bharata, there was a town named Koçavardhana. In it there was a Bráhman named Bhíma. He had two sons, named Devadharma and Devaçarman. Being afflicted with poverty,

* I have been much assisted in this passage by Muni Átmárám-ji, whom Dr. Hoernle kindly consulted for me. I have followed his Hindi paraphrase pretty closely.

the two brothers went to a foreign land in order to acquire wealth. They wandered from country to country, from village to village, and from city to city, and at last reached the town of Jayapura. In it there dwelt a king of the name of Arikeçarin, who had a daughter named Madanávalí. That princess went through a form of penance, named "the kindler of prosperity," and was at that very time concluding the penance. She had a proclamation made in the city by beat of drum, to the effect that two Bráhmans, who had never appeared there before,* young and handsome, and observing the vow of chastity, were to be summoned. Accordingly these two were summoned. She filled two golden vessels with wealth, jewels, and gold, and piled up on the top pastry, sweetmeats, and sugar, and gave them to the two Bráhmans. The two Bráhmans took the two urns and went to the river and feasted. They consulted together, and buried the wealth in that very place in a hole in the bank, and went to another country to earn more wealth. As they were going along, the heart of the elder brother changed for the worse. In a forest near Kauçámbí the elder brother sent his brother to look into a blind well. He said to him: "Brother, just see if there is water in this well, and come back, I am very thirsty;" and while the younger brother was looking to see if there was water in the well, his elder brother Devaçarman threw him into the well. As he was falling, he caught hold of the hem of the elder brother's garment, and so they both fell in and perished. After death they were born again as serpents. In the third birth they were born as mice. In their fourth birth they were born as deer, and killed by a hunter. In their fifth birth they were born as the sons of the Bráhman Mádhava, in the city of Kauçámbí, by his wife Vásantí, and were named Rudra and Maheçvara. One day the two went to the field to milk. They fell to quarrelling when they came over the place where the treasure had been buried, but were made to desist by the householders who were near them, and re-

* Compare the story of Vasudeva.

turned home. At home they were on the best of terms, but in the field they were enemies. One day they asked a saint, who possessed absolute knowledge, the cause of this. The saint told them of what occurred in a former life. Thereupon both the brothers were converted, and took upon themselves a vow. When they died they went to the world of the gods.'

The hermit went on to say: 'Now, Çrípati, for the sake of such an unsubstantial thing as this wealth, who would die an evil death, and make his birth as a man of none effect?' When Çrípati heard this, his conversion took place. He received consecration, and having become a perfectly instructed monk, wandered about alone. After some time, owing to the power of his penance, he acquired limited knowledge. As he was wandering about, he came in some days to Northern Mathurá, and entered the house of Samṛiddhidatta to ask for a dole. He saw all his own possessions, the bathing-tub, the *lota*, all the instruments used in the worship of the god, and the plate, the thirty-two spoons, and the thirty-two cups. He observed that the merchant was at that moment eating off the broken plate. The hermit looked round in all directions and beheld his own property. The merchant said: 'Holy man, why do you look about you in all directions?' The ascetic said: 'Merchant, did you have these bathing utensils, and this plate, and these cups, and so on, made for you, or were they made by the orders of your ancestors?' The merchant said: 'Reverend sir, they are inherited from my ancestors.' The hermit said: 'How can you eat out of one broken plate?' The merchant answered: 'I have not got the fragment of the plate.' Thereupon Çrípati took the fragment of the plate from his belt and put it near the plate. The fragment adhered to the plate, and the plate was mended. The hermit prepared to depart. Samṛiddhidatta prostrated himself before the hermit, and asked for an explanation. The hermit said: 'How can I assert that your statement is not true?' Samṛiddhidatta said: 'Inadvertently* I said what was untrue; and this property has been in my house for eight years.' The hermit said: 'All this belongs to me; I am the son of Açokadatta, Çrípati by name.' Samṛiddhidatta was delighted, and said: 'I bestow on you my daughter, marry her; I will make good all the gold and other property.' The hermit answered: 'Merchant, it is all yours; I have abandoned all worldly pleasures. Listen, merchant, to the story of our life in a former birth.' Then the hermit sat down and told the story of their life in a former birth:

STORY OF SAMṚIDDHIDATTA AND ÇRÍPATI IN A FORMER BIRTH.

'In the city of Çrípura, a merchant named Jinadatta had two sons, Padmákara and Guṇákara. One day, when he was at the point of death, he revealed to them the existence of a hoard buried in a field. Subsequently the two agreed to dig up the hoard when a favourable occasion presented itself. But one midnight the elder brother, Padmákara, went and secretly took possession of that hoard buried in the field. On a subsequent day the two went together, by appointment, to dig up the hoard. They dug up the place where it ought to be, but it had disappeared. Padmákara pretended to have an attack of faintness, and said: "Guṇákara, you have taken it."† He made his younger brother take a solemn oath that he had not taken the wealth. In course of time both of them died, and, owing to his deceitfulness from his birth, the soul of Padmákara was born as myself, and the soul of Guṇákara as you. Because in my former life I acted deceitfully, my wealth has come to your house in this life. Therefore no one should practise deceit.'

Thereupon the merchant became converted, and took a vow.

Here ends the story of Açokadatta, having reference to deceit.

* This rendering is based on a paraphrase by Muni Átmárám-jí.

† This story bears a slight resemblance to the story of Dharmabuddhi and Dushṭabuddhi ('Kathá Sarít Ságara' vol. ii. p. 40 of my translation).

Behold the strange drama of avarice,
Acted by all beings in the three worlds,
In which even the beloved of Lakshmí
Actually assumed the disguise of a dwarf.*

Crimes have avarice for their root, diseases have humours for their root;
Sorrows have affection for their root: avoid the three, and be happy.

Now for an example:

As a man's gains so is his avarice, by gain avarice is increased;
The acts performed in two months cannot be expiated in a crore.

STORY OF THE BRÁHMAN VASUDEVA.

In this very land of Bharata, in the village of Kuçasthala, dwelt a Bráhman, named Vasudeva; his father died while he was a child. One day he took leave of his mother, and went to the city of Champá to study learning. There he studied with a teacher named Kshírakadamba. He acquired fame among men as a student, and received alms even in the king's palace. Owing to too great intimacy, he formed a connection with a female slave belonging to the palace, and after some days she became pregnant. She said: 'Bráhman, when the time comes for me to have a child, how will my lying-in expenses be defrayed? Without money no affair can be brought to a successful conclusion. Therefore do you devise a means for obtaining money.' He answered: 'What means can I devise?' The female slave said: 'In the city of Çrípura there is a king of the name of Çrívardhana; that king gives every morning at daybreak a couple of *máshas* of gold to any Bráhman who appears before him for the first time. A couple of *máshas* of gold will be sufficient to tide me over the troubles of childbirth.' When the Bráhman heard this, he went to the city of Çrípura, and slept at night in a hut belonging to a native of that place. His avarice obscured his reason, and so, thinking in the middle of the night that it was morning, he went so far as to get up at that time to ask

* An allusion to the Vámana incarnation of Vishṇu. The god appeared before Bali and asked for as much land as he could step over in three strides. This Bali granted, and Vishṇu in two strides deprived him of heaven and earth.

for the couple of *máshas*. He said to himself: 'If I delay about going to-day, some other man will ask before me and carry off the gold, so I will go early.' But when he had got half-way, the police seized him and bound him, supposing that he was a thief, and took him in the morning to the king's judgment-hall. The king, seeing that he was a man of mild disposition, released him from his bonds, and asked him who he was, and for what reason he went about at night. He related from the beginning the affair of the female slave, and explained why he wanted the two *máshas* of gold. The king said: 'Then ask whatever present you like, I am pleased with you.' The Bráhman said: 'I should like to consider before I ask.' The king said: 'Then consider.' So the Bráhman went and sat alone in an elevated spot and considered, but found that a hundred, a thousand, a lakh—nay, even a crore—of *máshas* would not satisfy his desires. At that moment he saw a hermit sitting in the *padmásana** posture, who recited the following couplet:

> 'Every song is babbling, every dance† is deceit;
> All ornaments are burdens, all desires bring pain.'

When the Bráhman heard this couplet, he was filled with the spirit of asceticism, and said to himself:

> 'As a man's gains so is his avarice, by gain avarice is increased;
> The acts performed in two months cannot be expiated in a crore.'

When he had thus reflected, he plucked out his hair, and took a vow. He bestowed on the king a blessing on account of his having been the means of his conversion, and, after explaining the meaning of the couplet, he went to the forest a self-enlightened ascetic. So avarice is always to be avoided. Here ends the tale having reference to avarice.

In this very Bharata there is a city named Sáketapura. In this city once lived a king named Puṇḍaríka; his younger

STORY OF PRINCE YAÇOBHADRA.

* A particular posture in religious meditation—sitting with the thighs crossed, with one hand resting on the left thigh, the other held up with the thumb upon the heart, and the eyes directed to the tip of the nose.

† The word 'dance' must be taken to include acting.

brother was named Kuṇḍaríka, and he had a wife named Yaçobhadrá. One day the elder brother Puṇḍaríka was smitten in the heart with the arrows of love, and conceived a passion for the wife of his younger brother Kuṇḍaríka. Once on a time he said to his sister-in-law in private: 'Beloved, receive me as your husband.' She answered: 'Why do you speak thus?

'Many quickly enter the fire,
Lacerate with weapons their own bodies,
Perform severe self-mortifications,
But few conquer the enemy, the mighty champion, Mára.'

Again, the queen said: 'King, poison has sprung up in the nectar of immortality, the sun has brought forth darkness, the moon a rain of burning coals; from the quarter from which protection is expected comes danger; from water fire has arisen. If a man with good eyes wanders from the path, then who can blame the blind for doing the same?'

Let even the sight of a woman be carefully avoided, a woman impels and carries away;
The hermit Rávana had to be made war upon for the sake of Sítá alone.

The king menaced his sister-in-law with angry words. Another day, being beside himself with anger, and longing for the love of his sister-in-law, he gave poison to his younger brother Kuṇḍaríka, in order to slay him, for

An owl does not see by day, a crow does not see by night;
A wicked man blind with love sees neither by night nor by day.

When the king's brother Kuṇḍaríka was dead, his wife the princess said to herself: 'This villain will disgrace me by robbing me of my honour, so I will go to some foreign land in order to preserve it.' After reflecting thus in her mind, she started off at night, and went to the city of Çrávastí. There she entered the *posaha*-house of the female ascetic Suvratá, and hearing from her mouth instruction in the holy law, she conceived aversion to the world. Aversion having thus arisen, the princess took the vows. But she omitted to tell the saintly superior that she had become pregnant by her late husband, lest it should interfere with her taking the vows. The signs of pregnancy became more apparent, and the saintly Suvratá said to her: 'My child, what is the meaning of this?' The princess said: 'Reverend lady, I did not tell you the truth, because I wished to take the vows.' Then she was left in the house of a disciple named Sugupta, who had been fully instructed in the faith.* There her confinement took place, and she gave birth to a son, to whom she gave the name of Yaçobhadra. When he attained the age of eight years, he was dedicated and instructed by the priests. But when he became a young man, he was distracted, longing for the pleasures of the world, and continued in a state of bewilderment, like a mad elephant that recollects the Vindhya forest. He became out of health; he loathed food and loathed his vow, and observed his vow without heart, for

Honour ye that mighty Jina, who said, 'I have not tasted the pleasure of that love,
By whom Vishṇu, Çiva, Brahmá, Indra, and the hosts of gods and men have been conquered.
The demon of love is the origin of all demons, the great demon, tending to produce all crimes,
The evil-minded one by whom the whole world has been overcome.

Accordingly, on a certain occasion, he went and said to his mother: 'Mother, I cannot keep my vow; I will go to my own kingdom, I will assume the condition of a householder. After I have enjoyed pleasures, I will take a vow in my old age. At present I will rule by the side of my paternal uncle Puṇḍaríka.' His mother said: 'My dear child, then do what I ask:

'Though unable to keep your vow, yet out of regard to this my request
Remain here twelve years, and after that do what is fitting.'

He agreed to do what his mother asked him, and out of regard to her request he remained twelve years; he was detained twelve years also by the lady superior, twelve more by the request of his teacher, and twelve more by the injunction of his spiritual preceptor. So he was detained

* *Gitártha.* The Prakrit equivalent of this, *gíyattha*, is explained by Jacobi as *ein ausgelernter Mönch.*

forty-eight years in all. At the end of this period he departed, taking leave of all his superiors. When he was starting his mother gave him a jewelled shawl. He then took his way to the court of his uncle Puṇḍaríka, and reached the city of Sáketa at night. He said to himself: 'I will wait upon the king to-morrow morning early;' and so he carelessly seated himself to see a play acted at night in a temple. The king and many other persons were present to see the play, which was very interesting. After three watches of the night had passed an actress was exhausted. Her mother said: 'My child, when but a little difficulty has arisen, why do you allow your limbs to become relaxed?

> 'You have sung well, you have played well;*
> After lasting through a long night, do not be careless when the darkness passes away.'

When the hermit heard this verse repeated, he was filled with the spirit of renunciation, and he gave the jewelled shawl to the actress; the prince gave a golden bracelet studded with jewels; a lady named Çríkántá, who was a native of that city, gave a necklace of pearls; the driver of the royal elephant gave a driving-hook; the prime minister, named Jayasandhi, gave a couple of golden bracelets. All the presents taken together were worth five lakhs. The king's mind was filled with astonishment. He asked the hermit the cause of so unusual a gift. He answered:

> 'She has brought my mind to a state of composure, which my teacher could not do;
> As a candle in a cellar pierces the darkness which the sun cannot pierce.

King, this lady is my spiritual preceptor, and teaches me the true path; for this reason I gave her my jewelled shawl.' The king then asked Çríkántá. She said: 'King, I was purposing in my mind to murder my husband and take another, but I also have been converted by her words.' The king asked the driver of the royal elephant the reason of his gift. He answered: 'King, I wished to go to another kingdom, and I was purposing on the field of

* I read *váditam* for *viditam*.

battle to drive on the elephant, and carry you into the midst of your enemies.' It turned out also that the prince and the minister were engaged in the same plot to murder the king and seize the reins of power, but were converted by the words of the actress. It is said in the Ávaçyaka Siddhánta :

'You have sung the tune well, you have played it well, you have danced it well, O fair one ;
Since you have endured through a long night, let not sleep now make you careless.'

When the king had thus heard the real thoughts of them all he was pleased ; and seeing the emptiness of the world, all of them, and especially the king, were by the preaching of the hermit converted to the happiness of stability. The king placed the prince on the throne, and took the vows in the presence of the hermit as his spiritual preceptor, and, having maintained a blameless walk, went to heaven. The hermit Yaçobhadra also went to his spiritual preceptor, and having confessed his sin and promised amendment,* and once more maintained a holy walk, he acquired unlimited knowledge, and eventually dying a death of holy peace,† he went to blessedness. Hence it follows that :

A word spoken in season, a gift in season to living beings,
A shower in season, all these, though but slight, produce fruit by the crore.

Here ends the story of Yaçobhadra having reference to a word spoken in season.

Virtue is the one thing needful, and not high birth.
What is the use of high birth without virtue ?
Did not some men and a queen born in a royal family,
Firm of soul, by practising virtue, go to heaven ?

Sitá, afraid of ill repute, made her body an offering in the flame ;
In that the flame became like water, therein was displayed the might of her virtue.

---

* See note 155 in Dr. Hoernle's translation of the 'Uvásaga Dasáo.'

† Dr. Hoernle in the 'Uvásaga Dasáo' shows that *samâdhimṛityu* is practically a euphemism for a death by means of starvation.

Fire becomes water, water dry land, a mighty snake becomes the stalk of a lotus;
Poison becomes nectar, and the treacherous man sincere, the lion becomes a jackal;
And all other dangerous things become harmless to mortals; the power by whose lofty influence this happens
Is, as we have heard, a mighty providence arising from virtue, with wide-reaching splendour of fortune.

All hail to the honourable lady Madanarekhá divinely adorned,
Marked by beauty and loveliness, who made her mark in the world,
When her husband was killed, and his elder brother sought her love,
And the pride of the Vidyádhara who conceived a passion for her met with repulse.

STORY OF MADANAREKHÁ AND HER SON NAMI.*

Now, by way of illustration, follows the story of the very virtuous Madanarekhá. In this very Jambudvípa, in this very land of Bharata, in the province of Avanti, there is a city named Sudarçanapura. In it there ruled a king named Maṇiratha; he had a younger brother named Yugabáhu. Yugabáhu's wife, Madanarekhá, was exceedingly beautiful: she was an ardent votary of the law of the Jina, virtuous, auspiciously marked, full of blessed qualities. One day King Maṇiratha, the elder brother, having his mind bewildered by the beauty of Madanarekhá, said to himself: 'I must obtain possession of this woman by hook or by crook, through happiness or unhappiness, by fair or foul play.' Accordingly King Maṇiratha in his tenderness gave her flowers, betel, dresses, ornaments, and other things, in order to incline her mind to his wishes; but Madanarekhá took them all without being corrupted. Then the king sent a female messenger. She went and said to Madanarekhá, 'My good lady, the king, being attached to your good qualities, sends you this message by me:

'Receive me as your husband, and become the queen of this realm.'
Then the lady, detecting her object, spake thus the mind of the virtuous:
'By longing for other women, men go to the depths of hell,
Therefore be content, O king; relinquish the wicked grasping after pleasure.'
The female messenger quickly reported her words to the king.

---

* This is identical with the story of Nami in Jacobi's 'Ausgewählte Erzählungen in Mahárâshtrí.'

The king said to himself: 'As long as this Yugabáhu is alive she will not become my wife; therefore I will take steps to destroy Yugabáhu, and take her unto me to wife.' Now, one night Madanarekhá dreamed of the moon; she told her husband the next morning. He said: 'Princess, your moon will bring us prosperity; you will have a smiling-faced son.' Then in the third month, owing to her pregnant condition, Madanarekhá had a longing to bestow a gift for the purpose of divine worship. Prince Yugabáhu took care that that longing was satisfied. Then, in the season of spring, Yugabáhu went one day with Madanarekhá on a pleasure excursion. While looking at the festive sports of the townspeople, Yugabáhu entered an arbour of plantains. But when night came on, King Maṇiratha said to himself: 'Now is my opportunity, as Yugabáhu has retired to rest in the wood at night with a very small retinue.' Then King Maṇiratha, taking his sword in his hand, said to Yugabáhu's guards: 'Guards, where is my brother Yugabáhu?' They answered: 'Sir, he is sleeping in the arbour of plantain leaves.' The king said: 'I have come here out of anxiety, lest some enemy might overpower my brother in this wood.' With these words in his mouth the king entered the arbour. Yugabáhu, for his part, perceiving that the king, his elder brother, had come, rose up in a hurry. The king said: 'Come, my dear brother, let us go to the city; it is not advisable to remain here.' Then Yugabáhu bowed before the king and prepared to start, saying to himself: 'My elder brother is in a special sense my superior; I must not disobey him.' Then the evil-minded king, disregarding the fear of disgrace, smote his brother Yugabáhu with his sword on the shoulder. Then Madanarekhá cried out in her horror: 'Alas! an unknightly act!' Then the soldiers who were near, perceiving that Yugabáhu had received a sword-cut, ran to the place, exclaiming: 'What is this?' King Maṇiratha said: 'I was so careless that I let my sword fall from my hand.' Thereupon the soldiers, understanding the whole proceeding, took the king away to the palace by force. The facts were communicated to Yugabáhu's son Çhandrayaças, and he, exclaiming, 'Alas, alas!' came to the garden with surgeons, and had his father's wound bound up and all other necessary things done.

In a moment his voice stopped; his two eyes closed;
His body became motionless, and white from loss of blood;
Madanarekhá, perceiving that her husband was at death's door,
Going close to his ear, spake thus in a soft voice.

So Madanarekhá, summoning up all her self-control, brought about her husband's deathbed reconciliation* with all by uttering the following words: 'Noble sir, now attend carefully. This is a time for self-possession, do not indulge vain regrets; the operation of action is mighty; whatever acts a man long ago performed, to him those acts return; an enemy is merely the instrumental cause. Take with you the *viaticum* of virtue; condemn all wicked deeds; beg forgiveness of friends and enemies, relations and strangers; beg forgiveness of those animals that you afflicted in your animal births, those inhabitants of hell that you afflicted when in hell, and similarly of those gods that you gave pain to when a god, and of those men that you injured in your human births.

'Life, youth, fortune, beauty, association with dear ones,
Might, all these things are like a wave of the sea made to dance by the wind.
For living beings here, devoured by disease, birth, old age, and death,
Save the law revealed by the Jina, there is no other shelter.
Alien is the slaughter of enemies, alien corn, wealth, and so on,
Alien are relations to the soul; in vain is the fool bewildered.
What wise man would swoon with anxiety about the body, the home of impurities,
Filled up, as it is, with grease, blood, flesh, bone, liver, fæces, and urine?

'Have recourse to the *arhats* and other holy ones for refuge; remember the formula of adoration; avoid the

* I have translated *árádhaná* by 'reconciliation with all.' Jacobi gives 'content' as the equivalent of *áráhaná* ('Kalpa Sútra,' 114). Weber, in his 'Fragment der Bhagavatî,' seems to take it as 'attainment of the great object of life.'

eighteen causes of evil;* remember the law of the Jina; think of Çríyuga and the other Jinas.' By making this suitable composing address to him when dying, she induced her beloved to abandon his animosity against his enemies. Then Chandrayaças in his grief began to weep. Madanarekhá reflected earnestly: 'Alas, ill-fated that I am! I am ruined! Out on my beauty, since on beholding me the mind of even my respected superiors is disturbed! He who slew his own brother for my sake will certainly also seize on me, so it is not fitting for me to remain here:

'So I will go to some other realm, and attend to other affairs, those of the next world.
Otherwise, this villain will slay my son also.'
Having thus deliberated, she left that place, her son being oppressed with grief;
And wandering on in the night towards the eastern quarter, reached a great forest.

The night came to an end.

Alone on the second day, as the sun was setting,
She nourished her life there with forest fruits, and drank water.
Then, having rejected all luxuries,† wearied with the toil of her journey,
She slept at night, to dispel her fatigue, in a natural arbour of plantains.

The night descended on the forest, but through the might of the formula of adoration, tigers and other living creatures went far away. In the middle of the night she gave birth in the arbour of plantains to a son endowed with all auspicious marks. At the time of dawn she placed in the hand of her son a seal marked with the name of Yugabáhu, and wrapped him up in a jewelled shawl, and then went to a lake to wash her clothes. While she was bathing in it she was tossed up into the sky by a water-elephant. Then, as she was falling from the sky, Queen Madanarekhá was intercepted by a Vidyádhara, who was going to the island of Nandana. He took her to the Vaitáḍhya mountain. The queen said to the Vidyádhara: 'Noble sir, in

* See the translation of the 'Sarva-Darçana-Sangraha,' by Cowell and Gough, p. 62.

† Sanskrit *sákáram*. In the corresponding Prákṛit passage (Jacobi, p. 43), we have *ságáraṃ bhattam*, which Jacobi thinks may mean '*zubereitete Speise.*' *Naktam*, which follows *sákáraṃ* in the Sanskrit text, should probably be changed into *bhaktam*.

the night a son has been born to me. I left that son in an arbour of plantains, and went to a lake to wash my clothes and to bathe; but while I was thus engaged, a water-elephant, seizing me with the extremity of his trunk, tossed me up into the sky. As I was falling down I was intercepted by you. That child will be killed by some wild beast, or will naturally die for want of nourishment. Do me a favour; bring the child here, or take me to him.' The Vidyádhara said: 'If you accept me as a husband, I will do your bidding.' The queen said: 'Who are you?' He answered: 'On the Vaitáḍhya mountain, in a city named Ratnávaha, there was a Vidyádhara named Maṇichúḍa; I am his son, named Maṇiprabha; my father placed me upon his throne and took a vow; now that hermit is in the island of Nandíçvara, having gone there to adore the *chaityas*; as I was going to see him I beheld you. Moreover, that son of yours was discovered in the forest by Padmaratha, King of Mithilá, who had been run away with by his horse. He took the boy and gave him to his wife Pushpamálá, and she cherished him as her own son, and he is there in comfort. All this I have heard from the science named Prajnapti; now do you adorn my royal throne.' When Madanarekhá heard that, she said to herself: 'What device shall I adopt to save my honour?' Then the queen, having reflected in her own mind, said: 'First cause me to perform the pilgrimage to Nandíçvara; afterwards I will do what you say.' Then the Vidyádhara Maṇiprabha, pleased with her speech, took her to Nandíçvara, and enabled her to worship the everlasting *chaityas*. There Maṇiprabha and Madanarekhá bowed before the great hermit Maṇichúḍa, and both of them sat down in front of him. The hermit, knowing by his insight the behaviour of Madanarekhá, expounded the holy religion, and recalled his son Maṇiprabha to a sense of his duty. Maṇiprabha said to Madanarekhá: 'Henceforth you are my sister in the faith, and I am your servant, bound to execute your orders.' So Maṇiprabha was converted. Then Madanarekhá asked the hermit for tidings of her son. He related as follows: 'Long ago there were two princes; they died and became gods. One of them fell from his position and became King Padmaratha, the other became your son. Accordingly King Padmaratha, when run away with by his horse, gave your son to his wife Pushpamálá on account of his love for him in a former life. King Padmaratha made a great triumphal entry into Mithilá.' While the great hermit was saying this, there arrived a splendid deity, magnificently adorned, mounted on a heavenly chariot, delighting the heart with a charming exhibition of singing and dancing on the part of heavenly nymphs. He circumambulated Madanarekhá three times,* and bowed before her, and then did his reverence to the hermit and sat in front of him. Then Maṇiprabha, considering that his behaviour was out of place, said: 'If gods adopt this line of conduct, to whom can we speak? Why did you pass by a distinguished hermit, who possesses the four kinds of knowledge,† and whose conduct is blameless, and bow first before a mere woman?' But before the god could give an answer, the hermit said solemnly: 'Do not speak so; this god does not deserve blame. For King Maṇiratha murdered his brother Yugabáhu, because he was in love with this Madanarekhá; she made Yugabáhu's peace with all when he was at the point of death, and he became a god in the fifth *kalpa;* for this reason Madanarekhá stands in the relation of a religious instructor to this god; whoever establishes another in the true faith is his spiritual superior.' When the hermit had said this, the Vidyádhara implored the god's forgiveness; then the god said to the princess: 'Virtuous lady, what can I do to please you?' The princess said: 'To me salvation only is pleasing; nevertheless, take me quickly to Mithilá, there I will behold the face of my son, and afterwards devote

* The prevalence of this practice in many nations may be proved by a reference to the Index to my translation of the 'Kathá Sarit Ságara,' under the word 'Desiul.' It is unnecessary to dilate on the importance of the number three in all rites and ceremonies.

† In the 'Sarva-Darçana Sangraha,' p. 47, five kinds are mentioned. But perhaps the knowledge called *mati* is here disregarded.

myself to religious works.' The god (who was once Yugabáhu) then took the princess to Mithilá, where are the three kinds of knowledge of Mallinátha that produce happiness, namely, the knowledge of his birth, the knowledge of how he took the vows, and absolute, unalloyed knowledge. Therefore, in the first place, the two visited the *chaityas* of the Arhat, considering them holy spots. Then they saw a holy woman in a neighbouring nunnery and worshipped her. The holy woman preached to them the true religion. At the end of her instructive address the god said: 'Come with me, Madanarekhá, let me take you to the palace and show you your son.' Madanarekhá answered: 'What profit is there of natural affection, which is the cause of birth? The feet of this holy woman are my refuge.' When she said this, the god Yugabáhu bowed before the holy lady and returned to heaven. Madanarekhá took the vows; she received the name of Suvratá, and commenced a course of severe asceticism. In the meanwhile, owing to the power of her son, all kings were made to bow to King Padmaratha. Hence they gave her son the name of Nami. Being tenderly fostered by nurses, he gradually grew up. One day, when he had become a young man, King Padmaratha made Nami marry one thousand and eight maidens. After some days he put him on the throne, and himself destroying by severe asceticism the influence of actions, went to blessedness. Nami, subduing all kings, ruled the realm. Now, it happened that in the very same night in which Maṇiratha killed his own brother Yugabáhu, he was bitten by a serpent, and dying of the bite he went to the fourth hell. Then the ministers placed Chandrayaças, the son of Yugabáhu, on the throne, and he carried on the government. One day the well-bred royal white elephant of Nami, named Chaturdantin, tore up the post to which he was bound and started for the Vindhya forest. As the elephant was going along, he was seen by some people near the city of Sudarçana, and they told King Chandrayaças; the king tamed the elephant and brought him home, and tied him to an elephant-post. Nami, coming to hear of that, sent an ambassador to Chandrayaças in Sudarçanapura; the ambassador represented the matter to Chandrayaças. The king said to the ambassador:

> 'Fortune is not transmitted as a family heirloom, nor is she contained
> in a written edict;
> She should be won and enjoyed by the sword; the earth is for the
> enjoyment of heroes.'

Having said this, King Chandrayaças dismissed the ambassador. He went and told the whole story to King Nami, who flew into a passion. King Nami with his whole army arrived ready for battle at the city of Sudarçanapura. King Chandrayaças also was going out to meet him, but being warned by omens and dissuaded by his ministers, he barred up the gates of the main street of the city, and remained within the city while King Nami invested it. Suvratá found out this accumulation of evils, and went there to preach to both of them and to forbid the war. When Nami saw the ascetic lady on the field of battle, he rose up to meet her, and himself sat on the ground. The ascetic Suvratá admonished him, and said: 'King, whence this preparation for battle? Empty is the fortune of empire, enjoyments are terrible in their results; therefore turn away from fight, do not engage in strife. Moreover, what kind of a conflict can this be which is to be waged with your own brother?' King Nami said: 'Who is my brother?' Suvratá said: 'That very Chandrayaças is your brother,' and in order to convince him, pointed to the seal and the jewelled shawl. Nevertheless, he would not desist from war. Then Suvratá went to Chandrayaças. When he saw her, he said to himself: 'She is my mother, and also a great saint;' and he worshipped her with great humility. He gave her a seat, showing great devotion, and all the inmates of his harem honoured her. The king said: 'Noble lady, why have you begun this terrible penance?' When the king asked Suvratá this question, she told her own history. The king said: 'Well, where is that younger brother of mine now?' The noble lady said: 'He is outside the city, the very man who is besieging you.' Then

King Chandrayaças, highly delighted, went outside the city, and King Nami was delighted also when he found that he was his own elder brother. Both brothers hastened to meet one another. The elder brother rose up and embraced Nami, and said to him: 'My dear brother, ever since I saw my father's death I have had a loathing for the kingly office, but I have delayed so long because there was no one to hold the reins of government. Now do you adorn the throne. I will take a vow.' After exhorting King Nami with these words he anointed him king. So King Chandrayaças took a vow, and King Nami blazed with royal splendour like the sun. Once on a time King Nami contracted a burning fever that lasted for six months; it could not be alleviated by medicines, charms, or appliances; in short, a thousand expedients proved ineffectual. Then the queens themselves began to pound sandal-wood for his benefit. The tinkling of the many bracelets on their arms caused Nami great annoyance. Then by order of King Nami all the queens took off their bracelets one after another, but each kept one bracelet on her wrist for good luck. Then the king asked: 'Are the queens no longer pounding sandal-wood, as that sound is no longer heard?' The ministers said:

> 'All the queens, sir, are once more pounding sandal-wood;
> But the sound is not heard, as each has a solitary bracelet on her hand.'

Then a light flashed into the king's soul. As by many bracelets pain was produced, by few bracelets a little relief was produced; and so by this example it was shown that in the solitary state is great pleasure.

> 'Therefore, if ever this burning fever of mine should cease,
> Abandoning all attachment, I will become a solitary.'

With these thoughts in his mind, King Nami went to sleep, and in a dream he saw himself mounted on a white elephant. The next morning, having been woke up by the sound of conchs and drums, the king thought: 'Last night I had a notable dream.' While he was thus reflecting, he remembered his former birth—how in it he faithfully observed a vow, and became a god in the *práṇata kalpa*,* and how he fell from that position and became King Nami. So he placed his son on the throne and took a vow. The goddess that executes the orders of the Jina † gave him the dress of a monk, and he went out of the city. Indra determined to tempt him. He put on the appearance of a Bráhman, and came where he was. He stood before him, and spoke as follows: 'King, show compassion to living creatures. This city, without you, laments for that it is deprived of its ruler; this is not as it should be.' The hermit answered: 'Mankind receive the fruit of their own individual actions; so I attend to my own business. What is the use of troubling my head about other matters?' The Bráhman said: 'The city of Mithilá is in flames.' The hermit answered:

> 'In the burning of the city of Mithilá nothing of mine burns.'

The Bráhman said: 'Set up a rampart round the city.' The hermit said: 'Round the city of self-control I have set up the rampart of quietism, and mounted on it the engine of prudence.'

When Indra found that the hermit was no wise influenced, though plied with many speeches of this kind, he appeared in his true shape, bowed before him, and said:

> 'That family is praised whose virtue is ever undisturbed, O hermit,
> And thou who like a lotus-bud shalt never be defiled with the mud of infatuation.'

After the god Indra had praised the hermit in these words, and honoured him by circumambulating him three times, he flew up into the heaven, with his jewelled bracelets flashing.

Having thus rigidly observed his vow, Nami went to blessedness; and Madanarekhá also, having observed the

* The tenth world of the gods. Jacobi's translation of the 'Kalpa Sútra,' p. 271.

† Weber ('Ueber das Çatrunjaya Máhátmyam,' p. 43) informs us that each Jina has his Çásanadevi, or goddess that executes his orders.

rule of piety and virtue, went to heaven. Here ends the story of Madanarekhá concerning persistence in virtue.

Asceticism is the net in which all the senses are tamed like deer;
A myrobalan not dried up by action, that allays the fever of sin.

Now follows an example having reference to the subject of asceticism.

STORY OF NÁGADATTA.

In this very Bharata there was a city of the name of Kusumapura. In it there lived a merchant named Nágachandra; he had a son named Nágadatta.

A modest, ever-active, intelligent son, dear to his father and mother,
Who is full of merit, and naturally clever, is born by special good luck.

Once on a time that Nágadatta witnessed a religious celebration of eight kinds, which some pious man caused to be performed in the temple of the Jina. The son said to his father: 'Father, I also will acquire wealth with my own arms, and will perform such a ceremony, for

Who cannot increase the inherited property acquired by his father and transmitted by him to his children?
But seldom does a mother give birth to a man who without wealth is himself enterprising.*

Having gone through these reflections, he was anxious to go to a foreign land; so he sat down in the market-place. While he was there, a Bráhman was offering for sale for five hundred drachmas the following *çloka:*

That which ought not to be done is not to be done, even though a man's life be in his throat;
That which ought to be done is to be done, even though a man's life be in his throat.

Nágadatta bought this *çloka* for five hundred drachmas, whereat his father flew into a passion, and in his spite scolded him severely. Then Nágadatta went on a sea-voyage with five hundred ships. The ships, after sailing over the open sea for some days, fell into the hollow of the snake-encircled mountain. First one ship fell into the

* This closely resembles a verse on p. 82 of Dr. Schmidt's 'Çukasaptati.' I fear that my translation is only approximately correct.

hollow. When Nágadatta went on to the ship, a man there, who wished to commit suicide by starvation,* was restrained by Nágadatta, who taught him the formula of adoration. Now, five hundred parrots, who were natives of Suvarnadvípa, were residing in that place by order of their king, Sundara, in order to succour others. Whenever any one falls into a difficulty, they inform the king, and the king tries to devise a method for removing that difficulty. So one day Nágadatta fastened a letter to the foot of a parrot. The king, as soon as he read the story told in the letter, was unable to eat. He sent a crier with a drum round the city. A certain pilot who lived there touched† the drum, and said: 'I will, by means of an artifice, drive the ships out of the hollow of the snake-encircled mountain into the open sea.' The king gave him, by way of hire for his services, a lakh of gold pieces. The pilot embarked on a ship and went to the opening of the hole in the snake-encircled mountain, and said to Nágadatta: 'If one of you will do a daring deed, the ships will come out.' Nágadatta said to the old pilot: 'What is the nature of the daring deed?' The pilot replied: 'On the top of this mountain there is, in a palace of precious stones, an image of the lord Nemi, made out of a sapphire. In that palace are gongs of no‡ great size. If anyone climbs up this banyan-tree and sounds the gongs, crores of *bhárunḍa* birds§ will fly up, terrified by the sound of the gongs; the wind produced by the fanning of their wings will make the ships proceed on their way.' When the pilot said this, Nágadatta said: 'I will give a lakh of gold pieces to who-

* I have slightly altered the order of the words in the original.

† *Chhibitah*. The word is properly *chhivitah*, as Dr. Hoernle points out. It comes from *chhivai* = *spriçati*.—Hemachandra's 'Grammar' (ed. Pischel), iv. 182. I owe this reference to Dr. Hoernle.

‡ If the word 'no' were omitted the sense would be improved.

§ For enormous birds see the note on p. 221 of the first volume of my translation of the 'Kathá Sarit Ságara,' and the additional note on p. 630 of vol. ii. Some ships are released in this way in the 'Çatrunjaya Máhátmyam.' (See p. 31.) The 'Çatrunjaya' story is probably connected with the first part of *Der geraubte Schleier* (Kaden, 'Unter den Olivenbäumen,' p. 107). The jewel-collector is abandoned in both stories, in the Indian in a pit, in the European on a mountain.

ever goes there;' but, through fear of death, no one would go there. Then Nágadatta, wishing to benefit his fellow-creatures, being a hero of unparalleled audacity, climbed up on a branch of the banyan, and made his way there. He repaired to the temple of the lord Nemi, and, after worshipping him, sounded the gongs. Their sound made all the *bhárunḍa* birds fly up, and the fanning of their wings caused the ships to start. Then Nágadatta, having of himself acquired inward peace,* determined† on an eight days' course of self-mortification. At this moment a wandering hermit arrived to convert the eaters of human flesh. Nágadatta prostrated himself before the hermit with great devotion, and said: 'Reverend sir, give me a vow of starvation.' The hermit said: 'You have still some relics of action that must have enjoyment for their fruit.' Then the hermit converted the Vidyádhara,‡ and forbade the eating of human flesh, and flew up into the air. The Vidyádhara gave his own daughter to Nágadatta, and Nágadatta married her. The Vidyádhara gave Nágadatta sciences, spells, potent herbs, wealth, gold, jewels, and other things to his heart's desire, and preparing an air-going chariot, himself placed Nágadatta in it, and sent him home. When Nágadatta was thus reunited to his father and mother, he heard the good news§ that his ships had arrived. Then Nágadatta had a temple of the Jina built; he set up in it an image of the Jina, and he went three times a day to the temple that he had had made. There he performed worship to the image of the Jina, and did other virtuous acts. Here ends the story of Nágadatta having reference to the eight-day ceremony.

Now follows the story of the great hermit Sanatkumára, having reference to ascetic mortification:

* *Sámáyika.* See note 81 in Dr. Hoernle's translation of the 'Uvásaga Dasáo.'

† *Pratyákhyátam.* This word generally means 'rejected.'

‡ It is clear that there must be a lacuna somewhere. The Vidyádhara is now mentioned for the first time.

§ *Vardhápanakaṃ.*

In this very land of Bharata, in the district of the Kurus, is a city named Hastinágapura. In it lived a king named Açvasena. His wife's name was Sahadeví. One day there was born to them a very handsome son named Sanatkumára, whose birth was announced by fourteen dreams. A young Rájput of the name of Mahendrasiṃha, the son of Súraája, was a great friend of his. In course of time Sanatkumára learned all the accomplishments. One day, when he was entering upon the period of early manhood, Sanatkumára went to the wood at the time of the spring festival† to amuse himself with his friend. At that festival Sanatkumara beheld all kinds of interesting sights. Then a certain owner of horses presented the prince with a splendid horse. The prince mounted that horse. The horse ran away with the prince and carried him a long distance. The king proceeded in search of his son, but, though he looked for Sanatkumára, he did not find him. Then the father of Mahendrasiṃha asked King Açvasena to desist from the search, and Mahendrasiṃha himself went to look for his friend. He roamed about in a great forest for a year. Then one day he heard the cry of *sárasas*, and smelled the perfume of lotuses. He also heard a melodious sound. Going forwards, he beheld a lake, and in a bower of plantains near that lake he saw Sanatkumára recreating himself, followed about by crowds of ladies, and he heard the following laudatory verse being recited by a bard:

STORY OF PRINCE SANATKUMÁRA.*

> Victory to thee, the fortunate Sanatkumára, famed in the three worlds,
> The matchless jewel of the land of the Kurus, the son of King Açvasena!

When Mahendrasiṃha heard this verse being recited, he said to himself, 'Undoubtedly Prince Sanatkumara is in front of me.' On looking in front of him carefully, he

* This is identical with the second story in Jacobi's 'Ausgewählte Erzählungen in Maháráshtrí.'

† This appears to correspond exactly to the May ceremonies of our ancestors. See Chaucer's 'Knight's Tale,' 175-189 and 633-654.

recognised the prince. Mahendrasiṃha made a profound bow, and went to meet the prince. There was great joy on both sides, and Mahendrasiṃha was feasted with the utmost attention. The prince said: 'How are my father and mother?' His friend said: 'They are very unhappy, but tell me your own adventures.' The prince said: 'My wife, by name Vakulamatí, is coming; she knows the whole story by means of the Prajnapti science, and she will relate to you all my adventures.' When the prince had said this, he went to sleep.* Vakulamatí said: 'Listen, Mahendrasiṃha. When the prince was run away with by his horse, he was carried into a great forest; on the second day the horse was still galloping as fast as when he started; on the third day the horse was exhausted with hunger and thirst, and, lolling out its tongue, fell down. The prince got off. Then the horse died. Sanatkumára, for his part, with his eyes wildly rolling for want of water, fell senseless on the ground. Then a certain Yaksha that lived in the wood sprinkled him with water, so that he recovered consciousness. When the prince came to himself, he said: "Yaksha, where is such cold water to be found?" The Yaksha said: "It is found in the Mánasa lake." The prince said: "If I can bathe there, all the heat of my body will depart." The Yaksha took him to the Mánasa lake, and there he bathed and drank water; but while he was sitting on the shore of the lake he was seen by the Yaksha Asita, who was his enemy in a former birth. So a fight took place between the prince and the Yaksha.' At this point Mahendrasiṃha asked: 'What was the cause of the enmity between the prince and the Yaksha?' Vakulamatí said: 'I will tell you the cause of the enmity.

THE PREVIOUS BIRTHS OF SANATKUMÁRA AND THE YAKSHA.

'In a former period there was a king of the name of Vikramayaçás in the city of Kánchanapura; he had five hundred wives. In the same

* In the story as edited by Dr. Jacobi it is explained that the prince thought it unbecoming to be the narrator of his own exploits.

city lived a merchant of the name of Nágadatta; he had a wife named Vishṇuçrí, who was exceedingly beautiful. One day the king saw Vishṇuçrí as he was walking in the palace gardens. As his heart was fascinated with her beauty, he took possession of her, and introduced her into his harem. Nágadaṭta remained afflicted at being deprived of his wife, while the king, who had gained all he wished, passed his days in satisfaction. But one day the rest of the king's wives, being jealous of Vishṇuçrí, managed to kill her by means of sorcery. The king was exceedingly afflicted. He would not permit them to perform funeral rites with her body. But the chief men of the state, without the king's knowledge, cast the body of Vishṇuçrí outside the city. The king continued to abstain from eating and drinking, and all other bodily refreshments. The chief men of the city, hearing of the king's abstinence, took him on the third day to the park outside the city, and showed him Vishṇuçrí. When the king saw the evil-smelling body, he was filled with a spirit of renunciation, and took a vow. Having performed severe asceticism, he was born again in the third world of the gods. After the allotted period there was accomplished, he fell from it, and was born again in the city of Ratnapura as a merchant, of the name of Jinavarman. In the meanwhile, Nágadatta died from sorrow for the loss of his wife, and other ills, and was born in the city of Siṃhapura as the Bráhman Agniçarman. After the lapse of some time, the Bráhman Agniçarman took upon him the vow of a wandering mendicant with three staves,* and in the course of his ascetic tour he reached the city of Rájagṛiha. There he was invited by King Naraváhana to break his fast. It happened that at that very time the merchant Jinavarman came there, and was seen by that three-staved ascetic. He remembered his enmity in a former life, and said this to the king: "Sir, if I may be allowed to eat a pudding of rice and milk in a

* Professor Leumann, in 'Die Bharata-Sage,' p. 65, observes that the *tridaṇḍin* is a Bráhman monk. Of course the three bamboo staves were tied together.

copper vessel on the back of this merchant, I will break my fast, but not otherwise." The king ordered that that should be done. All the skin of the merchant's back came away, but he bore patiently that fruit of his actions in a former life. He worshipped the *chaityas*, and remained one month on the top of a lofty mountain in the statuesque posture, eating nothing; then he died, reconciled with all, and was born as Indra in the Saudharma world. The three-staved ascetic also died, and was born as Airávaṇa, the elephant on which Indra rides. He then fell from that position, and after various successive animal births, owing to the darkness of his ignorance, he was born as the Yaksha Asita. Indra, too, fell from his station, and was born as the Emperor Sanatkumára, in the city of Hastinágapura. Be assured that this is the cause of their enmity.

'Then a great combat took place between the Yaksha and the prince. The prince, being a skilful boxer, struck the Yaksha with his fist, but as the Yaksha was immortal, he could not die, but he fled. The Vidyádharas showered down a rain of flowers on the prince. Then Sanatkumára, proceeding further, beheld eight daughters of the Vidyádhara Mánavega. Mánavega bestowed them on him; the prince married them. After marrying them, he went to rest with the marriage bracelet on. Being somewhat wakeful [he heard a plaintive sound*]; on going forward after hearing that plaintive sound, he saw a palace on the Ratnaçṛinga mountain. Hearing the sorrowful lamentation of a woman in the palace, he went there, and conquering the Vidyádharas by his might, he married a beautiful lady named Sunandá, and he also married her sister, called Sandhyáyá.† He conquered the Vidyádhara Vajravega, and married a hundred maidens. And after this, at the time of battle, a discus was produced.'

While Vakulamatí was saying all this, the prince woke

* These words are inserted to make sense.

† Sandhyávali, in the form of the story edited by Jacobi. She is said there to be the sister of Vajravega.

up. Then he went, with a large retinue, to the Vaitáḍhya mountain; and thence, at the request of his friend, to Hastinágapura. Here follows the description, in detail, of his entry.* He was reunited to his parents, he obtained the nine treasures, and he conquered the six divisions of India. Now, about this time, it happened that a god named Sangamaka came from the heaven of Íçána to the court of Indra, the lord of Saudharma, and illuminated the whole court with his brightness. The gods asked this question: 'Is there any other god whose brightness is equal to that of this deity?'† Indra replied: 'Sanatkumára, in Hastinágapura, who wears a human form, possesses equal brightness. Then two gods went secretly, disguised as aged Bráhmans, to the court of the emperor to investigate the truth. The emperor asked them: 'Who are you, and whence did you come here?' They said: 'We have come to behold your beauty.' The Emperor Sanatkumára said: 'At present my body is smeared with oil, and there is no beauty in it. You must come when I give audience.' The gods went away, and came back when the emperor had bathed, and was sitting on his throne. When they saw his beauty, their faces became black. The emperor said: 'What is the meaning of your faces becoming black like this?' They said: 'We foresee the decay of your beauty.' The emperor said: 'How do you know?' They said: 'By the power of our divinity.' Then the two gods appeared in their real form, and, after praising him, went to their own place. The king felt a longing to renounce the world, and said to himself: 'Beauty, youth, and other things of the kind vanish in an instant; so what profit is there of this royal dignity, which is the cause of sin?' After going through these reflections, he took a vow in the presence of the spiritual teacher Vinayandhara, and,

* Jain writers frequently refer their readers to a common form, instead of repeating tedious details.

† This confusion between beauty and brightness is common in Hindu story-books. It is also found in European mythology. See my translation of the 'Kathá Sarit Ságara,' vol. ii., p. 133, note. See also the third note on the first of Miss Stokes's 'Indian Fairy Tales.'

having become a perfectly-instructed monk, he roamed about in accordance with the standard of solitary roaming.* After performing the abstinence of the sixth meal,† and of the eighth day,‡ he wandered about to obtain food, and once he was presented, through an error, with millet and rice. That bad food gave him seven diseases—dry itch, fever, asthma, cough, and rice-complexion,§ pain in the eyes, and pain in the stomach. All these seven diseases were very severe. For seven hundred years the kingly hermit bore the torture of these seven diseases, and did not use any remedies against them. One day he was praised by Indra before all his court. Accordingly, two gods assumed the form of physicians, and came to test the hermit. They bowed before the royal sage, and said: 'We are physicians that heal the body.' The hermit said: 'I do not try to get my external diseases healed, but the diseases of my internal part.' The physicians said: 'We know nothing about that; [we only heal the body].'‖ The hermit said: 'I also know how to cure that;' and rubbing with his spittle a finger that had fallen away, he restored it. The gods praised him, and returned to their own place. After completing such self-mortification, the royal hermit went to the third heaven of the gods. Here ends the story of the royal hermit Sanatkumára, having reference to mortification.

Then follows, by way of illustration, the story of Amarachandra, having reference to meditation.

> Meditation is the purifier of the whole world;
> It will be found to destroy the series of successive births;
> Meditation is indeed dear to the wise,
> Consuming the aggregate of all evil.

---

* This seems to be the eleventh standard. See Dr. Hoernle's 'Uvásaga Dasáo,' appendix iii., p. 43.

† Dr. Hoernle shows that this means fasting for two days and a half at a time ('Uvásaga Dasáo,' note 141).

‡ See Dr. Hoernle's translation of the 'Uvásaga Dasáo,' appendix iii., p. 39.

§ *Annaruchi* in the Sanskrit. Jacobi's Prákrit gives *bhattacchando*.

‖ I have inserted the words in brackets, as they seem to be required to make sense.

There never was, and there never will be, a female messenger equal to meditation,
For she brings about a union between men and immortal nymphs.

STORY OF PRINCE AMARACHANDRA.

In this very land of Bharata is a city named Ratnapura, and in it a king named Surasundara ruled his people justly.

In this city sticks were connected only with umbrellas, imprisonings with hair, and slaying of men was heard of only in chess;
Holes were picked in necklaces only; and hands paid the tribute of pressure only in marriage.*

So may the policy be described that prevailed in that city. The king had a wife named Vilásavatí, and a son named Prince Amarachandra, foretold by auspicious dreams. When he was twelve years old he was versed in the seventy-two accomplishments. One night, when Prince Amarachandra was reposing in his bed, he heard a plaintive sound of lamentation: 'Is there on the earth a man of Kshatriya lineage endowed with great courage? Is the earth bereft of heroes, that no one rescues me, though hearing such loud lamentation?' Prince Amarachandra, though nodding in drowsy sleep, when he heard the sound, like a bold Kshatriya, took his sword in his hand, and with a lightning-like bound sprang out of the castle and reached the open forest. Proceeding onward in the direction from which the sound came, he saw a man holding a woman by her braided lock and threatening her with a drawn sword. The prince called out to the man: 'You wicked and infamous ruffian! place yourself in front of me. Do you think to escape while thus attempting to kill this woman now that I have come? Let the helpless woman go, and fight with me.' The Vidyádhara said: 'You boy prince, white and tender, with mouth full of milk, do not presume to brave me. You will get no sweetmeats here. Go back; you are exceeding presumptuous.' The prince answered

* The whole passage is an elaborate pun. 'Stick' is also 'punishment' and 'the pressure of hands' means also 'oppressive taxes.' The other puns are obvious from the translation.

haughtily: 'You wicked ruffian, whither do you hope to escape, you infamous Vidyádhara?' While the prince was lashing the Vidyádhara with these bold words, a sudden flash of lightning came; and the Vidyádhara fled, terrified at the lightning. Then Prince Amarachandra said: 'Now, lady, who are you?' She answered: 'On the southern ridge of the Vaítáḍhya mountain there is a city named Gaganavallabha; in it dwells a Vidyádhara named Pavanagati, and I am his daughter, Chitralekhá by name. One day, as I was standing at a window, I was carried off by a Vidyádhara named Vásava, and he brought me here. Then you delivered me. He who now approaches must be my husband Kiraṇávali.' Thereupon Kiraṇávali asked Chitralekhá: 'My good lady, who is this man?' She answered: 'This man rescued me from the Vidyádhara.' Kiraṇávali was pleased, and gave the prince the power of entering another body.* He also gave him a necklace, and said: 'By the virtue of this necklace you shall escape defeat in the day of battle.' After this conversation they all went to their own place. The prince related the events of the night to his father. His father, pleased with his extraordinary courage, gave him the appanage of a prince.† At this conjuncture an ambassador arrived, and delivered respectfully this message to the king in open court: 'In the city of Çrípura there is a king of the name of Çríshena —his daughter Jayaçrí is approaching womanhood. One day the king said to her: "My dear child, what kind of husband would you like: an accomplished or a handsome or a rich husband?" His daughter answered: "A high-born and affectionate husband must be sought for." The king said: "My dear girl, how is he to be discovered?" He then went to bed at night full of anxiety about this matter, and while he was lying in a semi-wakeful condition, the goddess of his family said to him in a dream: "King,

* For a similar story see my translation of the 'Kathá Sarit Ságara,' vol. i., p. 22, with note. See also pp. 417, 418 of the same volume, and pp. 358 and 627 of vol. ii.

† *Kumálara bhuktiḥ*, perhaps for *kumára bhuktiḥ*. In the story of Metáryya a territory is given *kumára bhuktyai*.

you must construct a pavilion for the Svayamvara; the man who pleases her when she sees him must be her husband." Then I was sent here by the king. Now, send Prince Amarachandra.' Accordingly the prince was sent, and was conducted into the middle of the city with great pomp. Then, on the day of the Svayamvara all the princes, splendidly arrayed, sat down on elevated platforms; Jayaçrí entered, having adorned herself magnificently, accompanied by the female warder. She passed by all the other princes, and threw the garland of selection upon the neck of Amarachandra. The princes said: 'Prince Amarachandra, you must meet us before you celebrate your marriage.' When the prince heard this, he said to himself: 'I will first test the love or aversion of the charmer for whom all this effort is being made, for

'A loving lady gives life, but one full of hate takes it away;
Whether there be love or hate, a lover is apt to move anger in a woman.

Moreover, it has been said:

'His own queen* killed Vidúratha with a weapon concealed in her braid,
And an alienated wife killed the King of Benares with an anklet dipped in poison.'

The prince accordingly deliberated with his friend the minister, and spread the false rumour that he had a headache; then he employed his power of entering another body; the story went about that the prince was dead. When the princess heard this report she demanded firewood for her funeral-pyre; and did not desist, though her father and all the people and the princes did their best to dissuade her.† The princes asserted that Prince Amarachandra died of the fear which their threat had produced.

* Dr. Fitzedward Hall, in his introduction to the 'Vásavadattá of Subandhu,' informs us that this queen's name was Bindumatí. It is referred to in the 'Nítisára of Kámandaki,' vii. 54, and by 'Kullúka on Manu,' vii. 153, but no further details are given.

† For a similar test see my translation of the 'Kathá Sarit Ságara,' vol. ii., p. 12.

The princess dressed herself in white, and, mounted on a horse, approached the pyre which had been made for Amarachandra. Then the minister said: 'The princes assert that Amarachandra died from fear of them; now, in the family of our sovereigns a reproach like this makes even the dead live again.' The princes said: 'If you have the power, bestow life on Prince Amarachandra.' Immediately after this speech the prince recovered life by means of his previously acquired power. The princes said to him: 'Engage in combat before you celebrate your marriage, otherwise it will not be permitted.' Having made himself ready to battle, the prince, by the virtue of his necklace, conquered his enemies. Then Amarachandra celebrated his marriage, and returned to his own city, which he entered with great pomp.

In the meanwhile the joyful occasion was being celebrated by King Sundara with a dance of marionettes; a puppet was dancing there on a bamboo. At this moment a wandering hermit came flying through the air. He improved the occasion in these words: 'King, look at the puppet-show in your inner self; why do you gaze on an external puppet-show? For this continuance* of yours is the stage; your great name is the bamboo; the four migrations† of the soul are the four puppets; the four sins are the pegs, being anger, pride, delusion, and avarice; the eight actions are the drums; human forms are the attendants that tire the puppets; this intelligence‡ is the master of the puppet-show.' When King Sundara had in these words been instructed by the wandering hermit, he placed the prince on the throne and took a vow. Amarachandra with his consort Jayaçrí performed the functions of royalty. Now, the king was a slave to his passions. One day the king saw a man in Jayaçrí's palace. Having been called by the prince, he entered his hall of audience

* *Sthiti.* See the translation of the 'Sarva Darçana Sangraha,' p. 56.

† Into the bodies of men, animals, gods, and inhabitants of hell.

‡ *Jivo' yaṃ.*

to set his guards in readiness, and then he saw the very same man seated on the royal throne, and he exactly resembled the king himself.* The king left the city and went into the open country. In the meanwhile a minister named Kuruchandra was sent with a sword to kill the man. When the minister saw him he was astonished. He said: 'Who are you?' The man answered: 'I am King Amarachandra.' The minister questioned him about all the secrets of the government. He told them all. Then the two were made to undergo an ordeal. They both passed it successfully. The god, by virtue of his divine influence, made the king forget his power of entering another body. The king was banished by the minister, and went to a foreign land. He went up a mountain to commit suicide. He began to recite his wishes for the next birth. At that moment a hermit in a statuesque posture in a cave, foreseeing his future birth, said with a loud voice: 'King, do not act rashly.' When the king heard this he was astonished, and went and worshipped the hermit. The hermit said: 'King, why are you resolved on renunciation?' The king said: 'Holy sir, what is the cause of my being driven from my throne?' The hermit said: 'King, in a former age, in the city of Meghapura, there was a king named Megharatha. He had a minister named Priyankara, and a disbursing officer named Çubhankara. Priyankara was exceedingly correct in his conduct and discreet. One day he took a vow that he would restrict himself to a certain space at night. His vow was that he would not go to the door of his house at night. In the meanwhile the king sent to summon the minister. The minister declined to go. The king flew into a passion, and said that if he would not come he must give up the seal. He gave up the seal sooner than break his vow. The king said to Çubhankara: "You must take it." He answered: "No, indeed. In your majesty's service one cannot, even by the sacrifice of one's body, manage to

* A remarkably similar incident will be found in Longfellow's 'King Robert of Sicily.'

obtain a couple of *ghaṭikâs** time to devote to one's religious duties. So what profit is there of this royal service?" The king in his despondency said: "Then, what am I to do?" The minister said: "Give back the seal again to Priyankara with every mark of respect." The king went to the minister's house and conciliated him. The two ministers began to entertain a strong mutual regard. Finally they both took a vow. Çubhankara said to Priyankara: "At the favourable moment you must admonish me." Priyankara consented. Then they both went to heaven. Here is the god, the soul of Priyankara, that caused you to be banished from your kingdom, and you are the soul of Çubhankara, Amarachandra by name.'

Thereupon that god appeared in visible form in the very place where they were. The god said: 'I came to admonish you: you must not entertain unfavourable thoughts with regard to the queen.† The forms that appeared were assumed by me.' When the king heard this, recollection of his former birth arose in his mind. The god dismissed the king to his place. Amarachandra also, having established his son in his kingdom, and observed his vow faithfully, obtained salvation. Here ends the story of Amarachandra having reference to meditation.

People who offer worship to the mighty Jina with unbroken full dry grain,
Obtain an unbroken series of pleasures,
As a couple of parrots performing worship to the Jina with dry grain
Obtained unbroken everlasting happiness.

STORY OF THE COUPLE OF PARROTS.

Here follows the story of the couple of parrots, having reference to the offering of whole grain.‡

In this very land of Bharata is a city named Siddhapura. In a park outside the city is a *chaitya* sacred to the

* Some say that a *ghaṭikâ* is twenty-four minutes; some consider it equal to a *muhûrta*, or forty-eight minutes.—Monier Williams, s. v.

† This translation is conjectural.

‡ In the text there is an explanatory note on the above verses which I have omitted.

first Jina of the present *yuga;* in front of that temple of the Jina is a great fragrant mango-tree. In it dwelt a couple of parrots. Now, once on a time the hen-parrot said to her mate: 'Parrot, you must bring a head of rice from the rice-field; I am suffering from a longing for it.' The cock-parrot answered: 'My dear, this field belongs to King Çríkánta; if anyone takes a head of rice from this field, the king takes his head from him.' When the hen-parrot heard this, she said: 'Husband, there is no male in the world such a coward as you. You wish to see your wife die before your eyes in order to save your own life.' When the cock-parrot had heard this speech of the hen-parrot, he felt absolutely regardless of his own life, and brought some heads of rice from the rice-field. In this way he went on continually bringing heads of rice for his beloved before the very eyes of the keepers of the field. Then one day the king came to that field, and saw that in one part of it the rice had been devoured by birds. He said to the keepers of the field: 'How comes it, pray, that the field has been spoiled by birds?' Then the keepers of the field answered: 'King, a certain cock-parrot is for ever carrying off heads of rice; though we are on the look-out for him, he escapes like a thief.' Then the king, being angry, said: 'You must set nooses and catch that parrot, and bring him before me, in order that I may put him to death like a thief.' Accordingly, one day those men, in accordance with the king's order, entrapped in a noose and caught the cock-parrot; then they went with him to the king. Then the hen-parrot came after the cock-parrot lamenting. In the meanwhile those men produced the cock-parrot before the king, saying: 'Your majesty, here is that very cock-parrot that spoiled the rice-field.' The king drew his sword and prepared to kill him. Thereupon his wife, the hen-parrot, threw herself between the king and the cock-parrot, and said to the king: 'My lord, do not kill this husband of mine, the king of birds, that saved my life, but let him go free. This husband of mine counted his life but as straw to save mine; I, king, had a longing for your rice, and he satisfied it.' When the king heard that he laughed, and said to the parrot: 'Parrot, you are said to be a wise bird. How do you show your wisdom by throwing away your life for the sake of a female?' Then the hen-parrot said: 'My lord, a brave man disregards mother, father, and other relations, and abandons his life for the sake of his consort, as you, king, once on a time abandoned your life for the sake of Çrídeví. So wherein is this cock-parrot to blame?' The king was astonished at her speech, and vexed, and said to himself: 'How does this hen-parrot know my history?' He then said to her: 'Tell me, hen-parrot, how came you to use me as an illustration? Tell me the whole story; I feel great curiosity about it.' The hen-parrot said: 'My lord, long ago in your city there was a witch; she was full of many tricks and treacheries, and your wife paid her much attention. One day your wife Çrídeví made this request to the witch: "My good woman, I have become the most unfortunate of all the queens, so do you bestow on me some expedient by which I may become the king's darling." Then the witch gave her a fascinating spell. By the power of that spell she became the king's favourite, and was made the head queen, superior to all the ladies of the harem. Then she gave gifts, and enjoyed pleasures at will. One day that witch said to the queen: "Have you not, queen, gained all your heart's desires?" She answered: "Thanks to you, I have obtained them all. But I wish to test the affection of the king, whether he will make his life or death dependent on my life or death; this is the real test of affection." The witch said: "If this is your object, take herbs which are to be applied to the nose, in order that you may be as dead. Afterwards I will restore you to life with another root." The queen took the potent herbs, and the witch went to her own place. Thereupon the queen Çrídeví, having applied the herbs to her nose, lay down to sleep by the side of the king. In the morning she appeared to be dead. Accordingly in the king's palace a sound of lamentation arose. Everybody began to lament, saying: "The queen is dead—is dead." Then, by the command of the king, many people skilled in spells and amulets* came together to see her, but they also gave her up. Then the ministers said to the king: "Your majesty, let the last rites be performed to her corpse." The king said: "Let me also be consumed with fire along with her." The people exclaimed: "Sir, it is not fitting that a man should die for the sake of a mere woman." The king said: "What will not affection do?" So he quickly got together logs of sandalwood, and in spite of many similar remonstrances would not desist. Then, while the drums were beaten and the people shed tears, the king proceeded to the cemetery, and making a funeral-pyre, he prepared to enter the flame with his darling wife. At that moment a witch came running up, making a lamentation while still at a distance, and said to the king: "Sir, do not do that rash act." The king said: "Reverend lady, I wish to live with my beloved." The witch said: "If that is so, wait a moment, and I will restore your beloved to life, in the sight of all the people." When the king heard that, his heart became full of joy. Then she put another root into the nose of the queen, and she recovered. When the king saw her alive he danced with his arms in the air. Then the king returned into the city with Çrídeví, and bestowed on the witch the gift of five things. The king ruled with Çrídeví as his consort. The witch died, and was born again as a hen-parrot. Just now, when I saw Çrídeví at your side, I remembered my former birth.'

When the queen heard this speech of the hen-parrot, she said: 'Revered one, how comes it that you were born as a bird?' The hen-parrot said: 'Queen, owing to the power of actions souls go through all conditions.' When the king heard this he was pleased with the couple of parrots, and granted immunity from death to the cock-parrot. He said to the keepers of the rice-field: 'You must leave out every day near the field a *droṇa* of rice for this pair of parrots.'

* *Yantra.* The word may perhaps mean 'blunt surgical instruments.'

When the couple of parrots heard this, they flew away and went to the mango-tree. Then the hen-parrot, having had her longing satisfied, laid a couple of eggs; and at the same time her rival, the other hen-parrot, laid an egg in her own nest. While she went to get grain, the first hen-parrot carried off her egg out of jealousy. When she returned and looked for her own egg, lo! it was not to be seen. Then she fell unconscious on the earth. When the first hen-parrot saw her lamenting, she brought back the egg and laid it once more in the nest. After rolling on the earth, the second parrot returned once more to the nest, and saw her own egg, at which she was delighted. On account of this the former hen-parrot was doomed to suffer for her sins hereafter, but as in her repentance she returned the egg, she became liable to suffering in one birth only. From the two eggs sprang one cock and one hen-parrot; and the parent birds brought rice from that heap of rice that was placed for them by the king's orders, and so nourished their young ones. Now, one day there came to that temple of the Jina a wandering holy hermit, who possessed supernatural knowledge. The king went with a crowd of men and women to pay his respects to the hermit. Then, having done obeisance to the holy man, the king asked him the fruit of offering whole grain. Then the holy man said:

> 'Men who offer worship to the mighty Jina with unbroken full dry grain,
> Obtain an unbroken series of pleasures.'

Hearing this fruit of offering whole grain, all the people became eager about it, and kept offering whole grain. Then the parrots said: 'Let us also offer whole grain.' So both of them made that offering. One day they said to their young ones: 'Do you also place unbroken grain in front of the mighty Jina, that you may obtain unbroken felicity.' So all the four every day with great devotion offered whole grain to the mighty Jina, and when their allotted period came to an end, they died and went to the world of the gods. After enjoying the pleasures of the gods, the soul of the cock-parrot became a king of the name of Hemaprabha, in the city of Hemapura. The soul of the hen-parrot also fell from the world of the gods, and became Hemaprabha's wife, Jayasundarí by name. The second hen-parrot also, after wandering about in the course of mundane existence, was born as another wife of Hemaprabha's, Rati by name. The king had five hundred other wives also, but the two first wives were most dear to him, owing to the fact that affection had subsisted between them and the king in a previous birth. One day the king contracted a painful burning fever. At one moment he rolled on the ground, at another he anointed his limbs with sandalwood juice, and at another he rolled on the bed; still, he could not obtain any relief. Then physicians skilled in spells applied their remedies; but no one's remedy took effect on the king. Then an expiatory rite was performed; a great ceremony in honour of the mighty Jinas was performed in the Jaina temples; the deities of the clan were worshipped; but still the fever-heat in the king's body was not allayed. After all this, during the course of the night a certain Rákshasa appeared, and said to the king: 'King, are you asleep or awake?' The king said: 'How can I sleep?' The Rákshasa said: 'If one of the queens makes herself a victim and hurls herself into the sacred fire-pit you will recover; otherwise you have no chance.' When the Rákshasa had said this, he went to his own place. The king said to himself: 'Is this all a juggling delusion, or have I seen a dream to this effect owing to the suffering which has reduced me? No, this cannot be a dream, for I saw the Rákshasa before me in bodily presence.' So when the king woke up in the morning he told Sumantrin the occurrence of the night. He said: 'Let this expedient even be adopted to save your life.' Then the minister told the story of the Rákshasa in the presence of all the queens. Though they heard the story, all the queens remained with their eyes fixed on the ground out of regard for their own lives. Thereupon the queen consort Rati, with the lotus of her face expanded, said this: 'If the king's life is saved by the sacrifice of mine, I shall have attained all my objects.' Then the minister had made a window and under it a great fire-pit. The queen adorned herself, and said to the king: 'My lord, live by means of my life. I will enter the fire.' The king said: 'Queen, do not abandon your life for my sake; I will endure the consequences of my actions committed in a previous state of existence.' Then the queen said: 'My lord, if my life is to be lost for your sake, let it go.' Having said this, she ascended to the window and prepared to throw herself into the fire-pit. Thereupon the Rákshasa, pleased with her courage, said: 'My good lady, I am pleased with your courage, so ask your heart's desire.' The queen said: 'The king, Hemaprabha by name, who was given to me by my father and mother, is my boon,* so I ask for him; I do not require any other.' The Rákshasa answered: 'Nevertheless, ask one, since the appearance of a god should not be void of fruit.' The queen said: 'If the case is so, let my husband live for a long time free from disease.' The Rákshasa said: 'So be it;' and having said this, he went to his own place. Then the king was pleased, and said: 'Queen, ask a favour from me; you have bought me as your slave with the price of your life.' The queen said: 'If this is so, let the boon be laid up in store; when I ask for it, it should be given.' One day after this Rati was propitiating the family goddess in order to obtain a son, and she said: 'If I am blessed with a son, I will offer up the son of Jayasundarí as a victim in your honour.'† As fate would have it, both the queens had born to them sons endowed with many auspicious marks. The queen consort Rati was much pleased, and said to herself: 'The family divinity has bestowed a son on me; so how can I offer her the son of Jayasundarí as a victim?' While she was turning it over in her mind, she

* The word translated 'boon' also means 'husband.'

† For the subject of human sacrifices in India, see Dr. Rájendra Lál Mitra's essay referred to on p. 445 of vol. i. of my translation of the 'Kathá Sarit Ságara.' Many other references will be found in the index at the end of vol. ii.

hit on a device. She said to herself: 'I will do what I want by means of the king's boon.' Having determined on this, she watched her opportunity, and said one day to the king: 'My lord, do you mean to grant me the boon which you promised me some time ago?' Then, on the strength of that boon, she asked the king to give her the government of the kingdom for five days. The king consented. Then the queen began her five days' rule. So in the last watch of the night she had Jayasundarí's son brought; she gave him a bath, and worshipped* him with sandalwood, flowers, and grain, and laid him on a frame, and placed the frame on the head of a slave-girl; and so, surrounded with a train, and with drums beating, she went to worship the goddess. At this point a Vidyádhara named Súri, lord of Kánchanapura, who was travelling through the air in a sky-chariot, saw the boy on the frame; so he carried off the prince and put in his place another boy that was dead; he then returned to his own place and gave the prince to his own wife. Then the queen-consort Rati took the dead boy to the temple of the goddess, and dashing him down on the ground, accomplished her desire. Jayasundarí, deprived of her son, spent her days in great affliction. Then that Vidyádhara Súri, in the city of the Vidyádharas, gave that boy the name of Madanakumára. In time he acquired the magical arts of the Vidyádharas. One day, as he was roaming through the air in a chariot, he saw his own mother seated at a window afflicted at the loss of her son. Then Madanakumára, filled with great affection, seized his own mother and put her in the chariot; and the queen could not be satisfied with gazing on that prince. Then the queen's attendants, seeing that Jayasundarí was carried off, cried out with a loud voice. But though King Hemachandra was very brave, what could he do on the ground against a Vidyádhara? Then the king said to himself: 'This second calamity is like the rubbing of salt into a wound; first comes the death of my son, next the carrying off of

* The point that a human victim is also an object of worship is, I think, brought out by Mr. Frazer in the 'Golden Bough.'

my wife.' On this account he spent his days in sorrow. In the meanwhile the Vidyádhara Madanakumára had carried off his mother, and was with her in a garden of his own city, in the shade of a fragrant mango-tree near a tank. But the soul of the hen-parrot that was in the world of the gods, owing to its affection for the Vidyádhara in a former life, perceived by its limited knowledge what was going on, and said to itself: 'Oh! the nature of the universe! Here is my brother carrying off his own mother with the intention of marrying her; so I will admonish him.' Then she assumed two forms, that of a male and that of a female ape, and came to the mango-tree. Then the male ape said to the female ape: 'My dear, this is called the bathing-place of the aspirant: animals that plunge in this water attain the condition of humanity; men that plunge in here acquire, owing to the virtue of this bathing-place of the aspirant, the condition of gods; about this there is no doubt.* Now, there are two human beings sitting here in the shade of this fragrant mango-tree.' The female ape said: 'Think intently of their form, and leap into this well, that you may become a woman and I will become a man.' Then the monkey said: 'Fie! fie! who would mention the name of this man who has carried off his mother with the idea of marrying her? What desire have we for the form of that villain?' When they heard this speech of the monkey, both the Vidyádhara and his mother were astonished. The Vidyádhara said to himself: 'How can I be her son?' The queen said to herself: 'How can this Vidyádhara be my son?' While they were both engaged in these reflections, the Vidyádhara said to the male monkey: 'Great sir, how can this be true?' The monkey replied: 'It is indeed true: about this matter there

* Compare Jacobi's introduction to his edition of the 'Pariçishta Parvan,' p. 26. This incident is found in the story of Rájasimha in the 'Kathá Prakáça,' as appears from an analysis of a MS. of that work in the India Office Library, made by Professor Eggeling, which he has kindly lent me. A female monkey becomes a woman by throwing herself from a tree at the time of *sankramana;* but the male monkey, her mate, is afraid to imitate her example, and retains his simian nature.

can be no doubt; if you do not believe it, in this mountain-thicket there is a hermit, who possesses absolute knowledge, now performing austerities in the statuesque posture; go and ask him.' When the two monkeys had finished this conversation, they disappeared. Thereupon the Vidyádhara prince, accompanied by his mother, went into the mountain-thicket, and said to the hermit that possessed absolute knowledge: 'Revered sir, is the thing asserted by the monkey true?' The hermit replied: 'It is indeed true; but I will not relate the facts, for fear that it may impede my meditation. There is a man possessing absolute knowledge in the city of Hemapura, who will tell you the whole story.' When the Vidyádhara prince heard this, he humbly bowed before the hermit and went to his own city. He left his first mother in a solitary place, and went to his second mother, and said to her: 'Mother, who is my real mother, and who is my father?' Then the Vidyádharí said: 'My son, I am your mother, and this Vidyádhara is your father.' The prince said: 'No doubt, mother, this is true, but I have a special reason for asking.' Then the Vidyádharí said: 'Your father knows the real truth about it.' Then he questioned the Vidyádhara, and he told the story of the frame, and continued: 'Consequently, I do not really know who your parents are.' Then the prince said: 'The monkey and the hermit possessing absolute knowledge said that the woman I have brought here is my mother; so I will go to the hermit possessing absolute knowledge in the city of Hemapura and so remove my doubt.' When he had said this, he went with his mother to Hemapura, and there put a question to the possessor of absolute knowledge, while Jayasundarí took a seat in the midst of a crowd of women. At this moment King Hemaprabha, accompanied by his attendants, was receiving religious instruction from the mouth of his spiritual preceptor. Then the king, seizing a favourable opportunity, said to the possessor of absolute knowledge: 'Revered sir, who carried off that wife of mine, Jayasundarí?' The possessor of absolute knowledge answered: 'King, she was carried off by her son.' Then the king asked, with his heart full of wonder: 'Revered sir, whence has she a son? The only son that she had was devoured by accursed death. She never had a second son. Your speech is not true. It does not tally with facts.' Then the hermit, in order to remove the king's doubt, told the story of the family goddess, and Madanakumára also heard the tale. Then he was delighted at beholding his own father. So Madanakumára was reunited to his father, and great rejoicing took place. Then Jayasundarí said to the possessor of absolute knowledge: 'Revered sir, what deed brought about my separation from my son?' The hermit answered: 'Because in a former life, in your birth as a parrot, you took away the egg of your rival for sixteen *muhúrtas*,* therefore in this life you have been separated from your son for sixteen years. For

> He who causes joy or grief to another, even though it be no larger than a grain of mustard,
> Sows a seed in the fruitful field of the next life, and reaps abundant fruit.

When Jayasundarí heard this speech from the hermit she was afflicted with remorse, and asked the forgiveness of the queen-consort Rati, and Rati also asked her forgiveness. Thereupon King Hemaprabha said to the hermit: 'Revered sir, what merit did I perform in a former life that in this life I have obtained such a vast kingdom, with Jayasundarí for my consort?' Then the hermit said: 'In a former life, in your birth as a parrot, you, with your son and daughter, offered whole grain to the mighty Jina; then you died and went to the world of the gods; thence you fell and obtained a kingdom.' When the king had thus been instructed with regard to his former life, he gave his kingdom to the son of Rati, and he and Jayasundarí and Madanakumára became hermits; and after they had observed their vow for a long time the three died, and were born as gods in the seventh world of the gods. After they have fallen thence, they will be born as

* A *muhúrta* is properly a period of forty-eight minutes.

human beings and attain perfection. Here ends the story of the parrot, having reference to the offering of whole grain.

Worship that son of Nábhi* to whom the king of the gods gave his thousand eyes,
Whose two feet with their host of nails gleam as if with all the sciences;
The worship of the Jina is celebrated with sweet perfumes, incense, and dry whole grain;
With flowers, with choice candles, food-offerings, fruit and water.
A man obtains by the worship of the Jina with perfumes a sweet-smelling body, strength, and beauty;
Prosperity, and in addition surely the highest good.
As King Jayasúra, together with his wife, in his third birth,
Attained to salvation by worshipping the hermit, the mighty Jina, with perfumes.

Now follows the story of King Súra, having reference to worship by means of perfumes.

### Story of King Súra and his Wife, Çrutimatí, who were born again as King Siṃhadhvaja and Queen Madanávalí.

In this very Bharatakshetra, on the mountain of Vaitáḍhya, in the city of Gajapura, reigned a lord of the Vidyádharas, named King Súra. He had a wife named Çrutimatí. One day a god fell visibly from the world of gods, and became conceived in her. Then, having become pregnant, she was seized with a longing. After her longing had remained two days without being gratified, she became feeble of body. Then the king said to her: 'Queen, why are you so afflicted?' She answered: 'As I have become pregnant, there has arisen in me a longing to worship the gods in the holy place on the Ashṭápada mountain.' When she had said this, King Súra, accompanied by the queen, went to the Ashṭápada mountain. There the queen performed duly the ceremony of worship, with the sound of sharp-sounding kettle-drums, conchs, drums, and cymbals, and then with delighted heart offered sweet-smelling perfumes to the mighty Jinas. After she had performed worship, and fulfilled her longing, the king and she proceeded to

* *I.e.*, Ṛishabha.

descend from the mountain. When they came to a dense thicket of the forest, an intolerable smell was wafted towards them. The queen was astonished in her heart, and said to the king: 'King, what produces this evil smell in this wood, which is full of the perfume of flowers?' He said: 'Do you not see, queen, in an open space in front of us a great hermit standing in the statuesque posture* with arms uplifted? This evil smell arises from his body, heated by the rays of the sun, defiled with dirt, and afflicted with perspiration.' The queen said: 'My lord, the law of the Jina is to be revered, but if the hermit were to be washed with pure water, he would be more agreeable; therefore, let his body be washed with pure water, in order that his evil smell may depart.' Then, at the earnest request of his wife, the Vidyádhara king brought water in the hollow of a lotus and washed the hermit's body. Afterwards the two of them anointed the body of that hermit with sweet-smelling sandalwood perfume; then they bowed before him, and ascended their chariot to make a pilgrimage to another holy place. Then a swarm of bees, attracted by the sweet scent, left a tree† which was laden with a multitude of flowers, and settled on the body of that hermit. The hermit endured patiently the suffering caused by the bees also. At this juncture the Vidyádhara and his wife, having worshipped the holy places, came where the hermit was. The queen could not see the hermit, so she said to the Vidyádhara: 'My lord, here is that very spot where the hermit was, so how is it that I do not see the hermit there?' The Vidyádhara looked down, and saw what seemed a peg in the place where the hermit had been. They both descended from the region of the air and looked, and then they discovered that the hermit was being devoured by bees. They were both of them very much vexed, and said: 'Out on us!

* A hermit, while in this posture, does not bathe. See Dr. Hoernle's 'Uvásaga Dasáo,' appendix iii., p. 41.

† I have inserted the words 'a tree.' There is no corresponding word in the original.

Instead of doing the hermit a good turn, we have done him an injury.' Then they both joined to drive away the bees; and at that very moment, the effect of all former acts of injury to living beings, which had suffering for a result, having been destroyed, that hermit obtained limitless knowledge. Then the four kinds of gods came there, and in succession praised the *kevalin;** and then King Jayasúra and his consort said to the hermit: 'Prince of hermits, forgive our fault.' Then the hermit said: 'Do not be afflicted in your minds; every soul suffers the consequences of every act that it commits. But the person who, beholding a hermit defiled with dirt, exhibits loathing, becomes, on account of the sin of that act, an object of loathing in birth after birth, for—

> 'Those men are not really defiled who are defiled with dirt, mud, or dust;
> Those who are defiled with the mud of sin are truly defiled in this world.'

When Queen Çrutimatí heard this speech, she was terribly afraid, and said: 'Revered sir, I, wicked woman that I was, felt loathing for you on a former occasion;' so again and again she clung to the hermit's feet and begged his forgiveness. The hermit said: 'My good woman, do not be afflicted. By thus asking forgiveness you have destroyed the whole effect of your unholy deed; but in one birth you will have to suffer the due consequences of your action.' When they had heard this explanation, and afterwards an exposition of the law, Jayasúra and his consort returned to their own city. Then, after some time had elapsed, both of them took a vow. They died, and were born in Saudharma. When the period of his life in the world of the gods had expired, the king fell from heaven, and became a king of the name of Siṃhadhvaja, in the city of Surapura; the queen's soul became his wife, by name Madanávalí. Owing to attachment in the previous life, that Madanávalí became dearer to the king than any

* One who had obtained unlimited knowledge. The four kinds of gods are *bhavanavaï*, *vánamaṃtara*, *jotisa*, and *vemániya*.—Weber, 'Bhagavatí,' p. 203.

other lady of his harem. Now, it must be remembered that, owing to her disgust at the hermit in her former life, the guilt of an unholy act attached to her. That guilt began to display itself. An evil smell arose in the body of the queen. The people of the city fled, unable to bear that evil smell. The king, seeing her condition, showed her to the physicians. They said it was incurable, and they also abandoned her. Then the king had a palace built in the middle of the forest, and abandoned the queen there, causing her to be guarded by trusty warriors stationed at a distance. The queen said to herself: 'This is the result of my actions in a former life, so I must bear it with unflinching mind.' While she was going through these reflections, she saw a pair of parrots in a fragrant mango-tree. The hen-parrot said to her mate: 'My lord, tell me some wonderful story.' Madanávalí thought: 'I also will listen, in order that I may forget my grief.' The cock-parrot said: 'My dear, shall I tell you a fictitious tale, or something that has actually happened?' The hen-parrot said: 'Tell me something that has actually happened.' Then the cock-parrot told how there was a Vidyádhara of the name of Jayasúra, how his wife was named Çrutimatí, how they went to Ashṭápada, how they worshipped the hermit with perfume, how they went to the world of the gods, how they fell thence into the city of Surapura, and became King Siṃhadhvaja and his wife Madanávalí. Thus the cock-parrot related the whole story of Madanávalí from the very commencement. The queen said to herself: 'How does this bird know three lives of mine? Never mind, now I will hear what he has to say.' The hen-parrot went on to say: 'My lord, where is that Madanávalí now?' The cock-parrot said: 'You may see her sitting before you alone in this palace.' The hen-parrot went on to ask: 'My lord, is there any remedy for her complaint?' The cock-parrot said: 'This evil smell has attached to her in this life because in a former birth she showed disgust at a hermit; if for seven days she worships the mighty Jina three times a day with sweet-smelling substances, she will be relieved from this affliction in the form of an evil smell.'* Then Madanávalí, hearing this, threw down all her ornaments as a present in front of the parrot couple; but they, after holding this conversation, instantly disappeared. The queen, with her heart full of astonishment, said to herself: 'How does this parrot know my history? When I get a favourable opportunity, I will ask some hermit, that possesses supernatural knowledge, the story of the parrot; for the present I will do what the cock-parrot said. I will worship the mighty Jina with sweet-smelling substances.' Accordingly she worshipped the mighty Jina for seven days. After seven days her body became free from disease, and the evil smell left her. Then the soldiers, who were guarding her, brought the good news to the king that the evil smell had left the body of Madanávalí. Then the king was delighted, and put her on an elephant, and brought her to his own palace. Then he had great rejoicings celebrated in the city. At this conjuncture the man who took care of the public gardens said to the king: 'King, to-day there has arrived in the gardens the hermit Amṛitatejas, who possesses unlimited knowledge.' Thereupon Madanávalí said to the king: 'My lord, this is a cause of rejoicing, greater even than the cause of rejoicing we had before.' Then the king, accompanied by Madanávalí, went to pay his respects to the hermit. He bowed before him, and listened to his exposition of the law. Then Madanávalí, choosing a favourable opportunity, said to the hermit: 'Revered sir, who is that cock-parrot that instructed me when I had fallen into calamity?' The *kevalin* said to her: 'My good woman, your husband in a former life, being a god, descended from the world of the gods, and put on the form of a parrot, and came to you.' The queen again asked the *kevalin*: 'Revered sir, is that god present in this assembly of gods or not?' The hermit answered: 'It was that god that is standing in front of you, wearing a jewelled bracelet as an ornament.' The

* See vol. i. of my translation of the 'Kathá Sarit Ságara,' p. 25, and the supplementary note on p. 628 of vol. ii.

queen said to the god: 'Noble sir, when I had fallen into calamity, I was most opportunely instructed by you. What service can I render you as a return for that benefit?' The god said: 'My good woman, on the seventh day from to-day I shall fall from the world of gods, and become the son of a Vidyádhara; then you must admonish me.' The queen agreed to do what he said, saying: 'If I have the requisite knowledge, I will admonish you.' When the god had held this conversation he went to his own place. Then the queen said to the king, her husband: 'My lord, abandon your love for me; I will take a vow before the hermit.' The king said: 'Queen, when the proper season comes we will both of us take a vow.' Then the queen by great persistence broke the bond of affection, and took a vow. The king became a lay disciple, and returned to his own house. Madanávalí went on performing penance. Now, on the seventh day that god fell from heaven, and became the son of a Vidyádhara. They gave him the name of Mṛigánka. Gradually he grew up to man's estate. Now, one night it happened that Madanávalí, while engaged in meditation at the door of her convent, was seen by that prince Mṛigánka as he was roaming through the air in a chariot. Then he descended from his chariot, and told her of his supernatural power, and said to her: 'My good lady, why do you perform a terrible penance? If you are performing it for the sake of enjoyment, then listen to my words: I am a young Vidyádhara named Mṛigánka, and I am now going to marry Ratnamálá. But now that I have seen you, I ask you to ascend my chariot; I have no need of Ratnamálá. Come and enjoy with me the happiness of the Vidyádharas.' Though he said this, and uttered many coaxing speeches, Madanávalí did not swerve from her firm virtue. The more he exhibited the passion of love, the more engrossed with her meditation was Madanávalí. At last, while she was bearing patiently his persecution, there arose in her unlimited knowledge. Then the gods praised her. Then Madanávalí gave instruction in religion to that Vidyádhara named Mṛigánka. Thereupon the Vidyádhara asked: 'Lady,* how is it that I have an affection for you?' Then Madanávalí told him his three births, and said: 'Hence it is that you fell in love with me. Now, abandon passion, the cause of the ceaseless revolution of births and deaths. Strive to attain religion.' When the Vidyádhara had heard about his former births from the *kevalin*,† he resolved on self-renunciation, and took a vow. Having performed penance, he went to blessedness. Madanávalí also, having duly observed the way of life of a *kevalin*,‡ and having thus prevented future births, obtained salvation.

Here ends the story of Madanávalí, having reference to the offering of perfumes by way of worship.

Moreover, whoever offers in front of the Jina an offering of food,§ full of faith,
That man obtains the blessed happiness of men and gods, like the ploughman.

He who, endowed with much faith, brings an offering to the moon-like feet of the mighty Jina,
Enjoys the excellent enjoyments of gods, Asuras, men and snakes.

STORY OF THE PLOUGHMAN WHO BECAME A KING.

In this very land of Bharata there is a city named Kshemapurí; in it there was a king named Súrasena. Now, long ago there was a city named Dhanyá belonging to the family of that king, and in the family of the same king there was a king named Siṃhadhvaja. Now, in the entrance to that city a hermit practising a severe form of penance had established himself in the middle of the road in the statuesque posture. But the people entering the city thought him a nuisance, and saying, 'This man is of evil omen to us,' persecuted him. Therefore the god, who dwelt in the city, became enraged at this time with the citizens. In the meanwhile, as the hermit went on bearing patiently terrible persecution, unlimited knowledge arose in him, and at that

* In the original the masculine is used.
† The masculine form is used.
‡ *Kevaliparyáya*.
§ *Nevajjam*, this being a Prákṛit *gáthá*. In the Sanskrit passages that follow, the Sanskrit equivalent *naivedya* is used.

very moment he died. Then the god, who presided over the city, made up his mind to kill all the citizens, but was propitiated by the king by means of great devotion. Then the god said: 'King, remove this city, and settle it somewhere else, in order that there may be security.' Then the city was settled on another site, and thus arose the town of Kshemapurí. Now, that god held the true faith, and so he went and dwelled in the temple of Ṛishabha, in the form of a lion, though that temple was in the forest. He would not allow wicked people even to enter the temple. Now, at this time a ploughman was driving his plough in front of the temple, and his wife was bringing him his dinner* from the city of Kshemapurí. In this way he passed his days. Now, one day a wandering hermit came there to worship the Jina. Seeing the hermit, the ploughman also entered the temple. He bowed before the hermit, and said: 'Revered sir, how is it that I am so unhappy in this human birth?' The hermit said: 'In a former birth you did not give gifts to hermits—you did not make an offering of food to the Jina; it is for this reason that you are deprived of enjoyments.' When the ploughman heard this, he took a vow in the presence of that hermit as follows: 'From to-day I will set apart a portion of my own dinner, and, making it into a ball, will offer it as a food-offering in front of the Jina. Moreover, I will give gifts to the hermits to the utmost of my power.' The hermit said: 'My son, having taken the vow, do not neglect to perform it.' When the hermit had said this, he flew up into the air. Accordingly the ploughman every day, when his dinner came, presented a food-offering in front of the Jina. One day his food came late, when he was very hungry. He sat down to eat, and was lifting a morsel to his mouth, when suddenly he remembered his vow. Immediately he put down the morsel, and went into the temple of the Jina with the food-offering. As he was entering, he saw a great lion with a mouth terrible with teeth. Then the ploughman said to himself: 'How can I

* *Bhaktam*, probably boiled rice.

eat my dinner without presenting the food-offering? Whether I die or live to-day in the presence of the Jina, I must certainly give him the offering.' So he adopted a courageous course, and entered, and as he advanced into the temple, the lion kept receding with backward steps. The god was much pleased with this courage of his, and when he had fearlessly entered the temple of the Jina, the lion was not to be seen. After the ploughman had, with a heart full of a weight of devotion, offered the food to the august Jina, he returned to his own place. Then that very god, in order to test the virtue of the ploughman, appeared before him in the form of a hermit while he was eating his dinner.* Just as the ploughman was lifting a morsel to his mouth, the hermit appeared; so the ploughman, in pious joy, gave the hermit what he had taken to eat. Then he took another handful of rice, and was preparing to eat it, when again the hermit came in the form of an old man; to him also he gave rice. When he was again preparing to eat, the hermit came as a young man, so he gave him what remained of his meal. Thus he gave food to the hermit three times. Then the god was pleased with his virtue, and revealed himself in his divine form, and said to the ploughman: 'I am pleased with your entire devotion to the faith of the adorable Jina, so ask a boon.' Then the ploughman said: 'If you are pleased with me, my lord, then separate me from this herd.' The god said, 'So be it,' and returned to his own place. The ploughman related to his wife the whole story of his interview with the god, and she said: 'My lord, you are fortunate, in that by your entire faith you have propitiated the mighty Jina.' By thus welcoming his success she earned merit.

Now, at this time there was in the city of Kshemapurí Vishṇuçrí, the daughter of King Súrasena, an exceedingly beautiful girl. As the king could not find a suitable

* Compare the beginning of Grimm's No. 81, Bruder Lustig. St. Peter appears three times to him as a beggar, and Bruder Lustig gives him three-fourths of his loaf and three out of his four kreuzers.

husband for her, he proceeded to hold her *Svayaṃvara*, and summoned to it all princes. On the day of the *Svayaṃvara* all the kings, magnificently adorned, ascended platforms. Then Vishṇuçrí, decked with ornaments on all her limbs, came among the suitors; and at the same time that ploughman, having heard of the *Svayaṃvara*, came to see it. The female warder, having described in succession the families of all the kings, at last came with Vishṇuçrí near the door. She saw the ploughman standing on his plough. Being inspired by the god, the princess passed over all the princes and chose the ploughman. Then her mother and father were afflicted. They said: 'Unhappy is our lot, since our daughter has chosen a ploughman.' Then, too, all the kings were enraged. They said: 'Though we were present, this girl has chosen a ploughman. We cannot well blame the girl or the ploughman; the blame must fall on King Súrasena, the girl's father, because, after inviting us, he has given his daughter to a ploughman. So we will kill this ploughman and seize her.' Having said this, all the kings attacked the ploughman. The ploughman for his part, animated with the might of the deity, fought with them all, while they at once assailed him. Then the ploughman, whirling aloft his plough, cleft the foreheads of elephants, cut open the heads of horses, and dashed chariots in pieces. Then all the kings were astonished. They said to one another: 'Is this a god, or a Vidyádhara, or is he some Siddha hero, that such might is seen to be his? So let us propitiate him before he destroys us all.' Having said this, they joined together, with Chaṇḍasiṃha at their head, and tried to conciliate the ploughman, saying: 'O thou god, pardon the impropriety which we committed.' Then the father and mother, beholding such exploits performed by the ploughman, made their daughter marry him, and celebrated the ceremony with great rejoicings. They did honour to the kings and dismissed them. The ploughman enjoyed with Vishṇuçrí the pleasures of royalty. One day that god appeared before the ploughman in visible form, and said to him: 'Great sir, your poverty has vanished.' He said: 'Thanks to you, I have obtained all that is pleasant.' The god said: 'Whatever else you choose to ask I will immediately give you.' The ploughman answered: 'If it be so, my lord, let that city, which you made desolate, be again inhabited owing to your favour.' The god said: 'So be it.' Then he caused that city to be inhabited. The ploughman remained enjoying ever new pleasures with Vishṇuçrí. And inasmuch as, even in this world, the ploughman had obtained a kingdom by virtue of the merit attained by offering food to the mighty Jinas, knowing wéll the result of such a rite, he kept making the food-offering in front of the Jina with his two wives every day. Thus being immersed in happiness, he finds his days pass like those of a god in the *dogunḍika* heaven. Now, it happened that that very god, of whom we spoke above, fell from heaven, his period having expired, and became conceived in Vishṇuçrí. When the full time had come a son was born. The name of Kuṃsuda was given to him. Gradually he grew up to be a young man. On account of their affection in a former birth he was very dear to the ploughman-king. After some time had passed, he gave the kingdom to that son, and took a vow. When he died, owing to the merit of the food-offering, he became a god in the first world of the gods. He began to reflect by means of his limited knowledge what good deed he had done in a former birth to obtain such magnificence. Then he discovered that he had obtained such good fortune by means of an offering of food. Having thus discovered the action that he himself performed in a previous birth, he went every day to admonish his own son. In the last watch of the night he said to him: 'King, listen to my speech with an attentive mind. Because in a former birth I gave with great devotion a food-offering to the Jina, therefore this splendour has fallen to my lot. Moreover, it came about by your favour and the favour of the Jina, therefore do you also perform acts of worship to the excellent Jina. I, your father, have become a god in the world of gods by the fruit of an offering of food to the Jina, and I have come to admonish you on account of my love in a previous birth. Therefore, let the religion of the Jina be your refuge also.' After the god had in these words warned his son, he returned to the world of gods. Owing to the food-offering to the Jina, he will, after enjoying the pleasures of gods and men, obtain salvation in the seventh birth. Here ends the story of the ploughman, having reference to worship by means of a food-offering.

I will tell the story of that Gandhabhadrá, who, having with great devotion
Offered a candle in front of the Jina, obtained salvation.

Now follows the story of Dípaçikha, having reference to worship by means of a candle.

STORY OF DÍPAÇIKHA.

In this Bharata there is a city named Çvetámbiká. In it there was a king named Vijayavarman, and a female servant named Gandhabhadrá. One day she heard the fruit of the merit of worshipping the Jina with a candle thus described:

A beautiful body, a clear intellect, unimpaired senses,
Good eyes, long-continued strength, many auspicious marks on the body,
And supreme lordship, are the fruit of giving a candle to the great Jina.*

When she heard this, faith was produced in her. Then, at the time of lighting lamps, she offered a candle in the temple of the Jina out of her lawfully acquired earnings; and when her life's allotted period was terminated she died, and her soul was conceived again in that same city in Jayá, the wife of King Vijayavarman. At that moment the queen saw a flaming fire enter her mouth. The next morning she told the king. The king said: 'Queen, you will have a truly remarkable son.' Accordingly in the third month a longing came on. The queen felt a desire to worship gods and holy men, and to give gifts to the poor

* This passage is conjecturally translated. In two of the MSS. many words are omitted. In the Sanskrit College MS. some words seem to be repeated.

and wretched. The king had her longing satisfied, and when the days were accomplished a son was born. The ceremony of cutting the navel-string was performed, and the boy was called Dípaçikha, because from the day of his birth he had on his forehead a gem by way of a mark, and it resembled the flame of a candle in brightness.* This produced astonishment in the minds of all men. Now, at this time there was in Kántipura a king named Vikramasena; he had a daughter named Gandharvadattá. She was proud of her skill in playing the lyre, and so had a high opinion of herself; and she gave out that she would accept as a husband any man that could beat her in the accomplishment of playing the lyre. Then the king had a building for a *Svayaṃvara* constructed. All princes were invited. Dípaçikha also, having grown up to be a young man, came to the *Svayaṃvara*. When all the princes were seated on platforms, Gandharvadattá came into the midst of the guests assembled for the *Svayaṃvara*. When Dípaçikha saw her, he said to himself: 'O the skill of destiny in composing the universe!'

Then Gandharvadattá saw Dípaçikha. She said to herself: 'This man is a jewel among men, even if he does not possess skill in the pastime of playing the lyre. So I must marry him.' Thus the princess fell in love with Dípaçikha at first sight. And at this conjuncture a man of the name of Jálandhara† cried out in the middle of the guests assembled at the *Svayaṃvara*: 'Hear, all ye princes! The princess has made a vow that, if any one of the princes assembled here shall surpass her in playing the lyre, that man shall be her husband.‡ So now display, each of you, your knowledge of the lyre.' Then, having heard this, a conceited prince played the lyre. A mad elephant was placed near; the prince by playing the lyre quieted the elephant. Then the princess thought: 'These

* For parallels see the notes to Miss Stokes' 'Indian Fairy Tales,' p. 242 (Story of Phulmatí Rání).

† Or from Jalandhara.

‡ A princess, also called Gandharvadattá, makes the same promise in the 'Kathá Sarit Ságara' (vol. ii. of my translation, p. 431).

5

princes show themselves very clever in the accomplishment of music; but if I hear the one whom I saw first I shall be able to keep my promise.' Then another prince took up the lyre. A barren tree was placed near him. By playing the lyre he made the tree burst into blossom. Then another took the lyre, and by playing it sweetly attracted a distant deer.* Then yet another took it up. An elephant was placed near. A mouthful of sweet food was given to the elephant. By playing the lyre the prince made the elephant give up the mouthful when half devoured. All the princes exhibited wonderful feats of skill of this kind in playing the lyre. Then Gandharvadattá took the lyre and played it sweetly. Then the sound made a mad elephant come near from a distance. A deer also came from a distance. That same barren tree was clothed with flowers from its very root. An elephant was made to surrender entirely a mouthful it had taken. All the princes were astonished. They said to one another that the princess was hard to win. Then the lyre was given to Dípaçikha, and he played it. All the people there were eager to hear the lyre played by him; but he played it so well that everyone in the *Svayaṃvara* pavilion went to sleep. Seeing them all asleep, Dípaçikha took a seal-ring from the hand of the princess, and a gold bracelet from the hand of King Vikramasena; he took also the ornaments of all the others, and made a pile of them in the middle of the *Svayaṃvara* pavilion. In a moment the princes woke up and saw the heap of ornaments. In the astonishment of their minds they said: 'Oh, what wonderful skill in playing the lyre he does possess!' Gandharvadattá was delighted, and threw on his neck the garland of election. The marriage was performed with full ceremonial. After remaining there some time, the prince set out for his own country, accompanied by Gandharvadattá. As he was going along he reached the city of Pratishṭhána, and he encamped in a

* Compare Grimm's story of 'Der wunderliche Spielmann.'

garden in the suburbs. And at this time it happened that Lílávatí, the daughter of Karka, the king of that town, was bitten by a serpent. Saying that she was dead, they proceeded to carry her to the funeral pyre. Dípaçikha heard the sound of the bier.* He said to Gandharvadattá: 'My dear, they are carrying out a living person.' She said: 'How do you know?' He answered: 'I know by the peculiar sound.' She said: 'How can you tell by the sound?' He answered: 'By means of spells one can know all things.' She said: 'If it be so, then restore the corpse to life.' So he sent a messenger of his own and had the corpse stopped, and the ground near the pyre anointed. When this had been done, the prince went there, and was seen by King Karka. On seeing him the king was astonished, and said to himself: 'Certainly Lílávatí will be restored to life.' The prince fastened up his hair in a knot. Lílávatí was set down on the ground which the prince had anointed, and he, calling to mind the spell, thus addressed Lílávatí: 'Arise up, and, taking a golden vessel, give me water to rinse my mouth.' The princess rose up, and all the people were delighted. Great rejoicings took place. When King Karka found out that Dípaçikha was the son of King Vijayadharma,† he gave him his daughter Lílávatí, and the marriage was celebrated. After staying there some days, he again set out for his own country. As he was on his way, he came in due course to Ujjayiní, and, as fate would have it, encamped there. Now, at the time of twilight he saw a blazing pyre. The prince, when night had come on, went there without telling his wife, and approached the pyre sword in hand. While he was standing at the foot of a tree, an adept in magic arrived. He drew a circle‡ and beat a cymbal, muttering spells. Then a maiden came into the circle. The adept said to the maiden: 'Come now, call to mind

* *Váhitra.*

† He is called above Vijayavarman.

‡ See the word 'circle' in the index at the end of vol. ii. of my translation of the 'Kathá Sarit Ságara.'

your guardian deity, for your last hour has come.' When he drew his dagger and said this to the maiden, she began to weep. Then Dípaçikha was filled with compassion at hearing this lamentation of the damsel, so he drew his sword from the sheath, and said to the maiden, 'Fear not'; and presenting himself in front of the adept in magic, he said: 'You scoundrel, you worst of villains, are you not ashamed to kill this girl? I will cut off your head with this sword.' When the adept in magic heard this heroic speech, his whole body trembled with fear, and he forgot to repeat his spells. He said to the prince: 'Noble sir, you ought not to impede me when intent on performing magic rites. I am an adept named Bhárabhúti, and I have begun the employment of a spell for attracting a beautiful maiden. The previous rites lasted twelve months, and to-day, the crowning day of the whole ceremony, I have drawn here by the might of spells this princess for a sacrifice, so do not impede me.' Thereupon Prince Dípaçikha said: 'Noble sir, the slaughter of a woman is a disgrace to a man of honour, so think no more of murdering a woman, which involves great guilt. Moreover, you seem to be a man of a very attractive exterior, so the slaying of a woman is peculiarly unbecoming to you.' Then the adept in magic was ashamed. He said to the prince: 'Distinguished sir, right well have you admonished me. I am exceedingly wicked. So I abandon this wicked enterprise, and I will now return to my own place. You must give back to King Avantivardhana this maiden named Avantiní.' The prince said: 'I will do so.' Thereupon the adept went to his own place, and Prince Dípaçikha returned to his camp with the maiden. He related the adventure to his two wives, and in the morning he handed over the girl to the king, Avantivardhana, and related to him the circumstances. The king, Avantivardhana, was pleased, and gave his daughter to Dípaçikha. The joyful wedding ceremony was performed. After the prince had remained some time, he again continued his march by regular stages towards his own country. As he was travelling along, he came to the city of Padmávatí, and encamped in a garden outside the city. When King Mancha, the lord of that town, heard of it, he conducted him into the city with great pomp. Now, it happened that the following conversation arose in the court of that king. King Mancha said: 'When the gods enter the body of a human being, they do not say anything intelligible.' Dípaçikha said: 'King, do not say this. I assure you all this that you doubt does happen.' The king said again: 'How can a superhuman being enter a human body?' Dípaçikha said: 'If you feel any curiosity about it, I will myself show you.' Then the king summoned his own daughter, named Kámalatá. Prince Dípaçikha placed her in a circle, and thought on the spell in his own heart, and summoned the great hero Hanumán. Then the *medium** whirled round like a wind-smitten leaf† and said nothing. Then Prince Dípaçikha thought instantly on the spell, and then the *medium* began to speak. Dípaçikha said: 'Let other questions remain over for the present. First tell us why there has been so much delay about this matter.' The *medium* said: 'First, one has to look out for a suitable *medium*, furnished with all five senses unimpaired, because one has to speak by the senses of another. Then I went to the Himálaya and fetched the magic herbs; then I came here. This is the cause of the delay.' The lord of the city of Padmávatí asked other questions also. The princess answered them all. Then the king was satisfied, and Dípaçikha dismissed the deity. From that time forth Princess Kámalatá talked like Sarasvatí. Then Kámalatá was given to Dípaçikha. After the prince had remained there some days he went on with his four wives, and arrived at the city of Çvetámbiká. There he was reunited to his father, and great rejoicings took place. King Vijayavarman established Dípaçikha in his kingdom and took a vow. Dípaçikha governed the realm. One day he said in his heart: 'What meritorious act did I perform in a former life to acquire such happiness as I now have?'

* *Pâtraṃ.*

† Compare Virgil, 'Æneid,' vi. 46-51.

While he was intently reflecting upon this, there arose in his mind the recollection of his former birth. Then he saw that it was the fruit of offering a candle; so he practised religion with increased zeal. This is the story of Dípaçikha, having reference to worship by means of a candle.

By giving a gift in common there results to many a common advantage,
And in this case the highest fruit is a state of happiness, like that of Kuruchandra.

In illustration of this there follows the story of Kuruchandra, having reference to giving.

STORY OF KURUCHANDRA AND HIS FRIENDS VASANTADEVA AND KÁMAPÁLA.

In Jambudvípa, in this very land of Bharata, there is a city named Gajapura. In it there was a king named Kuruchandra. Now, once on a time the revered Çántinátha arrived in the garden of Gajapura. King Kuruchandra went out with great splendour to worship the revered Çántinátha. After he had bowed before him he listened to his preaching, and on obtaining a favourable opportunity, he asked the Jina the following question: 'By what merit, my lord, did I obtain such a kingdom? Moreover, owing to what action do five things, of which clothes and fruit are the principal, come to me as a present every day? As for those things about which I ask, if I do not give them to others, I cannot enjoy them myself. Tell me all this, my lord.' The holy one said: 'King, you obtained the kingdom by a pious gift. Now hear the act of merit by which you obtained that fruit of merit:

STORY OF KURUCHANDRA IN A FORMER BIRTH.

'In this very land of Bharata there is a city of the name of Çrípura. In it dwelt four merchants, who were friends, and they were known by these names—Sudhana, Dhanapati, Dhaneçvara, and Dhanada. All four of them went to Ratnadvípa to acquire wealth. The four had a servant called Dronaka, who carried their provisions. One day they all saw in a wood a great hermit in the statuesque posture, and they said: "Lo, a great piece of good fortune has befallen us, in that this hermit, like a treasure of quietism, has come within range of our eyes. So let us do ourselves a kindness by giving him something." It happened to be the time for the hermit to eat. So they all four said to Droṇaka: "Worthy Droṇaka, give this hermit something." So the hermit was relieved by Droṇaka, out of faith, with more food than they intended; and thus Droṇaka placed to his credit an action which would produce much auspicious fruit. Then, by the help of their good action, they arrived at Ratnadvípa, and having acquired wealth came back. By that very seed of merit they became successful on all occasions. Now, Dhanapati and Dhaneçvara were very deceitful. They traded with Sudhana and Dhanada on a system of subtle trickery. But Droṇaka was of a very guileless character. He was born as yourself, Kuruchandra, to King Duḥprasaha, in the city of Gajapura, by his wife Çrísundarí, having been foretold by a dream of the moon. In the meanwhile Sudhana and Dhanada died, and were born apart as sons of merchants, the first in the city of Kámpilya, and the second in the city of Kártika. One was called Vasantadeva, and the other Kámapála. As for those two deceitful merchants, Dhanapati and Dhaneçvara, when they died, their allotted period of life having come to an end, they were born as women on account of their deceitful nature, one in Çankapura, and the other in Jayantí. One was called Maillá, and the other Kesará. In course of time they all grew up to be young men and young women.

#### How Vasantadeva and Kámapála obtained their Wives.*

'Now, one day about this time Vasantadeva went from the city of Kámpilya to Jayantí to acquire wealth. There, on the great moon-

* This is identical with the story of the two Bráhman friends in book xiii. of the 'Kathá Sarit Ságara.' See the remarks of Professor Wilson, quoted by me in a note on p. 423 of vol. ii. of my translation.

festival of the eighth day,* he saw Kesará in the garden of Ratinandana, and she also saw him. Vasantadeva asked a native of Jayantí: "Who is this lady?" And then a young merchant named Priyankara, who had struck up a friendship with him, said: "My friend, she is the daughter of the merchant Panchanandin, and the sister of Jayantadeva, and her name is Kesará." Then Vasantadeva made friends with Jayantadeva. One day Jayantadeva asked Vasantadeva to a meal in his house. Then Vasantadeva saw that Kesará was exceedingly beautiful. Now, it happened that on this occasion Vasantadeva received flowers from the hand of Jayantadeva, and Kesará's nurse, Priyankará by name, thought that a very good omen. Then she said to Kesará: "You also ought to make some present to Vasantadeva." Kesará said: "Do whatever seems good to you." Then Priyankará gave to Vasantadeva, while in the garden of his own house, clusters of Priyangu and Kakkola fruits, and said to him: "My mistress Kesará sends you these sweets, sprung from the trees planted by Sundara with his own hands." Then Vasantadeva, knowing her feelings, was delighted, and said to Priyankará: "My good woman, you have done nobly; you must in the same way do another thing also, which it is suitable for you to do." Then Priyankará went and told Kesará the whole story, and Kesará was delighted. Now, it happened that in the last watch of the night† Kesará had a dream to the effect that she was married to Vasantadeva; Vasantadeva also had a dream that he married Kesará. In the morning Kesará told her dream with a glad heart to Priyankará, and while she was telling it the family chaplain happened to utter the words, "Even so shall it be."‡ Both of them rejoiced at hearing this utterance of the family chaplain, and Priyankará said to Kesará: "Be assured that

* See, for the meeting of two lovers at a religious festival, my translation of the 'Kathá Sarit Ságara,' vol. ii., p. 262, note.

† For the belief that such dreams come true, see my translation of the 'Kathá Sarit Ságara,' vol. i., p. 441; vol. ii., p. 482.

‡ Here we have an instance of belief in a φήμη. See Homer's 'Odyssey,' xx., l. 105.

Vasantadeva will be your husband." Kesará made the knot which it is usual to make on perceiving an omen. Then Priyankará related Kesará's dream to Vasantadeva, and Vasantadeva, for his part, related his own dream, and thinking from the tallying of the dreams that his object was as good as accomplished, he was highly delighted. In this way some time passed, while the mutual affection of that couple kept every day increasing. Now, one day Vasantadeva, while in his own house, heard the sound of festive drums in the house of the merchant Panchanandin. He exclaimed: "Ha! what is this?" and then a maid-servant said: "To-day Kesará has been given to Varadatta, the son of the merchant Sudatta, who is a native of Kanyakubja; hence this rejoicing." When Vasantadeva heard this he fainted. At this moment Priyankará arrived and comforted Vasantadeva, and said: "I have been sent by Kesará, and she sends the following message to you, 'You must not grieve. My mother, father, and relations, not knowing my heart, have begun all this business; but certainly you are my real husband. If I cannot obtain you, my only resource is to die.'" When Vasantadeva heard this he was satisfied, and his fainting-fit came to an end. Then Vasantadeva said: "My good woman, in this conjuncture my resolution is the same." Then Priyankará went and told this to Kesará; she was, so to speak, born again. Those two spent many days in thinking of a device for getting married. Then the troop of bridegroom's friends arrived. Then Vasantadeva said to himself: "To-morrow early the marriage will take place." Having heard this news, he went out of the city in despair, and, entering into the wood, said to himself: "Oh, the wanton sport of fate! That maiden promised to marry me, and now that her mother and father are giving her to another, she will commit suicide. So I had better abandon my life before I hear of her death." After going through these reflections he fastened a noose on the branch of an Açoka-tree, and tied himself to it. At that moment a man rushed forth from a dense thicket of the wood like a friend, and said: "Noble sir, do not act thus rashly"; and with these words he cut the noose. He took Vasantadeva under a Kinkilli-tree, and both of them sat down. The man said: 'Noble sir, why have you attempted an act reprobated by all excellent people?" Then Vasantadeva told his story. Then the man said: "Granted that things are as you say, nevertheless a discerning man like you ought not to act thus. In this case some artifice should be employed. If even by an artifice the object cannot be attained, death is our refuge in the last resort. Thus I, too, in the very same circumstances live, though afflicted. A living man sees hundreds of good chances; if the worst come to the worst, death is a refuge." When Vasantadeva heard this, he said: "Noble sir, who are you, and how are you unhappy?" He said: "I am the son of a merchant; I live in the city of Kártika, and my name is Kámala. Once on a time I started to visit foreign countries. As I was roaming about, I came in course of time to Çankhapura. It happened one day that all the people of that town assembled in a garden outside it to attend a festival in honour of the Yaksha Çankha, and I went there also. There I saw a maiden in a grove of fragrant mango-trees, and she also saw me, and immediately we fell desperately in love with one another. Then she offered me betel with her own hand. I thought in my heart: 'What shall I do? Shall I take it or not?' While I was thus reflecting, a mad elephant, that was roaming about at will, came there. Through fear of that elephant the girl's attendants ran away, but she did not run away herself. While the elephant was preparing to seize that girl, as she stood trembling in every limb, I struck the elephant with a stick behind. It left the girl and went away. Then the girl's attendants reassembled and praised me. At this moment the whole herd of elephants came up, and made the people fly in all directions, and I could not see what became of that girl. After I had roamed about for some days in that city, without getting tidings of that girl, I came here with an empty heart. I am deeply in love with that girl, but I cannot obtain her, as I cannot get certain news of her; still, I do not choose death. But there is an artifice by which you may obtain Kesará. She will be married to-morrow morning, so to-day she must perform worship to the god of love; this worship she will perform alone, such is the custom. So let you and me enter the city before she arrives, and go to the temple of the god of love. When she comes to the temple of the god, I will, with her consent, put on her dress and go to her house. But when I have gone some distance, you must take Kesará and make off as fast as possible." When Vasantadeva heard this, he said, "This is just like your nobleness," and rejoiced. Then he said to Kámapála: "My friend, my gain will be your ruin." At this moment somebody sneezed,* and Kámapála said: "By forwarding your business, I shall ensure my own prosperity also." At this moment someone near said, with reference to his own business: "There can be no doubt about that." Vasantadeva, catching the meaning of the omen, agreed to the proposal of Kámapála, and the two went into the city together. After taking food they went together at the time of evening to the temple of the god of love, and both of them remained concealed behind the image of the god. After a short time the sound of cymbals was heard. Both of them, hearing the sound, were delighted, as it showed that Kesará was approaching; and in a short time she arrived, thinking, from the throbbing of her limbs, that she was about to meet her beloved. Kesará got out of her litter, and entered the temple of the god of love. She took the instruments of worship from the hand of Priyankará, and Priyankará shut the door. Kesará performed her worship, and after the worship she thus addressed the god of love: "O lord, husband of Rati, thou seest into the hearts of all creatures; how is it, then, that, though knowing my heart, thou dost join me to a husband whom I have not chosen? My heart is not

* This seems to be a good omen, like the πτάρνυταί τις in Xenophon's 'Anabasis,' iii. 2, 9. See also Catullus, xlv. 8.

pleased with anyone but Vasantadeva. But now, what is the use of this reproach? Anyhow, by thy favour, let him be my husband in another birth." Having said this, she was proceeding to hang herself on the arch of the god's temple, but at that moment Vasantadeva rushed out and saved her life. When she saw him, she wondered where he could have come from. Vasantadeva said: "I am the lover for whom you asked the god of love. This is my friend. We entered this temple before you, and have devised a plan for carrying you off. Now, give your ornaments and other things to this friend of mine, in order that, wearing your clothes, he may return to your house, and we two may go to another country." When he said this to Kesará she gave her clothes to Kámapála, and taking the clothes of Kámapála, she herself remained hidden behind the image of the god. Kámapála for his part, in female garments, having his whole body wrapped up in them, and covering his face with the veil,* opened the door of the temple of the god of love and went out. He gave into the hand of Priyankará the vessel containing the implements of worship, and, holding her hand, got up into the litter. Immediately the servants lifted up the litter, and so he went to the house of the merchant Panchanandin without being discovered. Even Brahmá does not penetrate a well-laid plot.† When he had reached the house and got out of the litter he was taken to the bride's apartment. Priyankará said to him, "Call to mind the spell that produces union with the beloved," and went out. Kámapála, for his part, set himself to call to mind a spell for ensuring union with his love. At this moment the daughter of Kesará's uncle by the maternal side, Mairá by name, who had come there to be present at the wedding, and who had been seen on that previous occasion by Kámapála, entered the bride's chamber and

* *Nírangí*, which Hemachandra in his 'Deçínámamálá' paraphrases by *çirovaguṇṭhanaṃ*.

† I read here *dambhasya* for *daṃtasya*. See Böhtlingk's 'Indische Sprüche,' No. 7,112.

began to say as follows: "Friend, we have now an opportunity for talking together, therefore I will say something. Do not be distressed in mind, for fate is the cause of desirable and undesirable results to all living beings. When I was in Çankhapura I heard your whole story; your heart takes no pleasure in anyone but Vasantadeva. But, friend, you are lucky, since you have obtained the pleasure of seeing and conversing, and so on, with your beloved; but hear my sad story. One day I went to a garden outside the city with my attendants to witness a festival in honour of the Yaksha Çankha. There I saw a young maṇ resembling the god of love. I sent him betel and other things by the hand of a female companion. He saved me from a mad elephant; but I fled again from fear of the herd of elephants. I cannot find out the whereabouts of that young man, who has departed somewhither; though I have instituted a search for him in many quarters, I cannot find him. From that day forth I take pleasure in nothing. I have seen him in a dream, but I have never seen him in bodily presence. So I shall not be allowed by fate union with him, even by means of exchange of words; I alone can know what my grief is in this state of affairs. You are as dear to me as my life, that is why I have told you all this. So, my sister, abandon grief—be calm; by the help of favouring fortune all will turn out well." Then Kámapála said: "Gazelle-eyed one, I am that young man whom you saw on that occasion at the great festival of the Yaksha. By the help of favouring fortune Vasantadeva has been united with Kesará; in the same way our union also has come about, so dismiss anxiety." Then he showed himself in his true form, and Mairá, beholding him, was delighted, but was not able to speak for fear. Then Kámapála said: "My darling, cease this fear; show me a door by which we can go out." Then Mairá showed him a back door leading into the garden of the house. Then Kámapála went out into that garden with his beloved and met Vasantadeva, who had come there before with Kesará. The two arrived at the same instant.'

Then the Jina explained to King Kuruchandra that all five of them united in a previous birth in giving a gift to a hermit. 'For this reason,' said the hermit, 'five splendid things come to you every day as a gift. For this reason you cannot enjoy these five things unless you have given them to these people.'* When they had heard their former life thus described by the holy Çántinátha, recollection of it arose in all, and they remembered it perfectly. The king, after bowing before the Jina, took Vasantadeva and Kámapála and their wives to his own palace, and treated those two men as his brothers. With their help he ruled his kingdom. After he had cherished his realm for some time, he placed his son on the throne, and then all five took a vow. All five observed the conduct prescribed by their vow free from transgression, and went to heaven.

Thus ends the story of King Kuruchandra, having reference to a gift in common.

He who gives a gift to holy men, who are treasures of virtue,
Whose bodies are restrained with purity and penance, obtains happiness and is rich.

STORY OF THE FORTUNATE YOUTH DHANYA.

In this very land of Bharata there is a city named Supratishṭha; in it there was a king named Jitaçatru. Once on a time, a family that had formerly been rich, and had afterwards by the dispensation of fate become poor, left another city through shame, and settled in the city of Supratishṭha. The family was naturally well conducted, and a young son of it, who was devoted to giving, used to graze the calves of the citizens. One day there was a great festival in that city, and all the people went to the city garden, taking with them various kinds of eatables. That grazer of cattle, seeing what the citizens were about, felt a great desire to join in the festival. So he left the calves in the neighbourhood of the town and came home, and said to his mother: 'Mother, make preparations

* There is clearly some important omission either here or at the beginning of the story. As it stands it is unintelligible.

to enable me also to keep the feast.' His mother, when she heard what her son said, remembering the previous wealth of the family, began to weep with piteous sobs, as her throat was filled with a weight of woe; for women have no other resource than weeping. When the women who lived in the neighbourhood heard the mother of the grazer of calves weeping, they said to her: 'Why do you weep?' When they asked her, she told them her story. Then they felt pity for her, and, to satisfy the boy, gave her milk, rice, molasses, and clarified butter. Out of it she made a pudding, and then the boy took the food and sat down to eat it. His mother said, 'It is hot,' and covered up the pudding mixed with molasses and butter; so the boy remained patiently waiting. At that moment a hermit, with body dried up by mortification, who had conquered his senses and conquered all trials of patience,* came there to beg. The boy, when he saw him, thought in his heart: 'Fortunate am I, in that this saint, who is an eminent treasure of merit, has come here.' Then the noble-hearted boy relieved the hermit by giving him the pudding. Accordingly, by virtue of the gift to the hermit, he acquired merit that would ensure him one happy life as a man. He himself ate another pudding full of butter and molasses. At eventide the people said: 'Where have you left those calves?' Then he went out into the environs of the city to look for them. When he came back to the city, having hunted them up, he found the gates of the city closed. So he remained outside the city, and listened to the religious discourse of the hermit on the twelve vows against the killing of living creatures, and so on.† While thus engaged, his allotted period of life came to an end, and he died during the night. He was conceived again in that very city in the family of a certain merchant. From the day of his conception the merchant was blessed with an increase

* Hunger, thirst, cold, heat, stinging flies, etc. See Dr. Hoernle's note in the 'Uvásaga-Dasáo,' appendix iii., p. 47, where twenty-two such 'trials' are enumerated. The word in the original is *parísaha*.

† See Dr. Hoernle's 'Uvásaga-Dasáo,' appendix iii., p. 34.

of wealth. Then on an auspicious day a son was born that delighted the eyes of men. On the day that his navel-string was to be cut a great treasure was found full of jewels and gold. Then his father and mother made a great feast in honour of his birth, and for the sake of showing respect to the gods and spiritual teachers, and gave him the name of Dhanya.* When the due time arrived, he was sent to the school where reading and writing were taught, and he studied under a teacher of accomplishments. His four brothers were hostile to him, but his parents rebuked them. Then the brothers asked their parents why they treated him with so much respect. Thereupon their parents said: 'He possesses many great qualities, and therein you are not equal to him; for this reason we treat this son with so much respect.' The sons said: 'Then, put us all to the test.' Then they gave to each of them thirty-two rupees, and said: 'Trade with these.' So the sons set out to do their best. Dhanya, being clever in all accomplishments, bought a very strong ram, and made it fight for a stake of one thousand *dínáras* with the prince's ram, and it beat the prince's ram. So Dhanya came home immediately with a ram and a thousand *dínáras;* but the others gained no profit, as they had not acquired merit in a former life, and came home at the end of the day with downcast faces. The next day those four sons said: 'Father, try us once more.' So he gave sixty cowries to each of them. Those four sons went on buying and selling, but made no profit; on the contrary, they suffered loss. Now, it happened that in that very city there lived a merchant named Mahádhana, who was a thoroughgoing miser. He acquired wealth by various undertakings, but would not give half a mite of it away in charity, or help his relations in any way. To make a long story short, he would not spend even on his own person. When entreated by applicants, he flew into a passion, and when he saw others giving away anything, he spoke angry words to them. It happened that a fiery fever

* *I.e.*, Fortunatus. In many European stories one brother is more lucky in his undertakings than the others. See Grimm's No. 86.

seized him ; then in his delirium he filled a bed with that wealth, and put another bed on top of it and so slept. He did not abandon his bed at the moment of death, though everyone abandoned him. So he died on that very bed, and was carried on it to the cemetery. Then the keeper of the cemetery brought the bed to the cross-road, to sell it, but no one would buy it. However, Dhanya, owing to the luck that attended him, had the sense to buy it, and then he made it over to his parents. He took out the pegs of the bed and extracted from it the jewels ; so their treasure, already great, was increased. Then all the four brothers took counsel to kill Dhanya. But the wife of one of the brothers overheard their deliberations, and, being filled with compassion, told Dhanya. Then Dhanya said to himself : 'Alas ! these brothers are jealous of me ; and yet I have done them no injury, so why are they angry with me ? Anyhow, I cannot remain here.' After going through these reflections he went out of the city alone, and wandered about on the earth.

One day a householder saw him in a field near the road, and was delighted with him, thinking him a man of distinction. So he invited him to dinner, and told his wife to give him a pudding of choice rice. While Dhanya was eating his food, the householder, driving his plough, came on a jar full of *dínáras*. Then the householder thought : 'This piece of luck is due to the power of this man.' So he placed the jar in front of him, saying : 'It is thanks to your merit that I have obtained this treasure, so do you take it.' But Dhanya said : 'Take it yourself.' Then, leaving that place, he came in course of time to Rájagṛiha. There he rested in a garden outside the city under a fragrant mango-tree. Then he was seen by the gardener, named Kusumapála. He said to himself : 'Here is a most distinguished man,' and in his delight he carried him off to his own house, and he and his family treated him with the highest consideration, and Dhanya lived there in the utmost comfort. Now, at this time King Çreṇika was reigning in that city. One day his queen consort, Dhárinị by name, gave birth to a daughter. Then the king had proclaimed by beat of drum through the whole town : 'Whoever has a daughter born in his house to-day must report the same to me.' Now, there was a merchant of the name of Gobhadra living there, who had a wife named Bhadrá. She gave birth to a daughter that same day. Likewise a daughter was born in the house of that Kusumapála. Gobhadra and Kusumapála went both of them to the king's palace, and said : 'Your majesty, both of us have had daughters born to us to-day.' The king honoured them, and said : 'Both of them must be my daughter's companions.' They, after receiving the order of the king, returned home. The merchant Gobhadra named his daughter Subhadrá, and the gardener Kusumapála named his Pushpavatí. The king named his daughter Somaçrí. So the princess associated with these two companions. In time they all grew up. So they began to think who should be the husband of all three of them. One day Pushpavatí saw Dhanya, and fell in love with him. She said in her own mind : 'Truly this is a handsome man, and full of merit, for since his arrival trees, that had not a single flower before, have put forth flowers and fruit. So he will be a fitting husband for all three of us. Accordingly I must by some artifice let the princess know about him.' So she made Dhanya prepare a bouquet constructed with curious art, and going to the king's palace, she made it over to her companion Somaçrí. When she saw that bouquet, she said to her companion : 'Friend, who made this bouquet?' Pushpavatí said : 'My friend, there is a young man staying in our house who is in appearance like the god of love, and is skilful in all accomplishments ; he has sent you this bouquet to show his skill.' Then Somaçrí, hearing his name, thought : 'I will marry no one but him.' And from that day forth she remained thinking of him, with her cheek resting on the palm of her left hand, with her lower lip agitated with deep-drawn hot sighs, neglecting all other concerns. Then the king heard of the condition in which his daughter was from the attendants ; so he sent the warder and summoned

Dhanya from the house of the gardener Kusumapála. After Dhanya had made his bow, he was placed on a becoming seat. When the king saw that he was like a youthful god, he said to himself: 'My daughter has fixed her affection on a worthy object.' So he had the princess summoned, and said to Dhanya: 'I give you this maiden to wife.' Then Dhanya received her with a heart full of abundance of joy.' Thereupon Somaçrí bowed before her parents, and said: 'Let him also marry my two companions.'* Then the king said: 'If this thing pleases all three of you, let it be so.' Accordingly Somaçrí informed her companions, and the king caused the marriage of those maidens to Dhanya to be celebrated with great solemnity; and Gobhadra and Kusumapála also spent large sums on it. Dhanya lived happily with those three wives in a palace given him by the king. The king also gave him many elephants and horses, and much gold and raiment, and wealth of other kinds, so that he lived in comfort. One day Dhanya, while sitting at a window in his palace, saw his parents wandering about in the road in a miserable condition, with soiled garments. He sent some servants of his own, and had them brought to his house; then he made them take a bath, and had them dressed in splendid garments. They clung to Dhanya's neck and wept aloud. Then Dhanya made them sit on a seat of honour, and said to them, specially addressing his father: 'My father, how have you both suddenly become poor? How could such a splendid fortune fail?' His father answered: 'As soon as you left our house the whole of our wealth gradually disappeared. Some of our property was carried off by thieves; some of it was burned in a conflagration; some of it was seized by the king on account of a crime committed by my sons; all my wealth having thus been dissipated, we were ashamed to live at home any longer: I have accordingly come here; your elder brothers are outside.' Then Dhanya sent men, and brought his

* In the 'Kathá Sarit Ságara' (vol. ii., p. 471), Mandaradeví requests that Naraváhanadatta may marry her four companions.

brothers into his house. They said to him: 'Brother, our behaviour was unseemly; so, as you are a mine of virtue, pardon our fault.' Then Dhanya gave his brothers wealth, and sent them away to another city, where by his might they all became very rich. Then Dhanya made over all the care of his house to his father and mother, and lived happily with his wives. One day Subhadrá came to him weeping. Dhanya said: 'Fair one, why are you weeping?' She said: 'My beloved brother Çálibhadra has been receiving religious teaching from the hermit Dharmaghosha, and has become agitated in mind. He is desirous of undertaking a course of asceticism, but my mother said to him: "My darling boy, asceticism is difficult, and you are delicately nurtured; if you are resolved on a life of this kind, leave off luxuries gradually, in order that your body may grow accustomed to it." Accordingly, following the advice of my mother, he reduces his indulgences every day. Çálibhadra has renounced food, ornaments, beds, unguents, and similar luxuries, and is practising the *áchámla** penance; he sleeps on the ground with only one garment on; he will no doubt immediately take the vow of a monk. Know that this is the cause of my grief.' When Dhanya heard this he laughed, and said: 'Çálibhadra must be a coward if he cannot at once take upon himself the burden of self-restraint.' Then Somaçrí said: 'My lord, he is not a coward, but tender; he is gradually accustoming his body to difficult asceticism.' Dhanya replied: 'What is difficult to resolute men?' Then Subhadrá smiled, and said: 'If this is not difficult, then why do you also not do it?' Dhanya said: 'If you tell me to adopt a life of religion I will do it at once, and if I do not I will pay a penalty.' Then they said: 'If you will adopt a life of self-restraint, we also will take a vow at the feet of the Tírthankara.' Now, it happened that at that very time Çrívíra, who surpassed in attractiveness all the other Jinas, arrived in that

* *Áchámla* means the eating of dry food simply moistened or boiled in water. See Dr. Hoernle's paper in the *Indian Antiquary* for August, 1890, note 81.

city, and Dhanya's officers reported the fact to him. Then Dhanya was pleased, and went out with his three wives in a litter with great splendour, to do honour to Çrívíra. Çálibhadra also went out with great magnificence, glittering with jewelled ornaments like a god, in order to take the vow. Then both of them left their litters and entered where the Jina was, and after worshipping him, they sat down in a suitable place and listened to his discourse on religion. When Çálibhadra had heard the discourse, he tore out his hair* himself, and with his eight wives took a vow. Then Dhanya also and his three wives took a vow; and after these two men had performed severe asceticism for a long time, they had recourse to starvation at the latter end of their lives, and were born as two gods in the Sarvárthasiddhi abode. Here ends the story of Dhanya, having reference to giving alms.

Strive ever after the performance of faultlessly correct conduct, the root of true religion, and that will be acquired by honouring the Tírthankara, and the congregation, and by other similar observances.

Now follows the story of Árámaçobhá, touching the honouring of the Jina and the congregation.

STORY OF ÁRÁMAÇOBHÁ AND THE GRATEFUL SNAKE.

In this very land of Bharata, in the country of Kuçáḍhya, there is a village named Sthaláçraya. For a whole *yojana* round it there are no trees—nothing, in fact, higher than grass. In it there lived a Bráhman named Agniçarman, and he had a wife named Jvalanaçikhá, and a daughter named Vidyutprabhá. When the girl was eight years old her mother died. From that time forth Vidyutprabhá performed the household duties. She got up early in the morning and milked the cow; she cleaned and polished up everything, and took the cattle out to the pasture; in the middle of the day she drove the cattle home and gave her father his meal, and afterwards ate herself; then she went again to the forest to pasture the

* See Dr. Hoernle's 'Uvásaga Dasáo,' appendix iii., p. 30.

cows. At sunset she came home tired, and had to perform her household duties. As she worked like this every day, she became exhausted by the excessive burden of her family duties. One day, being quite broken down by the burden of household service, she said to her father : ' Father, bring to the house another mother, in order that I may be comfortable. When he heard this speech of his daughter's, he married another wife. She threw all the burden of the house on Vidyutprabhá, and gave her whole attention to anointing her body with unguents, bathing, and personal adornment.* Vidyutprabhá said to herself : 'Alas ! I got my father to bring another mother into the house with the hope of gaining relief for myself; but since this lady came I have been especially afflicted by increase of my labour, while this mother of mine sits with her feet crossed in perpetual ease.' Living a life of such hardship, she reached the age of twelve years. Now, about this time it happened that one day she threw grass before the cattle, and went to sleep. Then a huge black snake came near her in a state of the greatest terror, and, waking her up, began to say to her with a human voice : ' I am exceedingly terrified, and have come to you for protection. If these wicked snake-catchers follow me up, they will take me and throw me into a basket, so do you, my darling child, put me in your own lap and cover me up with your outer garment.' Then Vidyutprabhá fearlessly did as he said. Immediately the snake-catchers arrived with potent herbs in their hands. The snake-catchers said to the girl : ' Girl, have you seen a snake coming this way ?' The Bráhman's daughter said to the snake-catchers : ' I was asleep, so I know nothing about it.' The snake-catchers said to one another : ' This girl has seen the snake, and is frightened out of her life.' So the snake-catchers departed. She said to the snake : ' All the snake-catchers are gone, so dismiss your fear and depart.' Then the snake abandoned its snake body and became a manifest god, and said to that maiden : ' My

* The behaviour of the stepmother is of the true folk-lore type. Compare Ralston's ' Russian Folk-Tales,' p. 150.

dear girl, I am much pleased by the benefit that you have conferred on me, so choose a boon.'* She said: 'Make a shade over my head that I may pasture my cattle in comfort.' The god said to himself: 'This girl is foolish to ask for shade.' So he made a great garden to shelter her, and it was of the following nature:

> It was full of flowers and fruits that continued in every season; thick with leaves;
> Haunted by scent-loving bees; ever proof against the rays of the sun.

Then the god said: 'My dear child, wherever you remain, or wherever you go, this garden will always accompany you. When you are in trouble think on me.' Having said this, the god disappeared. So the garden remained sheltering her. At nightfall she went home with her cattle. Her mother said: 'Dear child, take food.' She answered: 'I am not hungry.' Then in the last watch of the night she went out with her cows. In this way she kept going backwards and forwards between her house and the field, and the garden always went with her. Once, when she was sleeping under the trees of the garden, the King of Páṭaliputra, having made the circuit of the regions, came to that forest. The king, seeing that that garden was in all respects charming, sat down under a fragrant mango-tree; then by the king's order the elephants and camels and other animals were fastened to various trees; the elephants' armour and things of that kind were hung on the branches of the trees. Then the girl was awakened by the cries of the soldiers, so she went to look after her cows, which were terrified by the elephants and other strange things. While she ran after her cows that were running away, the garden also ran with her, carrying the horses and other animals along with it. The king was bewildered to think what this could mean, and he said to his minister: 'Minister, what is this strange sight that I see?' The minister said: 'Un-

* In Kaden's 'Unter den Olivenbäumen' there is a grateful snake whom Lichtmess, in the story of that name, delivers from some boys. The snake was an enchanted princess, and he at length marries her. See also my translation of the 'Kathá Sarit Ságara,' vol. i., pp. 55 and 564, and vol. ii., pp. 107 and 633.

doubtedly it is the power of this girl.' Then the minister said to her: 'Do you go back, and we will bring your cows.' So she went back, and the garden went with her; while the grooms by the order of the king brought back her cows. The king, seeing her youth, fell in love with her. Then the minister, perceiving the desire of the king, said: 'My dear girl, accept this king, named Jitaçatru, as your husband.' The girl said: 'I cannot say anything about this; but the Bráhman, Agniçarman, who lives in this village, can say.' Then the minister went to that village by the king's order, and asked the Bráhman, saying: 'Bráhman, give this maiden to King Jitaçatru.' The Bráhman said: 'I would give even my life to the king, much more my daughter.' Then the Bráhman gave his daughter, and King Jitaçatru married her according to the Gándharva form of marriage. Wherever she went, a splendid garden flourished over her head, therefore the king gave her the name of Árámaçobhá. He then bestowed on his father-in-law, the Bráhman, twelve villages. Then the king put Árámaçobhá on an elephant and went to his own city, accompanied by the garden, that waved its trees over their heads. He entered his palace with great rejoicings. He then ruled in consort with Árámaçobhá, being sunk in great enjoyment. The garden shaded his palace. Now, it came to pass that the second wife of the Bráhman Agnimitra gave birth to a daughter. In course of time she grew up to be a young woman; thereupon her mother reflected: 'If Árámaçobhá were to die, the king would marry this daughter of mine.' So she began to devise a plot for killing Árámaçobhá. Accordingly, she said to the Bráhman: 'My lord, you never send any presents of food and so on for Árámaçobhá.' The Bráhman said: 'She is not in want of anything.' His wife answered: 'Although she may not be in want of anything, still, a daughter always longs for something sent from the home of her father.' Then she made some *siṃhakeçara** sweetmeats prepared of first-rate ingredients, but she took care to fill them full of

* Lion-mane.

poison.* She placed these sweetmeats in an undamaged pitcher, and said to the Bráhman: 'My lord, go yourself and give these to Árámaçobhá. You must also tell her from me that she is to eat these sweetmeats herself, and not to give them to anyone else; for these sweetmeats will meet with ridicule in the king's palace, on account of the clumsy way in which they are made, for what skill can be expected from rustic villagers?' Agniçarman, not seeing through her craftiness, put a seal on the pitcher and started off. In course of time he reached the city of Pátaliputra, and being weary, he slept under the shade of a banyan-tree in the garden outside the city. Now, it happened that that very snake-prince saw the Bráhman asleep, and possessing, from the union in him of merit and religion, the knowledge called limited,† he knew that he was the father of Árámaçobhá. He said to himself: 'Ha! I see what it is; that stepmother has given him food mixed with poison, and sent him with it to Árámaçobhá to bring about her death.' Having perceived this, he took out the poison. Then the Bráhman gave the food to Árámaçobhá.‡ She said to the king: 'My lord, look at this pitcher, in order that it may be opened.' The king said: 'Queen, no one is considered by me equal to you, so open the pitcher yourself.' Then the queen opened the pitcher, and a perfume unattainable in the world of mortals issued from it. Sweetmeats appeared in it resembling ambrosia. The king said: 'Queen, give one sweetmeat to each of the other queens.' Then, in accordance with the king's order, one sweetmeat was given to each of the queens. All of them, when they had tasted the sweetmeats, praised Árámaçobhá, and said: 'Truly her parents must be prosperous, since they send their daughter such sweetmeats, which even a king would find it difficult to obtain.' Then Agniçarman said to the king: 'My lord, let Árámaçobhá be sent to her father's

* Compare the cake which the envious sisters send to Maruzzedda in Gonzenbach's third tale ('Sicilianische Märchen,' p. 10).

† See Dr. Hoernle's 'Uvásaga Dasáo,' appendix iii., p. 44. It appears to extend to material objects only.

‡ I have here inserted one or two words to make sense.

house for a few days in order that she may see her mother.' The king said: 'What! do you not even know that kings' wives never see the sun?' Then the Bráhman, Agniçarman, went home, and told the whole occurrence to his wife. She said to herself: 'Alas! my scheme has not succeeded; so it is clear that the poison had no strength in it. I will send again, but cooked food this time, and I will put another and a terrible poison in it.' Then she made some delicious pastry, and putting in it a terrible poison, she sent it again by the hand of the Bráhman. Again the Bráhman went to sleep under the banyan-tree, and again the god removed the poison from the sweet pastry while he was asleep. This cooked food was praised in the king's palace like the sweetmeats. The Bráhman came back to his house as before, and told all to his wife. When she heard it, that wicked-minded woman was much grieved. One day she heard that Árámaçobha was pregnant. So she made some food mixed with *tálapuṭa* poison, and put it in the hand of the Bráhman, and again sent him off, saying: 'That daughter of yours is pregnant; you must certainly bring her to her father's house, that she may give birth to her first child there.' The Bráhman started off, and, as before, the god took away the poison while he slept on the way. He reached the king's palace and presented the food, which was praised as before. When the Bráhman was taking leave of his daughter in presence of the king, he asked that she might be sent to his house.* The king answered: 'Bráhman, kings' wives never give birth to children in their fathers' houses.' Then the Bráhman held a dagger to his breast, and said to the king: 'If you will not send her, I will involve you in the guilt of a Bráhman's murder.' The ministers said to the king: 'Your majesty, this Bráhman is obstinate. Some time or other he will involve you in the guilt of killing a Bráhman; so send the queen.' Then the king made great preparations, and sent her off with her father, and she went with him to his house. There she happily gave birth to a son. One

* I have here inserted some words which the sense requires.

day she went for some necessity to the back part of the premises, and her stepmother followed close behind her. Then Árámaçobhá saw a well, and said: 'Mother, since when has this well been here?' Her mother answered: 'My dear child, I had this well made.' While Árámaçobhá was looking at the well, her stepmother crept up behind her and pushed her into it. Then, as she was falling into the well, she called to mind the serpent-prince, and the serpent-prince himself held her up with his own hand. Then the god was very angry with that Bráhman's wife. But Árámaçobhá said, 'My lord, she is my mother,' and so pacified the wrath of the god. Then he made a palace in the well and placed her there. The garden also went with her into the well. Then the stepmother* arranged her daughter as a newly-delivered woman, and, after telling her what to do, placed her instead of the real mother near the son of Árámaçobhá. Now, it happened one day that her body was seen to be devoid of brilliancy. Then her ladies-in-waiting said to her: 'Queen, how is this? Your body seems to be devoid of brilliancy.' She answered: 'I do not know; for the last two or three days my body is not in good health.'

Then they employed various expedients, but none of them restored health to her body. Now, about this time the king sent a minister from the town of Páṭaliputra to fetch her. So the false Árámaçobhá set out. Then her slaves said to her: 'Queen, queen, why does the garden not come with you?' She replied: 'My garden is thirsty, and has gone into the well to drink water. It will follow me.' So the false queen went with her attendants to the city of Páṭaliputra. The king arranged for her a triumphal entrance. When he saw his son he was delighted. But when he saw that the body of the queen had lost its beauty,

* Here we have the well-known story of the substituted bride. A similar story is found in the 'Kathá Sarit Ságara,' vol. ii., p. 157 of my translation. For some European parallels see pp. 162 and 637 of the same volume. Grimm's eleventh story, 'Brüderchen und Schwesterchen' is an exceedingly close parallel. He refers us to some similar stories in his notes.

he said: 'Queen, what is this that has happened to your body?' Then her slaves said: 'The queen suffered from an unhealthy state of body.' Then the king was cast down, and said again: 'Why do I not see the garden with you, queen?' The supposed Árámaçobhá said: 'King, I have let it go to drink water. It will come after me as soon as I think of it.' Then the king said to himself: 'Is this the real Árámaçobhá, or some other woman?' On another occasion he said to the queen: 'Queen, summon that garden.' She said: 'I will summon it when a convenient season comes.' The king said to himself: 'Of a truth this is not the real Árámaçobhá; it is some other woman.' Then the real Árámaçobhá said to the god: 'My lord, separation from my son afflicts me exceedingly, so arrange that I may see my son.' Then the god said: 'By my power go and see your son, but you must come back quickly before dawn; if you do not, I will never grant you an interview again. Now, with regard to this matter, this shall be a sign to you: you shall see in your hair a dead snake.' She said: 'So be it.' Having said this, Árámaçobhá immediately went to the palace in which her son was sleeping. She took up her son in her tender hands,* and after playing with him a time, put him back comfortably in his place. Then she repaired to her palace below the earth, and threw all round the prince a heap of flowers and fruits coming from her own garden. In the morning the nurse of that son related this occurrence to the king. The king, hearing it, went and saw it with his own eyes, and said to the supposed Árámaçobhá: 'Queen, what is this that I see?' She answered: 'My lord, I brought all these flowers and fruits from my garden.' The king said: 'Then bring some now.' The queen answered: 'King, I can only bring them at night, but not in the day.' When the king heard that, he said to himself: 'Surely there is some foul play

* In Grimm's 'Märchen No. 11,' 'Brüderchen und Schwesterchen,' the real queen comes three times to nurse her child. On the third night the king speaks to her. See also Ralston's 'Russian Folk-Tales,' p. 184.

here.' On the second night, the whole thing went on just as before. Then, on the third night, the king stood with intent heart in a part of the room not lit up by the lamp, and beheld all the actions of Árámaçobhá; then he said to himself in the fulness of his joy: 'This is certainly the queen.' At that moment Árámaçobhá left the palace of her son. In the morning the king said to the sister of Árámaçobhá: 'To-day you must without fail summon the garden; there is no way out of it.' When the queen heard this her face became pale, and she said to herself: 'What answer can I give to-day?' Next night, when Árámaçobhá, after going through all the actions of the preceding night, was preparing to return, the king, who was lurking in a part of the room not lit up by the lamp, seized her hand, and said: 'Queen, why do you deceive me without cause?' Then Árámaçobhá said: 'King, I never deceive you; but there is a cause for my conduct.' The king said: 'What is the cause?' She answered: 'To-morrow I will tell you, but let me go now.' The king answered: 'You must tell me the cause now.' The queen said: 'When the cause is told you will regret all this.' But, though thus addressed by her, the king would not let her go. Then Árámaçobhá told the whole incident from the beginning, and at this moment the dawn appeared. When Árámaçobhá proceeded to bind up her hair that had become disarranged, a serpent fell from the god. When the queen saw the serpent stretched out in her hair, she was grieved, and she said: 'Ah, my father, am I, then, abandoned by thee?' When she uttered this lament in a loud voice, the king said: 'Queen, why are you so much afflicted?' Then she told the whole incident of the serpent-prince. Then the king was very angry with that Bráhman's wife, and had her summoned, and with his own hand chastised her with strokes of a whip; but Árámaçobhá fell at his feet, and entreated the king, saying: 'My lord, spare her.' So she brought about her release from further punishment. Then the king took from her and her husband the twelve villages that he had given them, and banished both of them from his land. The two consorts passed some time in mutual affection and loving intercourse; then one day the keeper of the park said to the king: 'My liege, to-day there has arrived in the garden of the sandalwood grove the saint Çrí Vírachandra, who possesses learning and knowledge.' Then the king went to adore him, surrounded by all his harem. He went and bowed before the great hermit, and sat down to hear his sermon. At the end of it Árámaçobhá said to him: 'Reverend sir, what act did I perform in a previous life?' Then the spiritual teacher said:

STORY OF ÁRÁMAÇOBHÁ IN A FORMER LIFE.

'In this very land of Bharata, in the town of Champá, there was a merchant named Kulandhara; he had a wife named Kulánandá. They had seven daughters—their names were Kamalaçrí, Kamalávatí, Kamalá, Lakshmiká, Çrí, Yaçodeví, and Priyakáritá—and they were all married in the houses of rich merchants. One day an eighth daughter was born, but she was utterly without promise of good fortune, so her father and mother were afflicted at her birth, and did not even give her a name. In time she grew up, but her father did not offer her in marriage. Then people said, "Why do you not marry your daughter?" Then the merchant, moved by the speeches of the people, began to look out for a bridegroom. One day there arrived in the exchange of the merchants a traveller with limbs begrimed with dirt. The merchant said to him: "Who are you? What kind of family do you belong to? What is your name?" He answered: "I am a merchant's son, and my name is Nandana, and I live in the city of Kauçalí. Once on a time, my wealth having been exhausted, I went to the land of Gauḍa to make money; but even there I could not make money, owing to my ill-luck. My feelings of pride made me return to my own country, and there I live by serving other men." When the merchant heard this, he said to himself, "This is a suitable bridegroom for my daughter." So he gave him his daughter. One day the bridegroom said to the merchant: "I will go once more to the land of Gauḍa." The merchant said: "Then take your wife with you." Then Nandana set out with his wife. As he was going along he came in due course to the city of Ujjayiní, and there they both of them entered a refuge for travellers at the time of evening. Nandana said to himself: "By thus travelling with my wife by short stages, I have already consumed a great portion of my provision for the journey. If the whole of my provision for the journey is consumed, I shall have to live by begging." So Nandana left his wife asleep, and, taking the provision for the journey with him, went off. In the morning she woke up, and said to herself: "Where is my husband gone? What can I do alone? If I go to my father's house I shall not be treated with respect." Then she lamented profusely, and at last, calming herself, she went into the house of a merchant named Maṇibhadra, in that very Ujjayiní, in order to preserve her chastity. The merchant said: "Who are you? Whose daughter are you? Who is your husband?" She said: "I am the daughter of the merchant Kulandhara; my husband is a man of the name of Nandana. As I was going with him to the land of Gauḍa, I was separated from the caravan." When Maṇibhadra heard this, he said: "My dear, I regard you as a daughter; remain in comfort in my house." Then she remained in his house, and performed household duties. Then Maṇibhadra went so far as to send out his own men to search for that caravan, but he did not succeed in clearing up the mystery. Then he sent a man to her father's house to interview the merchant Kulandhara. He went and said to the merchant: "Merchant, how many daughters have you? How many are married, and how many are unmarried? Tell me the facts of this matter, as I have been sent by Maṇibhadra with a proposal for the hand of an unmarried one." Then Kulandhara said: "I have eight daughters: seven of them are married in Champá, and the eighth has gone with her husband to the land of Gauḍa." Then the messenger returned to Ujjayiní and told the whole story to Maṇibhadra. Then Maṇibhadra, having learned the truth, treated Nandana's wife with great respect. Then that young woman performed with the utmost devotion in the Jaina temple—that Maṇibhadra had caused to be built—religious services, such as anointing with oil and decorating. By associating with holy women she became free from all connection with evil. Whatever valuable things Maṇibhadra gave her she disposed of; and she had splendid musical instruments made for the temple of the Jina. When she obtained much wealth, she had made three splendid umbrellas. She performed many penances, she caused many good works to be accomplished, and, according to her power, she exercised charity to the congregation. One day, seeing the merchant Maṇibhadra troubled with anxiety, she said: "Why are you anxious to-day, my father?" Maṇibhadra said: "My daughter, the king has presented to the god a garden full of fruit and flowers, but to-day it has suddenly withered up. Many devices have been tried, but it has not become fresh again. This is the reason why I am anxious." When she heard this, she said: "My father, do not be afflicted; I will restore the grove to its pristine freshness by the power of my virtue." When she had said this she meditated in her heart on the goddess, that executes the orders of the Jina, and refused food of all the four kinds,* and remained in the statuesque posture. Then on the third day the goddess, that executes the orders of the Jina, appeared, and said: "Virtuous lay-woman, the garden is afflicted by a demon, and almost withered, but by the force of thy virtue it shall be as good as ever to-morrow morning." Having said this the goddess disappeared. Then, morning having come, she related all the story of the night to the merchant. When Maṇibhadra heard that he went to inspect the garden. When he saw that it was full of flowers and

* See Hoernle's 'Uvásaga Dasáo,' p. 36, note. They are there enumerated as: *asana*, food, such as rice, curry, etc.; *pána*, drink, such as milk, water-gruel, etc.; *kh// áima*, delicacies, such as cocoa-nut and other fruits; *sáima*, relishes, such as betel, ginger, etc.

fruits, he said to the daughter of the merchant: "Daughter, it is by your power that my wishes have been fulfilled; now it is time for you to break your fast." Having said this, he got together a company of people and conducted her home amid the beating of drums with great rejoicing. That woman went home praised by all people; and after supplying the wants of the congregation, consisting of four classes,* she died a death of holy peace, and became a god in Saudharma; falling from that she became a Bráhman's daughter, Vidyutprabhá by name. Maṇibhadra also went to the world of gods; falling from that he became a man, then he died and became the serpent-prince who showed you such tenderness. Because in your former birth, being bewildered by falsehood, you did at first through ignorance do an unrighteous deed — owing to the influence of that deed you were born miserable. Because in a former birth, when living in the house of Maṇibhadra, you showed extraordinary piety in accordance with the law of the Jina— owing to the influence of that you obtained unequalled felicity. Because on that occasion you renewed again by your virtue the garden of the Jina—owing to the influence of that act, you have this garden given you by the god, which always wanders about with you wherever you go. Because in a former life you gave three umbrellas, therefore you are always in the shade. Because in a former birth you gave the implements of worship of the Jina, therefore you have had enjoyments. It is owing to your own religious devotion that the fortune of royalty has come to you. In course of time you will attain salvation.'

When the queen heard this, she fell fainting on the earth, and remembered her former birth, and beheld all her previous existence. At the end of her swoon, the queen said to the holy man: 'Reverend sir, let me separate from the king, and take a vow before you. You ought to remain here until this can be accomplished.' The king, too, said: 'You ought also to wait here until I can put my son on the throne, and come to you to take a vow.' Then

* Monks, nuns, and lay disciples, male and female.

the king placed his son Malayasundara on the throne, and, accompanied by Árámaçobhá, took a vow. Both of them observed in it a conduct without reproach, and obtained the happiness of heaven. When they fall from it, they will go through some births in succession and obtain salvation.

Here ends the story of Árámaçobhá.

Here begins the story of Ṛishidattá, having reference to virtue.

STORY OF ṚISHIDATTÁ.*

In this very Jambudvípa, in Bharatakshetra, is a district called Madhyadeça; in it was a city named Rathamardana, in which lived a king named Hemaratha. His wife was named Suyaças, and they had a gem of a son named Kanakaratha. At this same time there was in the northern quarter a city named Káverí; in it reigned a king named Surasundara, and the name of his queen was Vásulá, and they had a daughter named Rukmiṇí. In course of time she grew up. When her mother saw that she had recently attained womanhood, she adorned her with ornaments on all her limbs, and sent her into the presence of her father. She bowed before him, and then he took her on his lap, and said to himself in his heart: 'This girl is in the first bloom of youth; to what bridegroom must she be given? Ah! I know. King Hemaratha has a son, Prince Kanakaratha; he will be a deserving bridegroom for her, and no one else will.' After the king had determined on this plan with his ministers, he sent an ambassador to King Hemaratha; then the ambassador asked for Kanakaratha, and he, by the order of his father, set out for the city of Káverí. He advanced by forced marches, and had to encamp in the forest districts of the border. Then the loads were taken off the camels; the lines of tents were set up on all sides; the horses had the saddles removed from their backs and rolled on the ground; the elephants were taken to the binding-post by their

* This resembles very closely the story of Kadalígarbha in the 'Kathá Sarit Ságara.' See vol. i. of my translation, p. 286.

drivers. While this was going on, an ambassador approached Prince Kanakaratha, who had taken his seat on a throne under a fragrant mango-tree, and said thus to him: 'Royal sir, my master, Prince Aridamana, thus announces to you by my mouth: "Your entering within the borders of my territory will bring about your death; so, if you feel disposed to fight, meet me face to face; if not, submit to my authority, and return home."' When the prince heard this he knit his brows so as to assume a terrible appearance, and gave the ambassador this answer: 'Listen, ambassador! Go and tell that disgrace to his family, your master, that I, the prince, have come to kill him. I am delighted with the hope of combat, and ready armed to meet him, so send your master here at once.' Thereupon the ambassador went and delivered to his master the whole message as sent by Kanakaratha; and when Aridamana heard it, he went with his whole army to fight with Prince Kanakaratha. Then Kanakaratha, hearing from his swift horsemen that he was coming, went out to meet him. When the armies met, a terrible fight took place. At that moment the universe seemed to be all one cry, with the rolling of drums, the gallant shouts of warriors, the trumpetings of elephants, and the neighings of horses. Then the prince, galloping towards Aridamana, said to him: 'Here I am, you frog of the lake of battle, destitute of discernment; now fight!' Having said this, he dashed forward with the swiftness of lightning, and took him prisoner. He took him with him in his camp for some stages, and then let him go. Aridamana thereupon was filled with the spirit of renunciation, and abandoned his kingdom and took a vow; and having observed a conduct without transgression, he attained blessedness in the holy place of the Tírthakara Nami. The prince in his march came to a forest; and on that occasion the forest became like a city, owing to the prince's army settling down and encamping in it. It happened that, while the army was there, some men went out to look for water, and at the time of evening they returned and bowed before the prince. The prince said: 'How is it that you have been so long away?' They said: 'By the order of your majesty we went hence into a wood, and there we saw a lake like a sea; and while we were in that wood we saw a maiden, who surpassed in beauty the nymphs of heaven, amusing herself with swinging; but while we were looking at her, she suddenly disappeared. Then we searched that wood tree by tree, but we could not see her; it was for this reason that we were so long away.' When the prince heard it, he was agitated with the emotion of wonder. And just at this time the sun set. So the prince dismissed them, and said his evening prayer, and, folding himself in an eiderdown quilt, went to sleep. In the morning he washed the lotus of his face, and worshipped the gods, and ordered the victorious drum to be sounded for the onward advance. All the army, when they heard the sound of the drum, began to march. The prince himself, surrounded by some princes who were his friends, having the path pointed out to him by scouts, went forward to the lake. Thereupon the prince went to that place where the maiden was seen by those who went to look for water. As fate would have it, the prince saw the maiden in the very same spot. When the prince saw her, he said to himself: 'If she is a nymph of heaven, then the eyes of Indra alone are of any use to their possessor; if she is a snake-maiden, then the king of snakes is truly the prince of fortunate ones.* Such a pearl of women is not found in this world of mortals. Is camphor produced in a salt-mine?' While the prince was sunk in these reflections, the rear-guard of his army came up; and then the maiden, hearing the noise of the host, vanished. Then the army continued its march round the lake; and while the prince was searching for that fair-eyed maiden, having his heart drawn towards her by love, he saw a *chaitya*. Then the prince said to himself: 'That fair one will be in this *chaitya*;' so he went into it. And then the prince saw in that *chaitya* an image of the eminent Ṛishabha; so he

* The Sanskrit word that means 'snake' means also 'enjoyer.'

had an abundant supply of flowers brought, and himself made an offering to the excellent Jina. After he had made his offering, he composed this hymn of praise:

> 'To-day my eye is blessed, to-day my head is blessed,
> To-day my hand is blessed, to-day my foot is blessed,
> Since thou hast been propitiated, adored, worshipped and praised.'

Speaking thus, he bent before the chief of prophets again and again. Thereupon, at this very conjuncture, there arrived a hermit with heavy matted hair hanging down, with body broken with old age. When the prince saw this hermit, such as has been described, and saw that that very lady-love of his was carrying for him a large basket, his eyes were dilated with curiosity. The girl, too, seeing the prince, thought: 'Is this Indra, or the moon, or the sun-god? or is he the god of love himself, present in visible form?' Then the prince, having worshipped the mighty Jina, bowed before that hermit when he arrived. Then the hermit said to the prince: 'My son, what family is blessed by thee? What succession of letters is fortunate enough to form thy name? To what cause is the great happiness of thy arrival due?' The prince answered all his questions; in the meanwhile he saw the damsel, who was concealed by the hermit's weight of matted hair. Then the prince said to the hermit: 'Who caused this temple of the Jina to be built in this wood? Who are you? Who is this maiden? Tell me all.' Then the hermit said: 'My son, my story is long; first let us worship the god; so wait a moment.' Having said this, the hermit went in and worshipped the god; while the maiden looked at the prince, and the prince looked at the maiden. Then the hermit, having worshipped the god with lotuses, came out into the porch of the temple, and said to Prince Kanakaratha: 'Come to this hut of mine which is near, in order that I may show you respect.' Then the prince went into the hut in order to please him. The hermit said: 'Hear, my son, the story of the *chaitya*, of myself, and of this maiden:

'In this very land of Bharata there is a city named Amarávatí; in it there was a king named Harisheṇa, and he had a wife named Priyadarçaná; they had a son named Jinasena. One day a horse, that had been trained in an inverse manner,* carried off King Harisheṇa. He came to this very wood, and got rid of his horse, and gradually wandering about in the wood, the king reached a hermitage, and there he bowed before the abbot Viçvabhúti, sprung from the family of Kachchhamahákachchha. The hermit, knowing by his marks that he was a king, blessed him, and said: "Whence have you come hither? How is it that you are alone?" Then the king, being asked this question by the hermit, told the whole truth. In the meanwhile the army, that was following the king, arrived, and rejoiced when they saw the king. Then the army encamped outside the hermitage. The king remained there a whole month, courting the favour of the hermits, and he had this temple of Ṛishabha built. When he was leaving, the hermit gave King Harisheṇa a charm for destroying the effects of poison.† Then the king went to his own town. The people showed great joy when he made his entrance into the town. So he continued governing his kingdom. One day, as he was sitting in the hall of audience, a man came and said: "King, there is a city called Mangalávatí. In it there reigns a king named Priyadarçana, and he has a queen named Vidyutprabhá. They have a daughter named Prítimatí, who has been bitten by a serpent, and I have been sent by my master to inform you." When the king heard this, he travelled to that place by means of swift camels, and by means of that very poison-counteracting charm freed the maiden from the influence of the poison. Then her father gave her to him, and he married her, and returned with her to his own city. There he lived happily, and after the lapse of some time he committed the care of his kingdom to his son, and

STORY OF KING HARISHEṆA, WHO BECAME A HERMIT.

* *I.e.*, to gallop when it should stop, and *vice versâ*.

† Compare 'Kathá Sarit Ságara,' vol. i., p. 461.

with that newly-married wife went to practise asceticism. Both the king and the queen went to the hermitage of the abbot Viçvabhúti, and there engaged in asceticism. Then, while the Queen Prítimatí was practising asceticism, a pregnancy which was previously caused declared itself in the fifth month. When the ascetics saw her in such a state they were all shocked. Then King Harisheṇa said: "Queen, what is the meaning of this?" She answered: "This is a pregnancy previously caused, but I did not tell you of it when I ought to have done so, because I was afraid that it would interfere with my practising asceticism." Then all the ascetics who had previously occupied that hermitage left it, and went elsewhere. But Harisheṇa and his wife remained there. Those two passed four months in a state of extreme sorrow, blaming their own action. When the ninth month was completed Queen Prítimatí brought forth a daughter. Because she was born in the hermitage of the *ṛishis*, her parents called her Ṛishidattá. Then, as fate would have it, her mother Prítimatí died from the consequences of childbirth, and after performing Prítimatí's funeral the father tended and brought up the child till she attained the age of eight years. Then her father thought: "The beings that roam in the forest will see that my child is beautiful, and will carry her off." So he prepared a collyrium for her. The secret of this collyrium that makes invisible* was long ago communicated to him by the abbot Viçvabhúti. For that reason that daughter of his became invisible to those that roam in the forest.

'Know, O prince of auspicious aspect, that I am that Harisheṇa, and that this is my daughter.'

The prince looked at the maiden with such a loving glance, and she looked at him with such a loving glance, that they were 'both in either's powers.'† The hermit,

* Compare 'Kathá Sarit Ságara,' vol. ii., p. 221.

† I take these words from Shakespeare's 'Tempest.' I may, perhaps, draw attention to the fact that there is a certain similarity between the two stories.

perceiving in his own mind their desire, smiled and said to the prince: 'Prince, I hereby give you this daughter of mine.' The prince answered: 'I receive what you are pleased to give me, reverend sir.' Then the hermit said: 'Rise up, prince; go to your own camp and take food.' The prince said to the hermit: 'My lord, I will to-day eat with you, so come along with me.' The hermit said: 'My dear youth, your majesty makes it hard to refuse, but for hermits no other food but bulbs and roots is appropriate.' When the hermit had said this, he dismissed the prince, who went to his camp with his suite and took food. Then, in an auspicious moment, the prince married the daughter of Harisheṇa, Ṛishidattá by name, and lived there with her for some days. Then one day the hermit said to the prince with faltering voice: 'Prince, support of the world, why should I say much to you? Take care never to make my daughter an object of insult. This girl, who from living in the forest is wanting in experience of the world, is committed by me to your care; by living with you she will acquire many excellent qualities, since even dust that settles on the navel of a deer* becomes sweet-scented. But I now wish to enter the fire, as for people like me death is better than life.' Then the prince fell at the feet of the hermit, and said to that mighty saint: 'Do not even mention the word "suicide."' Then Ṛishidattá, weeping, said to her father: 'Show some compassion to me.' The hermit said: 'My dear girl, do not say this, but listen to my admonition. Be obedient to your superiors; observe the laws of virtue; do not be angry even with rival wives; do not turn aside from holiness in pleasure or in pain.' And then the hermit, having taken leave of Prince Kanakaratha and of his own daughter, and calling to mind the *mantra* of the five Parameshṭins,† entered the fire. Ṛishidattá, weeping and rolling on the earth, uttered the following lament:

* Or perhaps 'on musk.'

† Yugádíça, Çánti, Nemi, Párçva, and Víra. ('Weber über das Çatrunjaya Máhátmyam,' p. 15.)

'O father! father! devoted to boundless love of thy child,
To-day, without thee, I am wretched, like a plantain-tree deprived of its root;
I never beheld my mother; but thou hast been my mother;
So, thou being gone, both my hands have fallen to earth.'

Then Prince Kanakaratha, in order to admonish his beloved, said to her:

'Stay, stay, my beloved; do not stretch out weeping overmuch;
Of what profit is it that thou sorrowest over one gone to the other world?
Queen, thy father is not to be lamented, since he reigned as a king and observed his vows as a hermit.'

Then the prince performed his funeral ceremonies and made a saçrificial *sthaṇḍila* in the place of burial. Then the prince set out with his wife Ṛishidattá for his own city. And Ṛishidattá, as she was going along with her husband, kept sowing by the way a series of *sadáphala** fruits that her father had given her.† So the prince, travelling by continuous stages, reached Rathamardana, and entered it with great rejoicings. Then Kanakaratha, with his wife, bowed at the feet of his parents, and was welcomed by them. So Prince Kanakaratha lived happily with his wife. In the meanwhile King Surasundara, the lord of Káverí, heard that the prince had married the hermit's daughter, and his daughter Rukmiṇí, who longed for the prince, was much afflicted. Then one day she fell in with a witch named Sulasá, who was deeply versed in all charms and spells; and she managed, by giving her food and clothes, to incline the witch in her mind to undertake the task of disgracing Ṛishidattá in order that the prince might come to her. So she despatched the wicked Sulasá to Rathamardana. Then Sulasá, after a few days, arrived in the city of Rathamardana. And at night-time she went into the palace of Prince Kanakaratha, after administering a narcotic drug to all the inmates, and when she saw Ṛishi-

* Further on the word *sahakára* (fragrant mango) is used. *Sadáphala* means, according to Monier Williams, always bearing fruit: the cocoanut-tree, the glomerous fig-tree, the jack, the Vilva-tree.

† See the note on p. 290 of vol. i. of my translation of the 'Kathá Sarit Ságara,' and additional note on p. 576.

dattá sleeping by the side of the prince, she shook her head, and said in her heart:

'O the beauty, O the splendour, of this fawn-eyed fair one!
Happy indeed is the man whose beloved she has become.'

Then that witch smeared the face of Ṛishidattá with blood,* placed some flesh on her pillow, and, after killing a man, fled from the palace of the prince. Accordingly, in the morning the prince's retinue, seeing that a man had been killed, made a confused murmur. Hearing the murmur the prince said to himself: 'Alas! alas! I hear that a man has been killed in the night, so I wonder if this beloved of mine is a Rákshasí.' Then, seeing that the mouth of Ṛishidattá was stained with blood, and that flesh had been placed on the pillow—beholding, I say, his beloved in this position—he said to himself: 'Alas! the saying of the Çástras, that the gift of beauty is prolific of misfortune, is indeed true.' Having formed many ideas of this kind in his mind, and having again felt doubtful about them, he at once woke up his beloved, saying: 'Queen, rise up, rise up!' And then, seeing his darling aroused from sleep, he thus addressed her: 'Queen, I wish to ask you something. Are you, though born in the family of Harisheṇa, a Rákshasí?' She was terrified, and said: 'Royal sir, why do you talk in this way to me?' The prince said: 'My dear, last night a man was killed; there is flesh on your pillow; your mouth is stained with blood. These two things I have seen with my own eyes.' When Ṛishidattá heard this speech of her husband's, and saw the facts for herself, she said to the prince: 'Royal sir, if I have been a flesh-eater in the past, how could I, as I do, prohibit the eating of flesh? I know nothing about all this; it must have been done by some enemy, impelled by my deeds in a former life. But if you have any displeasure

* See p. 289 of vol. i. of my translation of the 'Kathá Sarit Ságara,' and the note on p. 631 of vol. ii. In No. 20 of Gonzenbach's 'Sicilianische Märchen,' the holy Francis takes away the three children of his god-daughter, and besmears her mouth with blood. She is accused of being a were-wolf. A similar incident will be found in Grimm's notes on No. 3 in his collection (Marienkind).

against me, put me to death.' When the prince heard this speech, he said to her: 'My beloved, you are innocent; do not be afflicted in your mind.' While the prince was saying this he himself removed the flesh, and washed her lotus-like mouth. In this way the witch went on continually bringing disgrace on her, and the prince, being deeply attached to her, continually went on palliating the disgrace. One day King Hemaratha said to his ministers: 'Alas! alas! every day there is a man killed in my city; do you know nothing about it?' They said: 'King, this is not the handiwork of a woman; this is all we know.' The king was filled with anger, and said: 'Then let all these sectaries* be banished from the city, whatever these men know or do not know.' Then, by the order of the king, all the sectaries, except the Jaina hermits, were banished. Now, at this very juncture the witch Sulasá came into the king's court, and said to the king: 'Royal sir, I had a dream last night, to the effect that a certain deity said to me: "To-morrow the king will expel all the sectaries, so you must go to him and tell him that the wife whom his son brought from the forest is certainly a Rákshasí, and that all this that has been done is her doing, so he ought not to illtreat the sectaries. Because the boar eats the sugar-canes the buffaloes are smitten." If, royal sir, you have any doubt about the truth of my statement, go to-night and look for yourself.' The king said, 'I will look,' and dismissed the witch. When night came, he made Prince Kanakaratha sleep near him, on the pretext that he had a pain in his limbs. While the prince was lying near his father, he thus reflected with himself during the night: 'Alas! now the disgrace of my beloved will be made manifest, since, on the one hand, it is not lawful for me to disobey my father's orders; on the other hand, my wife will be disgraced by my obeying them. On one side is a tiger, on the other a river.' Then, during that very night, Sulasá, the witch, smeared, as before, the

* *Páshaṇḍinaḥ.* The word has not generally a bad meaning with Jains. See Dr. Hoernle's translation of the 'Uvásaga Dasáo,' note 52.

mouth of Ṛishidattá with blood, and placed flesh on her pillow. King Hemaratha sent spies, who ascertained that fact, and in the morning they reported it to the king. Then King Hemaratha was angry, and said to the prince: 'Fie! how is it that, though you know this female to be a bloodthirsty Rákshasí, you still protect her? Depart, depart, husband of a Rákshasí! leave my territories; you have to-day stained a stainless race.' Then the prince folded his hands as a suppliant, and said to the king: 'Royal sir, this is all untrue. Be merciful to me; do not be angry with me.' Then the king said: 'Go yourself and look.' So the prince went in sorrow to his own house. There he saw his darling weeping, with her cheek pillowed on her left hand. The prince said: 'Queen, why do you rain down water with showers of tears? What are we to do? Yesterday a witch denounced you to the king as a Rákshasí, and early this morning the king sent spies, and discovered you to be so. Now I really do not know what will happen to you.' At this moment the king arrived, and, dragging the weeping girl by the hair, delivered her to the executioners, and gave them the following order: 'Take this wicked Rákshasí all round the city, and then remove her to the cemetery, and slay her quickly.' Thereupon Prince Kanakaratha began to gash his own body, but King Hemaratha prevented him by tying his limbs with his own hands. Then the executioners took Ṛishidattá, and entwined indigo with the seven locks of her hair. They encircled her neck with a garland of Nimba-leaves; they held over her a shoe by way of umbrella, on a lofty pole; they placed a piece of an old broom, by way of tuft, on her head; the whole of her body was stained with powder; she was hooted by the low people who had assembled, and so they led her, with dissonant cymbals, horns, and drums preceding her, in this condition through the city, in accordance with the king's order.* Then, while the citizens lamented, the execu-

* In this difficult passage I have been assisted by Átmárám Muni and Dr. Hoernle.

tioners took her into the cemetery, and at that very moment the sun went to his rest, as if unable to witness her miserable, pitiable condition, and immediately darkness was diffused all over the landscape. Then one of the executioners drew his sword, and said to Ṛishidattá: 'Bloodthirsty one, think upon some favourite deity, for you will this moment cease to be.' While, after saying this, he was brandishing his sword, Ṛishidattá, in her terror, fell on the ground in a faint. Then all the executioners, seeing that she seemed to be dead, said: 'What is the use of this slaying of the slain?' So they returned to the city. Now, in the evening twilight the cool breeze began to blow on her body, and she recovered consciousness, and seeing the cemetery, and not seeing the executioners, she fled to save her life, like a doe escaped from the net. And after she had gone a long way and reached an uninhabited forest, she lamented aloud: 'O my father! O my father! deprived of you I have fallen into the slough of calamity; so come and support with your hand your own child. If I had not been foolish enough to separate from you then, how would misfortune have come upon me now? O my soul! what sin did you commit in a former birth that such a disgrace should have befallen me, though I am innocent?' After she had uttered many lamentations of this kind, she walked on slowly towards the south, with the intention of repairing to her father's hermitage, and the way was made clear to her by the *sahakára* trees, which she had sown with her own hand on the path by which she had come after her marriage: so she followed that track, and in course of time reached the hermitage. When she saw the place where her father was burned, Ṛishidattá wept bitterly. She said: "Alas! father, here is your child returned. Where have you gone? Come and appear to me. Have pity upon me and comfort me, who am afflicted, downcast, solitary, and without a protector. Alas! father, in this uninhabited wood, deprived of you, with whom can I take refuge? where can I go? what can I do?' When Ṛishidattá had lamented much to this effect, she gradually got the better of her grief, and she remained living in her father's hut eating bulbs, roots and fruits, alone in that uninhabited forest. One day she reflected in her mind: 'How shall I be able to preserve my virtue in this lonely wood? Ah, I know. Long ago my father told me of a plant the virtue of which will turn a woman into a man.' Having resolved to make use of this plant, she went into the forest and fetched that plant and put it in her ear, and by virtue of it she immediately became a man.* Then she put on the dress of a hermit, and lived happily in that forest, worshipping the great Jina with sweet-smelling flowers three times a day. So she passed some time. In the meanwhile her beloved, though he enjoyed the pleasures of a royal station, felt his heart empty—like an animal that has been left behind when all its companions have been sold. Sulasá, thinking that she had triumphed, went and made the daughter of the King of Káverí happy with the joyful news. Then King Surasundara sent an ambassador to Hemaratha. The ambassador went and said to Hemaratha, King of Rathamardana: 'Royal sir, the King of Káverí sends you the following message: "The prince never came here. What is the reason?" So send the prince at once to marry the daughter of my master. Do not despise a good connection.' When Hemaratha heard this speech of the ambassador, he said to the prince his son in private: 'My dear boy, why do you thus perpetually grieve? Have you not heard the saying that one should not blame a deed that is done?† so, to please me, go and marry the daughter of the King of Káverí.' Then the prince, though unwilling, obeyed the command of his father, and set out to marry Rukmiṇí on a day fixed by the astrologers; then advancing gradually, he reached that very forest. When he saw that forest, the eyes of the prince were bedewed with tears, and he said to himself:

* Compare 'Kathá Sarit Ságara,' vol. ii., p. 302.

† The sense seems to be, 'It is of no use crying over spilt milk.'

'Alas! here is that very forest in which I married that fair-eyed one.

> 'Here are all the very same trees; here is that same lake;
> The whole landscape is the same, and in front of me is the temple of the Jina.
> What formerly gave me pleasure has now become a source of affliction to me!
> O Fate, what hast thou done to me, though I am innocent and alive to the vanity of the world?'

Being occupied with melancholy thoughts of this kind, the prince went with a few foot soldiers into the temple of the Jina. At this very moment his right eye throbbed violently;* then the prince said to himself: 'My eye throbs as if indicating a meeting with the beloved; but Fate has taken her away. Can this omen be ineffectual?'

While the prince was going through these reflections, Ṛishidattá came to him as a hermit, and offered him flowers. The prince took the garland of flowers from her hand, and looked again and again at the hermit with a look that indicated his perception of the resemblance to his beloved. Ṛishidattá the hermit said to herself: 'I wonder if my beloved has set out to marry Rukmiṇí.' The prince worshipped the Jina, and then went to his tent after summoning the hermit Ṛishidattá. He made the supposed hermit sit on a seat of honour, and feasted him, and after requesting him with great vehemence to accept the present, he clothed him in a suit of raiment. Then the prince said to that hermit: 'When did you come to this forest?' Then the hermit said: "Royal sir, in this hermitage there was a hermit named Harisheṇa; he had a daughter, named Ṛishidattá, who was exceedingly virtuous. Some prince or other married her, and took her away to his own city; as for her father, Harisheṇa, he attained the condition of a divinity by entering the fire. At that time I came here, after wandering over the earth, and from that day forth I worship Ṛishabha in this temple. While I have been dwelling here, five years have been completed, but to-day all my

* Compare 'Kathá Sarit Ságara,' ii. 128.

aspirations have been fulfilled by beholding you.' Then the prince said to the hermit: 'How is it, hermit, that my eye is never sated with gazing on you?' The hermit answered: 'Royal sir, one person is dear to one, and another to another. The *kumudas** rejoice in the moon, and the *kamalas* in the sun.' Then the prince said: 'Hermit, I have to continue my journey; but how am I to advance, seeing that my mind, being bound with the chain of love for you, cannot go forward? So come along with me; on my return I will leave you here.' Then the hermit said: 'Do not insist, royal sir, since intercourse with kings is to the detriment of ascetics.' Then the prince said once more to the hermit: 'What! do even people like you, my lord, refuse to grant petitions?' The minister also said to the hermit: 'Please do what the prince says.' The hermit, who was really Ṛishidattá, was induced to consent to all by their great persistence, and at this moment the sun went to his rest. The hermit and the prince offered up their evening prayer, and spent the night lying on the same couch. Then at dawn the prince set out, and, travelling by continuous stages, reached the city of Káverí, and then the King Surasundara, with his suite, came to meet him. The festive entry into the city took place amid universal rejoicing. A palace was prepared for the marriage; the prince was adorned. Then, on a day fixed by the astrologers, he married Rukmiṇí. One day, when Rukmiṇí was sitting on the prince's lap, she said to him: 'Lord of my life, what sort of a person was that unfortunate Ṛishidattá who captivated your soul?' Then the prince said: 'How can I describe in detail the perfections of that Ṛishidattá? In comparison with her beauty, the wife of the god of love is a mere slave girl, Menaká is only fit to be her mask, and the wives of the serpents are the dust of her feet. But since I am deprived of her by the decree of Fate, you have become dear to me. For if one cannot obtain a razor, is not

* These appear to be different kinds of lotus. The sudden affection that the prince conceives for the hermit reminds one of Cymbeline's feeling towards his daughter when she was disguised as a page.

even rubbing some alleviation?' Then Rukmiṇí flew in a passion, and revealed to the prince the daring deed that she had some time ago committed, and at that moment Ṛishidattá the hermit was delighted in her soul at the taking away of her reproach. When the prince heard this, he looked terrible with knit brows, and, flinging Rukmiṇí from his lap, scolded her severely in the following words: 'You wicked and cruel woman, you have hurled yourself and me into hell! Alas! of that accomplished and virtuous and beautiful woman that was, the memory only subsists, and this you have done. Why did you commit a deed detestable in the eyes of all men in order to serve your own interests?' While he was reproaching Rukmiṇí in these words, the day broke, and she fled weeping. Then the prince, afflicted at the loss of his wife, had a pyre built up in the court of the house, and, though his followers tried to dissuade him, he proceeded to ascend it. Then the King of Káverí came there with speed, and tried to dissuade him, saying: 'Prince, this womanish proceeding is not becoming to men like you.' But the prince did not desist from his persistent intention. Then the attendants said to Ṛishidattá, the hermit: 'Reverend sir, this prince will do whatever you tell him, so dissuade him from suicide.' The hermit, when entreated by those attendants, laughed, and said to the prince: 'Prince, why do you die for a mere woman? How comes it that you have forgotten the promise that you made when you brought me away from the forest? Moreover,

> 'Even the idea of union with your beloved will be impossible when you are dead,
> But if you live she will return from some place or other, and be reunited with you.'

Then the prince said to the hermit: 'Hermit, why do you deceive me? Does a dead person anywhere ever come back to life?' The hermit answered: 'Give the word, and, owing to this virtue of yours, Ṛishidattá, though dead, shall come back to life.' Then the prince said to the hermit: 'My lord, let me hear this again quickly: have you seen her anywhere with your eyes, or have you heard of her, or do you know by your knowledge that she is living anywhere, that you speak thus confidently?' The hermit answered: 'Prince, I know all about your beloved by my supernatural knowledge. As you see me, such is she in the city of Yama, the land of the southern region. So I will transport myself into the realm of Yama instead of her, and will bring that Ṛishidattá here for the sake of you, my friend.' Then the prince said: 'Hermit, if this be so, further delay is out of place.' The hermit answered: 'Prince, can one travel to the southern region with the momentary speed of thought? One would catch cold for nothing.' The prince said: 'Long ago I gave you my heart; now I give you my very self.' The hermit answered: 'Remain, prince, in possession of your own self; if hereafter I ask you for any boon, you must grant it me.' The prince said: 'So be it.' After this conversation, the hermit went behind a screen, and after remaining there a moment, during which she got rid of the form of a male hermit by means of a second herb, she appeared from behind the screen as Ṛishidattá, the daughter of Harisheṇa, and at that moment a troop of gods rained flowers on her head. When the people saw her, they said to one another: 'Rukmiṇí compared with Ṛishidattá is like brass compared with gold. So Prince Kanakaratha was quite right in his persistent intention; who would not die for such a woman?' As for the prince himself, he could not have enough of gazing at Ṛishidattá, whom he had not seen for such a long time. Moreover, Surasundara was exceedingly delighted when he saw her. Then King Surasundara placed Ṛishidattá and the prince on a huge elephant, and took them to his own palace; and there, to show his respect for her, he honoured her with a bath, with clothes, jewels and other things of the kind. Then the king had that wicked witch, Sulasá, mounted on an ass and led round the city. Cymbals and drums were beaten before her, the citizens abused her at every step, and at every step people beat her with sticks, fists and other things, and at last the king had both her ears and her nose cut off, and banished her from the city. And King Surasundara took his own daughter aside and reproached her bitterly. But Prince Kanakaratha, reunited with Ṛishidattá, was plunged in a lake of happiness. For some time he was simply bewildered with his joy; but one day he said to his beloved Ṛishidattá, who was seated on his lap, 'My darling, all has turned out prosperously, but my friend, the hermit, is suffering in the house of Yama.' Ṛishidattá laughed, and said: 'Prince, do not be downcast; I accomplished all this by means of a herb. But grant me the boon that you previously promised me.' The prince said: 'Well, then, what boon is to be granted?' Ṛishidattá said: 'Regard Rukmiṇí as you regard me.' When the prince heard this, he said to himself: 'How excellent is the feeling of her soul even towards one that is an enemy!' Having gone through these reflections, he said to his beloved: 'Be it so, queen.' When Ṛishidattá heard this, she herself summoned Rukmiṇí, and induced her to lay aside her shame. Then the prince took leave of the King of Káverí and returned with those two beloved ones to his own city. Then King Hemaratha came out to meet his son. When the prince saw that his own father had come, he bowed before him, and they entered the city. Then King Hemaratha, having heard the facts, being ashamed of his own misconduct, showed great honour to Ṛishidattá. In course of time Hemaratha placed Kanakaratha on his throne, and, repairing to Bhadráchárya, took the vows in his presence. Then Kanakaratha ruled his realm righteously, and had by Ṛishidattá a son, named Siṃharatha. One day the king, while sitting at a window with Ṛishidattá, saw a bank of clouds, which was immediately swept away by the force of a violent wind. Then, seeing that the cloud was dispersed almost as soon as it had gathered, the king became full of the spirit of renunciation, and he said thus to himself: 'Even as this bank of clouds appeared and disappeared, so in this revolving world transient are life, wealth and other blessings.'* While the king, with his beloved Ṛishidattá, was thus full of ascetic impulses, in the morning a keeper of the garden came and said to the king: 'My liege, there has arrived in the Kusumákara garden a teacher named Bhadrayaças, with his attendants.' When the king heard this, he bestowed on the gardener a gift consisting of five things, and he went to worship the sage. After he had worshipped him, he listened, in the company of Ṛishidattá, to his religious discourse. At the end of the sermon, Ṛishidattá said: 'Reverend sir, what deed did I do in a former life that I should have been thus falsely accused of being a Rákshasí?' The sage said:

STORY OF ṚISHIDATTÁ IN HER PREVIOUS BIRTHS.

'In this land of Bharata there is a city named Gangápura. In it there lived a king named Gangádatta; and he had a queen named Gangá, and their daughter was named Gangásená. In that very city there was an abbess of the name of Chandrayaças, from whom Gangásená received religious instruction. Then, after some time had passed, she† solemnly renounced in the presence of Chandrayaças all earthly pleasures as resembling poison. Now, it happened that in that very city a female lay disciple, named Sangá, was performing the penance of fasting for a whole month. Accordingly the people worshipped her, and published her fame abroad. When Gangásená saw how matters stood, she could not endure that Sangá should be praised, so one day she made the following imputation against the lay sister, that she was a Rákṣhasí, and devoured the flesh of corpses during the night, though she practised mortification during the day. Though Sangá heard the charge that had been brought against her, she endured it patiently, and did not bring a lying accusation against her rival. Owing to that deed Gangásená roamed through many births, and was again born as a princess in the city of Gangápura. Then she

* Compare Jacobi's Introduction to his edition of the 'Pariçishṭa Parvan,' p. 19.

† The Sanskrit has 'you,' which gives a kind of sense.

once more took a vow, and became angry and died without repenting of her anger, and became the wife of the lord Içána.* From that position she fell, and was conceived as the daughter of the hermit Harisheṇa, in the womb of his wife Prítimatí, and was born in the hermitage as Ṛishidattá; so, my good lady, it is owing to the influence of deeds in a previous birth that this grievous accusation was brought against you.'

When Ṛishidattá heard this account of her former existence from the mouth of the sage, she remembered all her births. When Kanakaratha heard that, he felt inclined to renounce the world; and both of them, after placing their son Siṃharatha on the throne, took the vows in the presence of the religious teacher Bhadrayaçaṣ. They performed the most terrible mortifications, and both of them obtained absolute knowledge.† This pair of *kevalins* enduring mortification, when the accumulated actions of a long existence had come to an end, having gained glory by destroying the enemy of the soul's peace, obtained the most blessed state abounding in the most exalted happiness.‡

Here ends the story of Ṛishidattá, having reference to virtue.

Now follows the story of Metárya, concerning compassion to living creatures.

STORY OF METÁRYA.

In this very land of Bharata, in the city of Sanketa, there was a king named Chandrávataṃsaka. He had two queens, named respectively Sudarçaná and Priyadarçaná. Sudarçaná had two sons, named Ságarachandra and Munichandra; whereas the two sons of Priyadarçaná were named Guṇachandra and Bálachandra. Then King Chandrávataṃsaka established Ságarachandra in the position of crown-prince,§ and gave Munichandra a

* One of the older forms of Çiva-Rudra (Monier Williams).

† *Kevalajnána*. The possessor of such knowledge is called a *kevalin*. See Dr. Hoernle's 'Uvásaga Dasáo,' appendix iii., p. 44.

‡ The state is, of course, *moksha*, or liberation.

§ *Yuvarája*.

kingdom in Ujjayiní by way of appanage.* One day, in the month of Mágha, King Chandrávataṃsaka was performing asceticism in the statuesque posture in his bedroom, and he formed the following resolution: 'I will not put an end to my painful posture as long as the lamp is burning.' Then the chambermaid, after each of the four watches, replenished the lamp with oil. At the dawn of day the king died, owing to the delicacy of his health, and went to the world of gods, and Ságarachandra reigned in his stead. One day he said to his second mother Priyadarçaná: 'Let your sons have the kingdom; I will take a vow.' But Priyadarçaná thought that the government could be carried on by Ságarachandra and by no other, and so she did not accept the kingdom for her sons. Then many days passed. One day Priyadarçaná saw King Ságarachandra adorned with royal splendour going to the amusements of a spring festival;† then, after the manner of the feminine character, she became angry with the king. She said to herself: 'Long ago, when he offered me the kingdom for my sons, I would not take it; now I should be delighted if my sons could obtain the kingdom in any way, so I must kill Ságarachandra by some device or other.' One day Ságarachandra was in a garden outside the city with his younger brothers, and as they all wished to eat something cool and refreshing, he sent a female servant to the cook to fetch sweetmeats. Priyadarçaná said to her: 'Why have you come?' She said: 'I have come to get some cool food for the king.' In the meanwhile Priyadarçaná smeared her hands with poison and stood in the path. In course of time she saw the female servant coming along with a single *siṃhakeçara*‡ sweetmeat. On pretence of examining it, she took it in her hands and rubbed it with her palms, and then gave it back into the hands of the servant impregnated with poison. The servant gave the sweetmeat to King Ságarachandra. The king said to

* *Kumárabhuktyai.* Literally, for enjoyment as a prince.

† Corresponding to the English May-games.

‡ Literally, lion's mane.

himself: 'There is only one sweetmeat, and my two brothers are hungry: it would not be fitting for me to eat while they are fasting.' So he gave each of them half the sweetmeat, and they ate it. Then it became manifest that they had taken poison, for their eyes were seen to be whirling round from the effect of it. The king sent for the physicians, and they made the princes drink a solution of gold.* That brought the princes back to life. Then the king said to the female servant: 'Who gave you the sweetmeat?' She answered: 'The cook gave it me; but as I was coming along the path, Priyadarçaná took the sweetmeat from my hand and then rubbed it.' Ságarachandra said to himself: 'This second mother of mine impregnated the sweetmeat with poison, and sent it here to put an end to my life.' When he had mastered the situation, the king reflected: 'When I offered her the kingdom on that occasion she would not take it; now she behaves in this way.' So he became filled with the spirit of renunciation, and took the vow of a hermit, making over the kingdom to the sons of Priyadarçaná. One day some holy men came from Ujjayiní. The hermit Ságarachandra asked them: 'Are you free from persecution in Ujjayiní?' They answered: 'In that city the son of the king and the son of the chaplain oppress the hermits.' Then Ságarachandra, hearing the conduct of his own brother's son, went to Ujjayiní. He rested under some tree or other. When the time for begging came, the hermit Ságarachandra was invited by the hermits who lived there. He answered: 'I must break my fast on the food which I have myself obtained; I cannot eat food brought by another. So point out to me the houses where hermits are relieved.' Then a certain hermit pointed out the house of the chaplain. The hermit Ságarachandra went there, and proclaimed in a loud voice the advantage of religion. Then the ladies came out, making a great disturbance. The hermit said with piercing accents: 'Lay sister, what is the meaning of this?' Thereupon, hearing the tumult,

* Compare Shakespeare's 'Henry IV. *B.*,' IV. v. 163.

the son of the king and the son of the chaplain came to the spot. Both of them, when they saw the hermit, shut the door, and said: 'Come, hermit, dance.' The hermit said: 'How am I to dance without music? So you two must play music in an agreeable manner, in order that I may satisfy your desire for seeing dancing.' Then the hermit laid aside his begging-bowl and began to dance. Then the hermit said: 'You two do not know how to play music properly.' This enraged the company. The son of the king and the son of the chaplain said: 'We are at home in the accomplishment of fighting, but we do not profess the accomplishment of music.' The hermit said: 'Then fight with me.' Then the hermit began to fight with them. Then the hermit vanquished them in fight, and, paralyzing the limbs of both of them,* opened the door and departed. Then Ságarachandra the hermit went to the garden to engage in religious meditation. Munichandra heard what had happened, but he could not find the hermit Ságarachandra, though he looked for him everywhere. Then he asked the hermits. They said: 'To-day a guest came, but he has gone somewhere, and we do not know where; however, he was seen to-day standing in the garden.' So King Munichandra went there and reproached the hermit. The hermit reproached the king, saying: 'King, does this contempt for hermits become you, of all people?' The king was ashamed, and went on to say: 'My lord, do me a favour: release the prince and the other young man.' The hermit said: 'If they will take a vow I will release them.' The king agreed to that. Then he gave back to both of them the use of their limbs, and they both of them took a vow. The prince duly observed his vow under his uncle Ságarachandra, but the chaplain's son became disgusted. Then they died and went to the world of the gods. There they both made this mutual agreement, that whichever of them first fell from the world of the gods was to be admonished by the other. So the soul of the chaplain

* *Gátrabhangaṃ kṛitvá.* I suppose their limbs were put out of joint.

fell from the world of gods, and, owing to the effect of the disgust shown in a former birth, he was conceived in the womb of an elephant-driver's wife. Now, it happened that a woman of the merchant caste, the wife of a merchant, who lived in that city, was a great friend of that elephant-driver's wife. She gave her own son to the woman of the merchant caste. Then the woman of the merchant caste kept continually laying him at the feet of the elephant-driver's wife. They gave the boy the name of Metárya. In course of time Metárya grew up. At night the god came from the world of gods and admonished that Metárya; but he would not receive his admonitions. And about this time Metárya was seen by the elephant-driver adorned with fresh youth, returning to his house in a chariot, after marrying eight daughters of opulent men. Then the elephant-driver said: 'If my son were alive, I also would perform for him the ceremony of betrothal.' Then the wife of the elephant-driver, being inspired by the power of the god, revealed all her conduct to the elephant-driver, and said: 'This is my son.' When the elephant-driver heard that Metárya was his son, he dragged him out of his chariot, and saying, 'The marriage of people of inferior caste with people of high caste is not commendable,' flung him into a dungeon in his own house. After twelve years the god came there. The god said: 'Friend, do you recognise me?' Metárya said: 'I do not recognise you.' Then the god appeared in his true form, and said: 'I am your friend in a former life. I have frequently come from the world of gods to admonish you, but you will not receive my admonitions. It is I that have brought about all the present state of affairs.' Metárya said: 'Then bring about my release.' Then the god gave him a goat. That goat went on producing jewels continually,* and the elephant-driver regularly made over those jewels to King Çreṇika.

* This goat resembles the ass in Gonzenbach's 'Sicilianische Märchen,' No. 52, and still more closely the ass in Kaden's 'Unter den Olivenbäumen,' 'Schuhflicker im Glücke.' See also Grimm's No. 36. More parallels will be found on pp. 8 and 453 of vol. ii. of my translation of the 'Kathá Sarit Ságara.'

The king said to the elephant-driver: 'Tell me, what can I give you?' The elephant-driver said: 'Give your daughter to my son.' So the elephant-driver went on presenting jewels. One day Prince Abhaya said to the elephant-driver: 'Whence have you jewels in your house?' The elephant-driver answered: 'A goat gives them to me.' Then Prince Abhaya asked the elephant-driver for the goat. The elephant-driver gave it to him, and it was brought to the king's palace. There the goat produced no jewels; it only produced evil-smelling things. Then it was given back to the elephant-driver, and in his house it produced jewels as before. King Çreṇika thought: 'This goat possesses divine powers.' One day the king asked the god to make a chariot-road to the Vaibhára* mountain. The god made it. On another occasion the king asked the god for a rampart of gold. The god made a rampart of gold. Again the king said to the elephant-driver: 'Bring the sea here, in order that your son may bathe in the sea and be purified.' The god performed it. Then the king gave his own daughter to the son of the elephant-driver. Moreover, the eight daughters of rich men, who had before been married by the elephant-driver's son, came to him also. Then he remained living in his house for twelve years with those nine wives, enjoying the pleasures of the world. Again the god admonished him. Then the wives of Metárya asked the god to grant them twelve years more of their husband's society. So Metárya took a vow at the end of forty-nine years. He was initiated by Mahávíra. He then roamed about in accordance with the standard of solitary roaming.† One day, as he was wandering about from house to house in the city of Rájagṛiha to beg food, he went to the house of a goldsmith. Now, it happened that at this moment the goldsmith had placed some grains of gold on a cloth, by way of a weight, and gone into the house. At that very instant a heron came and swallowed

* A very holy place of pilgrimage. See 'Weber über das Çatrumjaya Máhátmyam,' pp. 22 and 38.

† I take it that this is the eleventh standard. See Dr. Hoernle's 'Uvásaga Dasáo,' appendix iii., p. 48.

the grains of gold, thinking that they were barley-corns. The goldsmith came out of the house and looked about for the grains, and could not find them. Then he said to himself: 'This hermit here has taken the grains.' Then he asked the hermit: 'Hermit, did you take the grains?' The hermit, in order to save the life of a living being, did not say anything. Then the goldsmith said: 'If you took the grains, give them up; or if anyone else has taken them, say who he is.' The hermit adopted the statuesque posture and remained silent. Then the goldsmith, wild with anger, placed melted lead round the head of the hermit. The hermit endured it all, but did not say that it was the heron that swallowed the grains. Then the goldsmith knocked out his two eyes with a blow from a wedge.* That Metárya, remaining engaged in pure meditation, gained absolute knowledge, free from impediments, and after gaining it attained salvation. Thereupon a servant of that goldsmith let fall suddenly a bundle of faggots; that frightened the heron, and made him bring up the grains. When the goldsmith saw that, he and all his family took a vow. Here ends the story of Metárya, having reference to compassion for living creatures.

Many other great-hearted men also distinguished for religion, Ratnaçikha and others, engaged in pure devotion, have become partakers of good fortune and altogether prosperous.†

In this Jaina religion, many souls, such as Çrídarçana the merchant, and others, by the might of the five principal beings, have become partakers of good fortune. Among these the advantage which Prince Ratnaçikha obtained by the formula of adoration is specially spoken of.

It was as follows:

Here follows the story of Ratnaçikha, having reference to the formula of adoration.

* Two of the MSS. read *pháchara*. The one which I call 'B' reads *páchara*, which appears to be a Marathi word for a wedge.

† This sentence is in Prákṛit.

In this very Jambudvípa, in this very land of Bharata, there is a village of the name of Çáligráma. In it there lived a householder named Sangata, who was simple by nature, but very poor. One day he gave shelter in his house to a hermit. The hermit instructed him in religion. He said: 'O Sangata, everywhere does the flower bear fruit: for

STORY OF RATNAÇIKHA.

'By religion one may obtain prosperity, wealth, glory, to an equal extent, and by religion renown,
Intellect free from stain, well-conducted sons, a virtuous daughter, and well-established wisdom.'

The householder said: 'Mighty sir, how can people like myself, who live in continual poverty, practise religion?' The hermit said: 'Virtuous sir, learn from my mouth the great formula of adoration.' The householder said: 'What formula of adoration? What is got by reciting it?' The holy man said: 'Hear the peculiar efficacy of the formula of adoration:

'After committing thousands of sins and slaying hundreds of men,
By duly repeating* this formula, even animals have gone to heaven.
Those who have attained, and those who will attain, and those who are attaining the highest beatitude,
All of these, by continually calling to mind the formula of adoration, have gone to heaven.'

When he heard the efficacy of the formula described in these words, he learned the formula of adoration from the mouth of the hermit. The holy man said: 'You must repeat this formula with your prayers every day at morning, noon, and evening.' After saying this, the hermit in the morning continued his wanderings. The householder went on repeating the formula of adoration at morning, noon, and evening of every day, with pure mind. After some time his allotted period of life came to an end, and he died. Now, in this very land of Bharata, in the country of Sandarbha, in the city of Nandipura, there was a king named Padmánana; and he had a queen named Kumudiní. In her womb the soul of the householder became

* *Samárádhya.* In classical Sanskrit the word would mean 'having propitiated.'

incarnate. In her sleep she saw a heap of jewels. So when the son was born, they gave him the name of Ratnaçikha. Being tenderly cherished, he became, in course of time, expert in all the accomplishments. When he became a young man, his father united him in marriage to the daughter of the King of Koçalá, named Sukoça. One day King Padmánana saw a grey hair* on his head, and filled with the idea of renunciation, he anointed Ratnaçikha as ruler in his kingdom, and himself, with his queen, went to live in the forest. So King Ratnaçikha ruled the kingdom. Now, that king took great pleasure in stories, but he showed special favour to anyone who told him a story of a man of great virtue.

One day a certain person began the story of Vírángada and Sumitra, saying, 'Hear, O king!—

STORY OF PRINCE VÍRÁNGADA AND HIS FRIEND SUMITRA.

'In this very land of Bharata there is a city called Vijayapura. In it there was a king named Surángada; his son was a prince named Vírángada. Now, that son was a wishing-jewel† of wealth to petitioners, and to those who desired protection a cage of adamant, and to the wretched and afflicted a paternal mansion. That prince had a great friend in Sumitra, the son of the prime minister. One day the prince had a conversation of this kind with Sumitra. The prince said: "My friend, we must go to another land; without going to another land how can we test our merit? how can we acquire fresh knowledge? So let us start for a foreign land, after informing our fathers and mothers of our intention."

'Thus they deliberated, and remained thinking over a means of starting. One day, while the prince was amusing himself in the garden, a certain thief adorned for execution, with eyes rolling with fear, fell at his feet,

* See my translation of the 'Kathá Sarit Ságara,' vol. i., p. 67; vol. ii., p. 628. See also Professor Jacobi's preface to his edition of the 'Pariçishta Parvan,' p. 14, note.

† See my translation of the 'Kathá Sarit Ságara,' vol. ii., p. 8.

crying out: "Protect me." In the meanwhile the executioners arrived in pursuit of him, running at full speed, and said to the prince: "Prince, this wicked robber was seen by us to-day coming out of the house of the merchant Sudatta with the plunder that he had taken. Accordingly, by order of the king, he was taken away to the place of execution to be impaled. Now he has escaped and fled to you. So permit us to carry out the orders of the king." The prince said to himself: "It does not become great-souled men to surrender suppliants, and yet it does not become them to protect thieves; so what shall I do?" Then he thought: "Let him be what he will, it is incumbent on one to protect suppliants." So the prince said: "As long as I live, no one can slay him. I will certainly not surrender him, even in the destruction of the world. Go and tell my father so." The executioners went and informed the king. The king was angry, and ordered the prince to be banished.

'Then the prince was delighted,* and went with Sumitra to another land. After he had crossed many realms, in the course of his wanderings, he came to a great forest, and went to sleep in the shade of a banyan-tree to dispel his fatigue; while Sumitra kept watch to protect him. Now, it happened that a Yaksha was dwelling in that tree. So, being attracted by their beauty and other good qualities, he said to himself: "I will show these two some hospitality."† Accordingly he became visible. Sumitra, saying to himself, "This is some god," rose up to honour him. Then the Yaksha said: "Sumitra, I am the Yaksha that inhabits this banyan-tree." Sumitra bowed before him. The Yaksha said: "Auspicious sir, you two are to-day my guests; tell me, what hospitality can I show you?" Sumitra said: "The mere sight of you is hospitality enough." The Yaksha said: "Nevertheless, the sight of

* For the same reason Mrigánkadatta is delighted at the sentence passed on him ('Kathá Sarit Ságara,' vol. ii., p. 147).

† In the 'Kathá Sarit Ságara,' vol. ii., p. 82, a Yaksha entertains two Bráhmans.

a god should not be without fruit. For this reason receive these two jewels." Sumitra asked the properties of the jewels. The Yaksha said: "This, which is a sapphire, if worshipped for seven nights, will give the kingly dignity; this other one, which is a ruby, will give you more provision for the day than you can possibly desire.* You must give the sapphire to the prince." Sumitra received the two jewels, and then the Yaksha disappeared. Sumitra thought: "How great is the power of the prince's merit, that even the gods assist him in this way!" Then the morning broke, and the two set out on their journey. The prince became hungry, and was preparing to eat some fruits, but Sumitra forbade him. Then, about noontide, they reached the city of Mahâçâla, and encamped in the park surrounding the city. Then Sumitra made over the sapphire to the prince. The prince said: "What is this?" Sumitra replied: "Prince, worship this jewel in order that you may become a king." The prince said, full of astonishment: "How did you obtain this splendid jewel?" Sumitra answered: "By the power of your merit. When you have obtained a kingdom I will tell you all." The prince said: "Friend, how can I obtain a kingdom?" With this thought in his mind, he sat down in the shade of a fragrant mango-tree. Sumitra, for his part, went aside, and worshipped the wishing-jewel, and asked for food for the day. At that moment shampooers arrived. The shampooers respectfully shampooed the two young men with perfumed oil. Then females of celestial beauty approached with fragrant unguents in their hands, and anointed and perfumed the bodies of the two young men. Then they went into a bathing pavilion to bathe, and there they were made to sit on costly golden seats, and were douched by means of pitchers filled with perfumed water by a company of heavenly nymphs. Then they were clothed with magnificent dresses of a cotton material fit for gods. Then the nymphs put flowers on their heads, and perfumed their

* This is the well-known story of 'Tischchen deck dich.' See my translation of the 'Kathá Sarit Ságara,' vol. i., p. 14; vol. ii., p. 627.

bodies with sandalwood, and served them with a banquet; and after the banquet was over all the preparations disappeared. Then the prince said: "Sumitra, what is the meaning of this extraordinary wonder?" Sumitra answered: "This, prince, is due to the power of the sapphire." Now, it happened that at this time the king of that very city of Maháçála died without a son. Then the barons had recourse to the five ordeals of the elephant, the horse, and so on. The elephant came into the city park trumpeting. There he sprinkled the prince, named Vírángada, with the water of inauguration, and, taking him up in his trunk, placed him on his forehead. All the barons and the chief ministers and the other ministers, and the crowd with them, bowed before him, and exclaimed: "Long live the king!" The ministers hailed the king as lord, and prayed him to establish himself in the city. The king was astonished, and his friend was delighted. Sumitra said to himself: "Let my dear friend have the kingdom; I will amuse myself in the city as I please, without the knowledge of the king." After forming this intention, Sumitra disappeared, and went into the city. The king looked for him everywhere, but could not find him. Then the king said to the barons: "Look for my dear friend, and bring him here." Then the king entered the city, and began to rule there. He married eight princesses. So King Vírángada administered his realm without opposition. Sumitra, for his part, roamed about at will in the city. One day a *hetæra* in that town, named Ratisená, was sitting at a window. She saw that Sumitra was very handsome. She said to herself: "Surely this man is exceedingly blessed by fortune; so it will be a good thing if I can bring him here by some device." So she sent a female servant, who brought Sumitra to the house. Ratisená showed him great affection, and Sumitra was much pleased with her beauty. Then he remained in her house, and while there became much attached to her; but he did not give her a corresponding amount of wealth. So her affection for him diminished. One day Sumitra said to himself: "This woman will not be satisfied with a small gift." So on an auspicious day he propitiated that wishing-jewel, and by virtue of that jewel he was enabled to give her enormous wealth. The *hetæra* was pleased, but out of avarice asked again for money. Sumitra, by virtue of the jewel, gave her abundance. As fast as the *hetæra* asked for wealth, Sumitra supplied it. Then, one day the *hetæra* said to herself: "Surely he must possess a wishing-stone, else how could he have the power of giving so much? So I will get possession of that stone." One day, when he was engaged in bathing,* she took the jewel from his garment. When Sumitra looked for the jewel, he could not find it. He said to himself: "Surely that *hetæra* has taken the jewel." So he asked her. Then she feigned anger and said to Sumitra: "I want no more of your gifts; but do not cover me with false reproach in the presence of my hired servants." When Sumitra heard this, he said to himself: "There can be no doubt that she has taken the jewel; otherwise how could she utter such a contumelious speech, as if she had got all she wanted?" Then Sumitra left her house. He was so ashamed that he did not dare to tell the king; so he went to another country. Sumitra said to himself: "Oh, how foolish I was to be cheated by a mere woman! Now I must, somehow or other, think of a device for doing her some injury. Moreover, in that way I shall exhibit my own valour:

'"For out on the manliness of that man who is not able
To recompense the benefaction of benefactors and the enmity of enemies!"

Roaming in another country engaged in these thoughts, he beheld a great city † adorned with splendid gardens, forts, and temples. When he beheld the delightsomeness of the city, he was much pleased; but when he entered into the city he observed that it was altogether deserted. He saw troops of monkeys gibbering joyfully in the temples; he saw tigers roaring in all the houses, and serpents hanging

* Literally, sitting down in the act of bathing.

† Indívarasena finds a similar city in the 'Kathá Sarit Ságara,' vol. i., p. 385.

from the arches of the gateways. Wandering from house to house in the city, Sumitra at last reached the palace; there also he did not behold a single human being. Then he went up to the seventh story of the palace. There he saw a couple of female camels with their bodies streaked with saffron colour, with their heads whitened with abundance of camphor, with their slender necks adorned with garlands of sweet-smelling flowers, and their two feet fettered with iron gyves. Sumitra said to himself: "This is strange! How did these female camels get into this deserted city? Moreover, how did they ascend to this seventh story?" While he was thinking over this, he saw in a window two vessels; in one vessel was white collyrium, in the other black.* He also saw in the same place a collyrium pencil for the eyes. Sumitra thought: "Surely this is collyrium that possesses some wonderful magical properties. Someone has touched with the white collyrium the eyes of the camels, and from being women, they have become by its application female camels."† Thereupon Sumitra touched their eyes with the black collyrium, and by virtue of the collyrium they became two girls of unexampled loveliness. Those girls said to Sumitra: "How have you come to this deserted town?" Sumitra said: "My good fortune was in the ascendant. But I have great wonder in my heart: how did you, wearing the form of women, arrive in this town?" They proceeded to tell their story as follows:

STORY OF THE HYPOCRITICAL ASCETIC AND THE TWO MAIDENS.

'"In this very land of Bharata, in the northern quarter, on the bank of the Ganges, is a town named Subhadra. In it there lived a merchant named Gangáditya, and he had a wife named

* In the second story of the 'Panchadaṇḍachattraprabandha' we find a cat and black ointment. When anointed with this, she turns into a lovely princess. When first discovered in her feline form, her eyes were seen to be smeared with white ointment (*anjana*).

† See the index at the end of my translation of the 'Kathá Sarit Ságara,' under the head 'Animal Transformation.'

Vasudhárá. He had two twin daughters born to him in addition to eight sons, and their names were Jayá and Vijayá. In course of time they grew up to womanhood. Now, at this time there lived in that neighbourhood in a forest on the sands of the Ganges a handsome ascetic* with matted hair, named Suçarman, who was a sweet speaker, quick in inventing answers to suit the occasion, and skilled in the science of prognostics. One day our† father respectfully invited the ascetic to dinner. When the time for dinner arrived, our† father washed his feet and made him sit down to eat; and then splendid food of delicacies, relishes, and sweetmeats were served up. In the meanwhile we two maidens fanned him with a fan. Then that ascetic, as he was eating his food, observed our beauty, and was overcome with love; and while under the power of love that hermit said to himself:

'"'Disappointing is the terrible vow, O ascetic, the taking of which is to be accomplished by discipline of the heart;
I must abandon the crowd in the city of Çiva, that holds in hand the spear of that thunderbolt-bearing god.
If one does not care for pleasure in the society of beautiful maidens,
Then, I think, one may certainly be considered to differ not at all from a madman.'

While absorbed in these reflections he forgot to eat his dinner, and, remaining silent like a devotee, he pretended to be engaged in contemplation. Then the merchant said to him: 'Great sir, eat; it is not proper to meditate now; the food will get cold.' When he said this, the ascetic, though absorbed in contemplation, took a little food. At the end of the meal the merchant said: 'Great sir, what is your grief that prevails so that you have even forgotten your food?' The ascetic said: 'Merchant, I cannot feel the smallest grief as long as there are persons like yourself devoted to me; but I cannot bear to behold your evil fortune.' When the ascetic had said this he went

* This story is found in the 'Tantrákhyána.' See the paper by Professor Bendall in the Journal of the Royal Asiatic Society of Great Britain and Ireland, vol. x., part 4, p. 482, where some parallels are given; among others, the tale beginning on p. 102 of vol. i. of my translation of the 'Kathá Sarit Ságara.'

† The Sanskrit has 'my.'

to his own place. The merchant said to himself: 'Of a truth this hermit is a great authority on prognostics; so there can be no doubt that by virtue of his knowledge he has seen some calamity impending over me.' So our father, disturbed in mind, went to his cloister and questioned him in private. Then the ascetic said: 'What can I do? On one side is the tiger, on the other side the river. You are a very pious patron of ascetics, and I cannot neglect your interests. It is not fit for ascetics to speak of such things; nevertheless, as you are so devoted to holy men, I will tell you the truth. When I sat down on that occasion to eat in your house, I beheld all the marks of your daughters, and saw that they involved the destruction of the paternal side of the family. Being absorbed in anxiety with regard to this, I neglected my food; but at last I took some to please you.' Then the merchant, being distracted with fear, said: 'Reverend sir, is there any means of averting this?' The ascetic said: 'There is an expedient, but it is difficult to carry out. Nobody would consent to the abandonment of these two daughters, so dear to their family.' The merchant said: 'On the principle that one should abandon one for the sake of the family,* I will do whatever you command.' The ascetic said: 'If this be so, then deck these two maidens with ornaments on all their limbs, and put them into a wooden box without anyone knowing of it, and send them to float down the stream of the Ganges, and afterwards have performed a ceremony for averting calamity; and if you do this, all will turn out well.' When he had said this, the merchant took the following steps in order to preserve his family. First he had a great box made. Then he made his two daughters bathe and put on all their ornaments, and he put them into the box. He put food into the box, and fastened up its openings with wax.† Then the father set the box afloat on the stream of the Ganges, and returned home. Then the ascetic performed a ceremony for averting calamity. Afterwards he

* See Böhtlingk's 'Indische Sprüche,' No. 2,627.

† MS. *A* has *meṇa*, which means 'wax' in Marathi.

returned to his own cloister, and said to his pupils: 'Hear, pupils: to-day the holy goddess Gangá has brought from the Himálaya mountain a wooden box full of instruments of worship, in order to ensure the success of my spells. You must go to the lower bathing-place and bring that wooden box. You must not open it. If you open it, the success of my spells will be impeded.' The pupils thought: 'Oh, the excellence of our abbot!' and all the pupils were beside themselves with wonder. Then the abbot said: 'That bathing-place is two *kos* distant.' Then the pupils started. In the meanwhile that wooden box had been seen by King Subhíma, the lord of that city, while amusing himself in the river. Being full of curiosity, he took possession of it and opened it, and saw the two maidens.* When the king saw the beauty of the maidens, he was over head and ears in love, and said to the minister: 'Oh minister, behold a marvel: for

'" 'Are they maidens of Pátála, or daughters of Vidyádharas,
Or nymphs of heaven, or children of kings of men?'

The king asked one of the maidens who they were, but they answered not a word. Then his friend, perceiving the king's wish, said: 'King, no one abandons maidens thus adorned without a reason; so you may be sure that some-one has put these maidens into the Ganges as victims, in order to attain some object. So let the king put another pair in their place and take them.' Another said: 'Put a pair of females.' So they brought a couple of female apes from the wood and put them into the box, and sealed it up as before. Then the wooden box was sent floating down the stream of the Ganges, and the king returned to his town in high spirits. The king went on attending to the affairs of his kingdom. Now, it happened that those pupils of the ascetic, wandering along the bank, as fate would have it, after a long time found the wooden box, and quickly took it and made it over to the ascetic. The ascetic

* A similar incident will be found on p. 220 of Kaden's 'Unter den Olivenbäumen.' A king finds two maidens set afloat in a box. In the twenty-second story of Basile's 'Pentamerone' a king marries a maiden whom he finds floating about on the sea in a box.

was delighted. Indeed, this wicked abbot was in such a state of expectation that the sun seemed to him slow in setting. However, it did set at last. Then the ascetic said to his pupils : 'Hear : to-day you must lock the doors of the monastery and remain outside ; even if you hear loud cries, you must not enter until the sun rises ; you must not by any means show yourselves my enemies by thus interfering with the success of my spells.' Then the ascetic shut the doors of the monastery, and himself remained inside. Then the ascetic proceeded to say : 'Women, the fruit of your good luck has to-day reached its climax, in that you have obtained as husband myself, a god that dwells in heaven ; so you must not humiliate me.' When he had said this, he used his two hands to open the box. But the moment he opened it that wicked ascetic was seized by the two female apes, wild with hunger. The two apes reduced him to such a state that,

'"Having his limbs torn with sharp claws, his ears split, and his cheeks scratched,*
And his nose taken off by the female apes, with their teeth, in despair he exclaimed,
'Run here, run here, my pupils ; I am being devoured by Rákshasís.'
Thus lamenting continually, he fell suddenly on the ground.

Though his pupils heard his piteous cries for aid, they did not come to help him, for they had been specially forbidden by him ; so, by the appointment of destiny, he died, and became a very terrible Rákshasa. By his knowledge he knew all about his death in his previous state of existence, and he became a very ill-conducted being. He knew that King Subhíma had carried off his wives, and that by the instrumentality of that king his own bad death had been brought about, so he became very angry with King Subhíma. So that ascetic, who had now become a Rákshasa, and remembered his former birth, killed the king, and exterminated all the inhabitants of the city, except us two girls."

* In Kaden's 'Unter den Olivenbäumen,' p. 75, a similar incident will be found. A girl is taken out of a sack, and a big dog put in. When the sack was opened the big dog sprang out, '*und zerriss sie alle beide.*'

'Then the two ladies said to Sumitra: "This, great-hearted sir, is our history: the device of collyrium has been arranged by that Rákshasa. By the application of the white collyrium human beings become camels; by the application of the black they again become human beings. This is our history. So it is owing to our good luck that you have arrived; we are tired of dwelling in this uninhabited forest; release us from this affliction."

'When Sumitra, who was tender-hearted and incapable of refusing a request, heard this, he said: "Where is the Rákshasa now? At what time does he come to visit you?" The girls said: "He comes here from the island of the Rákshasas, sometimes after two days, sometimes after three—just as he likes. Sometimes he stays a fortnight, sometimes a month, but he will certainly come to-day. So during the night-time you must go into the splendid tank adorned with jewels on the ground-floor, and so save your life. In the morning you must act as seems expedient." Then Sumitra made the two girls camels again, and remained concealed in that very place. So at eventide the Rákshasa arrived, exclaiming: "How is it that there is a smell of humanity* here to-day?" The two ladies said: "We are human beings, and it is our smell that is diffused through the air." So the Rákshasa remained there that night. In the morning the two girls said to the Rákshasa: "Sir, we are terrified at remaining alone, so you must come back quickly. . . ."† Having said this, the Rákshasa went away. Then Sumitra took the vessels of collyrium, and, turning those two camels into women again, he brought them down from the seventh story, and then he again turned them into camels, and, loading them with a burden of jewels, set out for the city of Mahaçála. After some days he met with a man skilful in the conjuring of

* This is common enough in European tales. It is, perhaps, sufficient to refer to Grimm's No. 29, where the Teufel exclaims, 'I smell human flesh.' See also the second story in the 'Panchadaṇḍachattraprabandha,' and Ralston's 'Russian Folk-Tales,' p. 103.

† It is clear that some words have fallen out here. Probably the Rákshasa said when he would come back.

demons. To him Sumitra related his exploit. He said: "Do not be afraid, Sumitra." And so that man skilled in magic science cheered up Sumitra. And at that moment the wicked Rákshasa arrived, having assumed a terrible form, uttering a loud laugh, scaring all animals. Immediately the man skilled in magic fixed the Rákshasa motionless. Then the Rákshasa, pleased with the wonderful might of his spells, said to the conjurer: "Mighty magician, people have a saying that there are remedies even against Rákshasas. You have proved the truth of this; so let me go; I will do whatever you command." The magician said: "If this is so, then abandon your feelings of hostility against this hero Sumitra." The Rákshasa answered: "If this is to be so, then make him give up my two darlings." The man skilled in magic said: "By associating with the wives of another man you will certainly incur a painful and terrible death; and after you have died you will go to hell. Moreover, you are of divine nature, and these are human females; so, as you are of divine nature, how can you entertain deluding passion for human females? By all means let these women go. Your present conduct is suited only to the lowest beings." When the Rákshasa heard this speech of the man skilled in magic, he was pleased, and gave the two women to Sumitra; then he went to his own place. Then Sumitra was delighted, and said to the man skilled in magic: "O man of noble nature, of great courage and great compassion, there is no other benefactor of his neighbour in the world like you, since by force of spells you have conquered such a wicked Rákshasa." The man skilled in magic answered: "Sumitra, how am I courageous? You are really courageous, since you have carried off the two wives of a Rákshasa without the force of spells." When they had thus exchanged friendly speeches, they both set out for their own destinations. The magician went to his own home, and Sumitra, with his two wives, went to the city of Maháçála; there he had a delightful palace built for himself, and lived happily, sporting with his wives. In the meanwhile Ratisená became depressed by the loss of Sumitra. For three nights she refused nourishment; no wealth came from her jewel; then she became still more depressed, and, though she was admonished by her aged mother, she did not give up her attachment for Sumitra. So Ratisená said to the old *hetæra*:

'"Though pain embrace my terrified body, my speech is certain, and my opinion is this:
No other man even comes near Sumitra in nobility.

I will immediately enter the fire. I will never again love any man except Sumitra." She remained resolute in this intention which she had formed.

'Now, one day, as Ratisená was sitting at the window, she saw Śumitra beautifully adorned. So she went out in haste and politely conducted him into her house. She showed him great affection. Then the old *hetæra* said to Sumitra: "My dear fellow, where have you been absent these many days? From the day on which you left our house, this daughter of mine has been in danger of her life, on account of losing you." Then Sumitra said to himself: "Ah, she has again planned a piece of treachery, so I will remain some time in her house, otherwise I shall never get the jewel out of her." Having thus considered, he remained in the house of the *hetæra*. After some time had passed, Sumitra said one day to Ratisená: "My dear, I will show you an extraordinary marvel if you will not be angry." She said: "Show me that marvel." Then Sumitra turned Ratisená into a female camel, by employing the collyrium as before described. Then he went himself to his own house. Meanwhile, when the maid came to call Ratisená at meal-time, she looked, and lo! there was no Ratisená, but a female camel. Then she was terribly frightened, and said to all the attendants: "Undoubtedly our mistress has been devoured by a Rákshasa; otherwise, without the intervention of a Rákshasa, how could a female camel get up into this palace?" Then the attendants came there also, and every one of them was astonished, and they said to one another: "What lover has visited her lately?" The maid said: "Indeed, a man versed in every accomplishment, who has come from a foreign country, has been her lord, so undoubtedly this is his doing. Accordingly, let the king be informed of it, before he manages to escape to a distance." Then the old *hetæra* went to the king's palace and informed him. The king said to himself: "Undoubtedly, no one else but my friend Sumitra could have performed such an achievement." Then the king said to the old *hetæra*: "My good woman, how much time has passed since he came into your house?" Then the *hetæra* said: "This man came into my house on the very day on which your majesty obtained the sovereignty of this town. Afterwards he went to another land; now he has returned, and a fortnight has passed since his return." When the king heard this he ordered his servants to search for his friend immediately. Then the old *hetæra* pointed out Sumitra to the king's servants. They brought him to the king. Thereupon the king, even when he saw his friend Sumitra coming at a distance, rose up. When he came face to face with him he embraced him warmly, and the two sat down and asked after one another's health. King Virángada said: "Is my cunning friend Sumitra well?" Sumitra answered: "In everything he is well off, thanks to the favour of your highness." The king said: "Now tell me the rest of your adventures. Why did you turn the daughter of this *hetæra* into a camel?" Sumitra answered: "In order that she might easily browse on the shoots of the trees, for she has not money enough to procure other food." Thereupon the maid said to Sumitra: "Bring this confidential conversation to an end, and relieve my mistress from her deformity; we have seen your skill in accomplishments." Sumitra answered: "You wicked woman! Do you call this skill in accomplishments? Why, I will turn you also into a female donkey, and make you browse on all the dirt in the town, in order that there may be no offensive smell in my lord's city. If you do not want me to do this, give up my wishing-stone." Thereupon the king said: "My friend, what is your wishing-stone?" Sumitra answered: "That by the power of which I provided all the dinner arrangement for you in the forest." Then the king's eyes became red with anger, and he said: "You wicked harlot! you manifest thief! you have stolen the jewel of my friend." Then the *hetæra*, terribly alarmed, fell at the feet of Sumitra, exclaiming: "Protect me!" Sumitra appeased the king Vírángada, and took back his wishing-stone. He then restored Ratisená to her proper shape. She was desperately in love with Sumitra. Then the *hetæra*, perceiving it, bestowed Ratisená on Sumitra. So Sumitra, being married to three wives, passed his time in the enjoyment of the pleasures of the world. On a subsequent day the king said to Sumitra: "Sumitra, after you left me on that day, how did you manage to disappear for so long a time; and what pleasure or pain did you experience? How did you obtain the couple of jewels that you mentioned before? This circumstance excites my curiosity." Then Sumitra related the whole story exactly as it happened, beginning with his obtaining of the jewels. When the king heard the story of Sumitra he was astonished, and said to him: "Oh, the excellence of your perseverance! for

'"From good conduct comes respect, from perseverance the attainment of the prosperity proposed,
From diet freedom from disease, from religion heaven and also happiness."

Then Sumitra said: "King, what is the use of perseverance to men? Merit acquired in a previous life is of primary importance. Without perseverance, by means of merit every happiness is acquired. For

'"Though a friend may be hard to obtain, far off, and situated in impassable regions,
In the power of others, and detained by wicked men long prepared,
Nevertheless, when thought of, that friend is certainly acquired by a man with ease,
If he possesses, as his trusty helper, even an atom of merit previously gained."

'Having stated religious truths in these and similar utterances, the two friends ruled in that town.'

Now we go on with the story of Ratnaçikha.

> Display thou perseverance as a calf produces excrement,
> But a man obtains joys by merit, like King Virángada.

King Ratnaçikha, having heard this story from the mouth of a bard, said to himself: 'Wonderful are the exploits of determined men. For

> 'The real greatness of a man, like that of gold, is manifested
> When he is severely blackened* in the vessels of a thousand trials.'

King Ratnaçikha thus reflected: 'Without travelling to a foreign land one does not obtain glory, fame, knowledge of accomplishments, or anything. So I will certainly go to a foreign land and make trial of my merit.' Having thus reflected, he told the whole story to his minister, named Púrṇabhadra. He said: 'King, who can hinder your wishes? But still I must represent to your majesty that foreign countries are difficult to traverse, the tracks are full of dangers, enemies are on the look-out for weak points, and the kingly body is unable to endure hardships; so having obtained the kingdom, let the king cherish it as the fruit of his merit.'

Though the minister addressed many remonstrances of this kind to the king, he would not desist. Then the king formed a secret plan, and at the end of night he left the city, with his sword for his only companion, and went towards the north. Then, beholding many marvels in villages, assemblies, towns, and cities, relying everywhere on the power of his own merit, the king at last entered a terrible wood. That forest was of the following kind:

> It was full of bamboos, banyans, ratans, and *kuṭajas*;[1]
> It was rich in *ankolla*, *vilva*,[2] *çallaki*,[3] *kṛitamála*,[4] *tamála*,[5] and *çála*[6] trees;

---

* This seems to be clearly the meaning of the Prákṛit words; but gold ought not to turn black when tested in the fire.

[1] Wrightia Antidysenterica.
[2] Ægle Marmelos, Bel.
[3] Gum olibanum tree, Boswellia Thurifera.
[4] Cassia Fistula.
[5] Xanthochymus Pictorius.
[6] Shorea Robusta.

It was densely crowded and terrible with *nimba*-trees,[7] mango-trees, *udumbaras*,[8] jujube-trees, and *kapilas*;[9]
It was skirted with *pipals*,[10] *paláças*,[11] reeds, *nílas*,[12] *bhillas*,[13] and *bhilloṭas*;
It was diversified with rose-apples, *kadambas*,[14] tamarinds, and *kapitthas*;[15]
It was closely packed with *tíndukas*,[16] *varuṇa*-trees,[17] with *çirishas*,[18] and *çriparṇi*-trees;[19]
It contained marsh-date-trees, palm-trees, *çimçapá*-trees,[20] *çami*-trees,[21] and silk-cotton-trees, which were all massive and touched the sky with their towering tops;
It was covered with lines of whistling canes, being continually split asunder.*

When he had advanced some distance in this wood, the king saw an infuriated elephant resembling Airávaṇa. He said to himself: 'How is it that there is an elephant of this kind iṇ this wood?' In the meanwhile the elephant lifted up its trunk and came near King Ratnaçikha. Then the king, skilled in the art of managing elephants, tamed the elephant. At that moment a garland of flowers fell from the sky on the king's neck. The king was astonished. He heard in the sky this exclamation of heavenly nymphs: 'Hail to his heroic powers!' Then the king mounted on the elephant, and set out towards the north. Then he became thirsty, and, looking round for water, he descried a large lake. The king got down from the elephant and drank water. When the elephant had drunk water it would not come out of the lake. Then the king left the elephant and went on. As he advanced a woman presented him with garments of heavenly stuff and of great value. Then she gave him ornaments for every limb and joint,

7 Azadirachta Indica.
8 Ficus Glomerata.
9 A kind of Çiṃçapá, or perhaps Aloe Perfoliata.
10 Ficus Religiosa.
11 Butea Frondosa.
12 A kind of fig-tree.
13 Symplocos Racemosa.
14 Nauclea Cadamba.
15 Wood apple-tree, Feronia Elephantum.
16 Diospyros Embryopteris.
17 Cratæva Roxburghii.
18 Acacia Sirisha.
19 Premna Spinosa.
20 Dalbergia Sisu.
21 Acacia Suma.

* I have omitted the names of some trees which I have been unable to identify. Atmárám Muni is of opinion that some of the names are local. I gladly acknowledge the help that he has given me in this difficult Prákṛit passage.

and, in addition to an unguent of flowers, betel-nut mixed with camphor, cardamoms, and *kankola*, and said to him: 'Welcome, king!' The king said: 'My good lady, who are you?' The woman said again: 'Welcome, matchless monarch!' The king said: 'My good lady, why do you say "matchless monarch"?' The woman said: 'Indra and the other gods, when worshipped for a long time, may perhaps give and may perhaps not give, but my friend propitiated you, and you gave her her desire.' The king asked: 'Who is this friend of yours? When did she see me?' When the king asked this question, she said: 'In the northern direction from this place there is a mountain called Vaitáḍhya. On it there is a city named Sagaya,* in which lived a king of the name of Súraṇa. He had two daughters, named Svayamprabhá and Mahāprabhá, and two sons, named Çaçivega and Súravega. One day King Súraṇa established Çaçivega in his kingdom, and took a vow in the presence of a wandering hermit named Ravitejas. Then Súravega, beholding the enjoyment that the royal dignity bestowed, conceived a desire to obtain it. Thereupon the Vidyádhara Súravega made his maternal uncle, Vasuvega by name, his ally, and came to fight with Çaçivega. Çaçivega for his part, perceiving that Súravega possessed great force, by the advice of his ministers left his city with his army and elephants, and has built a city in this forest. He has a daughter named Chandraprabhá. One day the king was informed by a soothsayer, on seeing Chandraprabhá, that the man who was destined to marry her would enable him to recover his kingdom. King Çaçivega asked the soothsayer how he was to recognise the man. The soothsayer answered: "He who shall tame a mighty elephant† belonging to the lord of the city of Sugríva, while roaming about in this wood in a state of madness, shall become the husband of your daughter, and restore to you your kingdom." From that day forward

* Or Ságara, according to two of the MSS.

† Literally a smell-elephant. According to Monier Williams, it is an elephant of the best class, supposed to emit a peculiar smell.

the mighty elephant was guarded by Vidyádharas every day; but it rebelled against its driver, tore up the pillar to which it was fastened, and entered this wood.* For this reason Chandraprabhá, the daughter of Çaçivega, being in the sky with her friends, threw the garland of election eagerly round your neck, and sent you these garments, with betel and other presents.' While the Vidyádharí was saying this to the king, there came from some quarter or other a chariot drawn by horses. The king was astonished. Then a groom bowed before him, and said to him: 'Where is now that man who tamed the mighty elephant? Our master wishes to have an interview with him, and inquires after his health.' Then the Vidyádharí said: 'Did that man, such as we see him to be, go off with the elephant?' The groom answered: 'Even so; say no more. My master is pleased with him, therefore he desires an interview with him.' Then the Vidyádharí said: 'Can a great elephant, terrible as death, be tamed by a mere man? So it is clear that this person is of the nature of a god; let your master, therefore, himself come and see him!' When the groom heard this he was astonished, and told it to King Vasutejas. He reflected: 'Inconceivable are the developments of merit;' then he sent his own minister to summon Ratnaçikha. In the meanwhile the Vidyádharí had returned to her own place. Then the minister won over King Ratnaçikha by showing respect in all kinds of ways, and took him to the Vidyádhara king. The elephant was taken by the head elephant-keeper. Then King Vasutejas, having accomplished his object, went to the city of Sugríva, and there he made King Ratnaçikha marry eight maidens, and kept him near himself. One day King Vasutejas said to King Ratnaçikha: 'A man possessing absolute knowledge, Púrṇasumangala by name, came into my town. I was converted by his preaching; I became disgusted with this royalty, which is the cause of hell. Thereupon, as I had not a son fit to bear the weight of the kingdom, I asked Sumangala, the

* There seems to be an omission here.

man of absolute knowledge, what course I ought to take. He said: "The man who shall subdue your mighty elephant shall inherit your kingdom." So release me, and receive my kingdom, in order that I may take a vow.' Then King Ratnaçikha consented to the proposal of Vasutejas, and Vasutejas established him in his kingdom. Then King Ratnaçikha remained in that kingdom in the enjoyment of pleasures. In the meanwhile the Vidyádhara Çaçivega heard that Ratnaçikha had succeeded in obtaining the kingdom. So he came there in person and gave him his daughter Chandraprabhá, and the science named Invincible, with a thousand other sciences. When the Vidyádhara Suvega heard that circumstance, he came there in the form of an elephant, and remained in the garden of the city of Sugríva. Thereupon King Ratnaçikha came to that park, with a small escort, out of curiosity. After he had for a long time made that wild elephant run about, he tamed it. Then the king got up and sat on the elephant's back, and, lo! the elephant flew up into the air. Then the king struck the elephant on the head with a blow of his fist, which resembled a blow from a rod of adamant. Then the Vidyádhara, having his body paralyzed by this terrific blow, forgot his spells, and fell on the surface of the earth, displaying his real form. Then the Vidyádhara rolled on the ground, saying: 'Honour to the Jaina saints!' King Ratnaçikha said to himself: 'Oh! he remembers the sacred formula when he is in difficulties, so he is fortunate.' Thereupon he sprinkled him with water. When Ratnaçikha had restored him with fanning, he said to him: 'Great sir, pardon my offence.' Then the Vidyádhara said: 'King, as you did not know my real nature, you committed no offence; it is I that committed an offence in this, since, though I knew the facts, I acted thus treacherously against a great brother in the faith.' The king asked the Vidyádhara: 'Great sir, who are you?' The Vidyádhara said: 'I am a Vidyádhara named Suvega, the lord of the city of Chakrapura. Through partiality for Súravega, the son of my sister, I drove Çaçivega out of his kingdom, and established Súravega in it. Thereupon I heard from a soothsayer that you would restore to Çaçivega his kingdom. So I assumed the form of an elephant and came here to kill you. But I have been vanquished by you. Now I am disgusted with this sea of existence; take my kingdom. I will first crave the pardon of Çaçivega, and then carry out my intention.' While he was saying this, Çaçivega suddenly came to the spot, and the Vidyádhara Suvega said to him: 'Çaçivega, establish as sovereign in my kingdom my relation Ratnaçikha.' But Ratnaçikha and Çaçivega said to Suvega: 'Great sir, rule your hereditary kingdom; afterwards, when you are old, you ought to perform asceticism.' Though they said this to him, Suvega would not desist from his intention. He took a vow in the presence of his spiritual guide. Ratnaçikha and Suvega went to the city of Chakrapura. Ratnaçikha became king in Chakrapura. Súravega, hearing the story of his uncle, became inclined to renunciation and took a vow. He gave back his kingdom to Çaçivega. So Ratnaçikha, having attained felicity, held the government of the mountain of Vaitáḍhya. He had built numerous temples to the Jinas; he gave gifts to deserving persons, and caused the law to be preached at holy places. One day he saw a Tirthankara, named Sujasa, who had arrived in the city of Sáketa. Then, with all the hairs on his body standing on end from joy, joining his hands on his forehead, he thus praised the mighty Jina:

> 'Hail, thou that art loving to men, whose countenance is pure as a cloud, whose eyes and mind are impartial,
> Who increasest joy, who lookest with equal mind on wealth, gold, and jewels.'

Having praised the mighty Jina with laudatory utterances of this kind, and worshipped the hermits of his retinue, King Ratnaçikha sat down near the Jina and listened to his sermon, which ran as follows: 'Prosperity is changeful as a wave of the sea; youth lasts for three or four days; life is fleeting as an autumn cloud. What is the use of riches? Practise blameless virtue.' When the king had heard this exhortation, he inquired from the holy man about his former life, and the holy man told him that he had obtained such a kingdom owing to the power of the formula of adoration. When he had heard this about his former birth, and the wonderful power of the formula of adoration, King Ratnaçikha became more devout than ever; and after a short time had elapsed he became inclined to renunciation, and made over the kingdom to his son, and, having observed a blameless walk and conversation, he attained absolute knowledge, and reached final emancipation. Here ends the story of Ratnaçikha, having reference to the formula of adoration.

Now begins the story of Amaradatta and Mitránanda, having reference to sin.

STORY OF AMARADATTA AND MITRÁNANDA.

In this land of Bharata there is a city called Suratilaka; in it there was a king named Makaradhvaja, and he had a queen named Madanasená. One day the queen saw in a dream a lake adorned with a multitude of lotuses. When the time was fully come, a son was born. Then they gave that prince the name of Padmakeçara, and in course of time he was appointed crown-prince. One day, as Madanasená was combing out the hair on the head of Makaradhvaja, she saw a gray hair. She said by way of joke, 'My lord, here is a messenger of religion come to you,' and placed the white hair in the king's hand.* When he saw it his face became black. Then he placed Prince Padmakeçara on the throne, and going to the forest with the queen, became an ascetic. When he had gone there and was practising asceticism, a child that had been previously conceived by the queen began to grow. Then the king asked the queen: 'Queen, what is this?' The queen said: 'King, the fact that I had previously conceived this child was not revealed by me, as I feared that it would be an impediment to my vow.' Then the king told that

* See 'Kathá Sarit Ságara' (my translation), i. 67; ii. 628. Compare also the note in Jacobi's Introduction to his edition of the 'Pariçishṭa Parvan,' p. 14.

fact to the abbot, and then when the due time was come, the queen gave birth to a son. Though the other female ascetics attended the queen, she, being oppressed by the exhaustion of child-birth, died for want of proper remedies. At this conjuncture, a merchant, of the name of Devadhara, a native of Ujjayiní, arrived in that forest of ascetics with his wife Devasená, on their way back from Harshapura. This merchant was devoted to ascetics. He saw that the abbot's face was black. The merchant said: 'Why is your face black?' The abbot told him the whole occurrence. The merchant said: 'Then give this boy to me, reverend sir, in order that I may give it to my wife, who has recently been delivered. A girl has lately been born to her. So this boy and the girl will drink milk at her breast, and so thrive comfortably.' The abbot then gave the boy to the merchant Devadhara. The merchant said to his attendants: 'My wife has given birth to twins, a boy and a girl.' They gave that boy the name of Amaradatta, and the daughter the name of Sundarí. In course of time Amaradatta struck up a great friendship with Mitránanda, the son of a merchant who was an inhabitant of that city. One day in the rainy season they went to amuse themselves in the public garden of Ujjayiní, on the bank of the river Siprá, near a haunted banyan-tree. They were playing the game of ball between them. Then, while Amaradatta was throwing the ball, and Mitránanda catching it, it fell into the mouth of a corpse hanging on that banyan-tree. The corpse said: 'As that ball has fallen into my mouth, so shall it fall into thy mouth when thou art hanging upon this very tree.' When Mitránanda heard this, he was terrified, and said to Amaradatta: 'My dear friend, enough of play. Let us go to our own house.' Amaradatta answered: 'As this ball has fallen into the mouth of a corpse, let us play with another.' Though Amaradatta said this, Mitránanda would not consent to play. Then both of them went to their own rooms. After eating, the two were sitting together. Then Amaradatta said: 'Mitránanda, why does your face appear black?' Mitránanda related the whole circumstance. Amaradatta observed: 'My friend, a corpse cannot speak, but this is the sport of a demon. Whether it be true or false, this obstacle may be overcome by displaying valour; as in old times Jnánagarbha, by exerting himself, warded off the calamity impending over him.' Then Mitránanda said: 'Who was this Jnánagarbha?' So Amaradatta told his story:

STORY OF THE WISE MINISTER JNÁNAGARBHA.

'In this very land of Bharata there is a great city named Champá; in it thero was a king of the name of Jitaçatru, and a minister of the name of Jnánagarbha. The minister's eldest son was named Subuddhi. He had also many other sons. One day, when the king was sitting in his court, a certain great soothsayer, who could predict the future, came there. The king caused a seat to be given to him, and said: "Tell me, soothsayer, what do you know?" He said: "King, I am a soothsayer that predicts according to the appearance of eight parts of the body." The king said: "Then what will happen to these courtiers within a fortnight?" He considered, and said: "Within a fortnight this minister Jnánagarbha will die with his whole family." When Jnánagarbha heard this, he dismissed the assembly, and went home with the soothsayer. There he questioned him in detail. The soothsayer said: "Your eldest son will be your ruin." When he heard this, he dismissed the prophet with gifts, and told the circumstance to his eldest son. Then the minister, in order to save his family, put his eldest son into a chest, making provision in it for food and natural necessities, and after putting a padlock on it, he had it sealed with the king's seal, saying: "This is my household treasure." Then he deposited the chest in the king's palace, and he himself, going home, proceeded to worship the shrines in his own house, taking care to have it guarded on every side with cavalry and infantry. Now, on the fifteenth day from this, the following cry was raised by the female slaves in the king's inner apartments: "Run, run, the son of the minister has cut off the hair of Ratnavatí, and is escaping." Then the king was angry, and sent a body of troops to kill the minister's son. Thereupon the minister, being in his house, said to the commander of the force: "Wait until I have an interview with the king, to whom I am willing to go surrounded by your servants." He agreed. The minister went to the king, and said to him: "My lord, wait until I open that chest." The king consented. The chest was opened, and in it he saw the minister's son with scissors and a braid of hair in his hand. The minister said: "King, this is the doing of some demon, who was my enemy in a former birth." When the king and the minister had seen that occurrence, they both of them became disgusted with the world, and after placing their respective sons in their places, they both took a vow. In the same way I also will overcome this obstacle by some device, and will deliver my friend Mitránanda.'*

Mitránanda said: 'Then let us leave this place.' When they had thus deliberated together, they went out on the pretence of sleeping in their rooms, and immediately departed. One day they reached a garden in the suburbs of Paṭaliputra. There they saw a great temple. In that temple Prince Amaradatta beheld a statue. Seeing that it was very beautiful, he was afflicted with the arrows of Cupid, and was not able to move a step from the spot.† When Amaradatta beheld the statue thus beautiful, he said to himself: 'Is this some heavenly nymph turned to marble by someone's curse?'‡ While the prince was thus deliberating, Mitránanda said to him: 'My friend, shall we enter the city?' Amaradatta answered: 'Mitránanda, wait a moment, that I may behold the beauty of the statue.' When he said this, Mitránanda waited. After a moment or two he said again: 'My friend, rise up, let us go into the city.' Then Amaradatta threw aside his bashfulness, and

* This translation is conjectural. The passage seems to be corrupt.

† In the 'Kathá Sarit Ságara' (vol. ii. of my translation, p. 600), Vikramáditya falls in love with a statue, which turns out to be that of Kalingasená, the daughter of the King of Kalinga.

‡ See vol. ii. of my translation of the 'Kathá Sarit Ságara,' p. 578.

said: 'My friend, I cannot leave this statue; and if you try to separate me from it by force, my life will certainly leave me.' When Mitránanda heard this, he wept, and Amaradatta wept also. At this moment a native of the place, a merchant, Ratnaságara by name, came into that temple. The merchant asked: 'Why are you two distracted with grief?' Mitránanda told the merchant, though with difficulty, the case of Amaradatta. The merchant said to himself: 'Oh, the might of Cupid triumphs! There is in his mind a passion even for a stone image.' Then Mitránanda said to the merchant: 'My lord, who had this temple made? Who was the workman employed on it? Who had so much artistic skill? Did he make this statue by his own artistic invention only, or did he carve it to represent some person?' The merchant said: 'I had this temple made. It was made by an architect residing in the city of Sopára, named Súradeva.' Mitránanda said: 'I will go to that city.' Then Amaradatta said: 'Without you I cannot support my life.' Then Mitránanda fixed a limit of two months for his absence, and gave instructions to Ratnaságara to take care of his friend. Then Mitránanda crossed the sea, and went to the city of Sopára. There he put on a splendid garment, and, taking a present in his hand, went to the architect's house. The architect showed him great regard, and asked the cause of his coming. Mitránanda said: 'I wish to have a temple built in honour of a god, therefore I have come to you. So show me a model of a temple.' The architect said: 'I made the temple in the garden outside Páṭaliputra; this is the model of it.' Mitránanda said: 'Was the marble statue in that temple devised out of your own head, or is it the likeness of any lady?' The architect said: 'The statue is copied from Ratnamanjarí, the daughter of King Mahásena in Ujjayiní, and is not the product of my own artistic invention.' When Mitránanda heard this, he said: 'I will come to you again in an auspicious moment;' and thereupon he journeyed to Ujjayiní. He arrived there at the time of sunset, and went to the house of a *hetæra*. And while he was there, he heard at night-time the following proclamation by beat of drum: 'A rich merchant will give a thousand *dínáras* to whoever will guard until dawn this man who died a violent death.' When Mitránanda heard this, he asked a man: 'Why is this corpse to be guarded?' The man answered: 'This corpse is very difficult to protect from the Lamia.'* When Mitránanda heard this, as he was desirous of money, he touched the drum, and took five hundred *dínáras* by way of advance, and then guarded the corpse through the night. When the morning came, the relations of the dead man refused to give him the other five hundred *dínáras*, and took the corpse away from him by force. Mitránanda said: 'I will inform the king of this unjust proceeding.' Then he bought a respectable dress for a hundred *dínáras*, and went to the house of Vasantatilaká, a principal *hetæra*. Then he gave four hundred *dínáras* to the mother of Vasantatilaká; then he was bathed and feasted in the most splendid manner by the old *hetæra*, but as he was intent on his friend's interests, he remained indifferent for three watches of the night, thinking of nothing else. Then the old *hetæra* said to Mitránanda: 'Why do you thus cheat my daughter of your society? Is she neither affectionate nor good-looking, that you will not speak to her?' Mitránanda answered her: 'Mother, I will do all your bidding, but I ask you one thing: have you the *entrée* of the apartments of the princess, or not?' She answered: 'This daughter of mine is always entering the apartments of the princess; Ratnamanjarí is a great friend of my daughter's.' Then Mitránanda said: 'The next time you enter Ratnamanjarí's

* I translate Mári by Lamia. We find further on that the Mári assumes the form of a beautiful woman. The story may be compared with 'The Soldier's Midnight Watch' and 'The Headless Princess' in Ralston's 'Russian Folk-Tales,' pp. 271-283. In an article in the *Globe* newspaper of September 18, 1894, on 'Funeral Superstitions,' I find the following sentence: 'Readers of the "Golden Ass" will remember the weird and dismal superstitions with which the ancient world surrounded the corpse of the departed, and how heavy a bribe was needed to induce the student Telephron to watch beside a dead body previous to its interment.' This passage will be found in the 'Metamorphoses of Apuleius,' lib. ii., c. 35 and ff.

private apartments, you must say to her that I have been sent with a message to her from her beloved Amaradatta.' When the old *hetæra* heard this, she was delighted, and went herself to the apartments of the princess. When Ratnamanjarí saw her, she said: 'Mother, you seem to be very merry to-day.' She told Ratnamanjarí all that cunning fellow's doings. When the princess heard this, she was rather pleased. She said: 'Then let me have an interview, mother, with that bringer about of interviews.' When the *hetæra* had heard this, she came home, and told Mitránanda all that had taken place. At night-time she went with him to the chief gate of the palace, and said to him: 'How will you manage, my dear boy, to enter this pavilion of Ratnamanjarí, that is surrounded with seven ramparts?' As she said this, she pointed out the pavilion of Ratnamanjarí with the tip of her finger. Then he leapt with the speed of lightning, and, bounding over the seven ramparts, reached the pavilion of the princess. He lighted in a window there, and saw Ratnamanjarí. The *hetæra* said to herself: 'This must be some heroic being* to possess such might;' so she went home with this thought in her mind. The princess, seeing a man suddenly arrive, was struck with amazement; however, she pretended to be asleep, in order to see what he would do. At this moment Mitránanda drew his dagger and made a mark on her right thigh; and then he took the bracelet from her left hand, and returned to the house of the *hetæra* by the very same way by which he had come. The princess bewailed her ill-luck in not being addressed by that heroic being, and kept awake all night; however, at the end of that night she fell asleep. Then Mitránanda appeared the next morning before the gate of the palace, with a bundle on the end of a bamboo, making a great panting. The warder informed the king, and Mitránanda was called, and the king said to him: 'Why do you look as if you were out of your mind?' Mitránanda told him the ill-treatment he had received

* *Vírapurusha.* I remember reading in the newspapers that this very term was used by a Bengali of an English aeronaut.

from the merchant. The king summoned the merchant, and said to him: 'Why do you not give this man the money you ought to give him?' The merchant said: 'My lord, for three days I remained absorbed in mourning according to the custom of the world, therefore I did not give him the money I ought to have given him; so I will give it now.' Having said this, the merchant went home. The king then said to Mitránanda: 'How did you guard the corpse?' Mitránanda answered: 'King, I girded up my loins firmly and drew my dagger, and remained on the alert, looking about me in every direction. Accordingly, in the first watch the tribe of jackals arrived. In the second watch terrible vampires* came. In the third watch the congregation of witches arrived. In the fourth watch a charmingly-dressed fair one came near the corpse. I knew that she was a Lamia,† so I seized her by the left hand. Then she slipped from my grasp, but as she went I marked her on the right thigh with my dagger,‡ and when she slipped away, her bracelet remained in my hand. The king said: 'Then show me the bracelet.' Mitránanda drew the bracelet from his zone and put it in the hand of the king. The king saw that it was the bracelet of Ratnamanjarí, marked with her own name. His face became black. He said to himself: 'Poison has been produced in nectar, since this Ratnamanjarí has acquired the reputation of a Lamia.' Then the king went into the pavilion of Ratnamanjarí. There the king beheld Ratnamanjarí, clothed in transparent garments, sleeping heavily, with no bracelet on her left wrist, and with a bandage wrapped round her right thigh. Then the king said to himself: 'I will myself arrest that girl, who disgraces my family like a witch.' Having thus deliberated, he returned to his own dwelling. The king said to Mitránanda: 'As you displayed courage in guarding the corpse, do you know any other charms and spells that will avail in other similar cases?' Mitránanda said: 'I am a master of spells.' The king said: 'That fair

* The word translated 'vampire' is Vetála. † Mári.
‡ Compare the 'Kathá Sarit Ságara,' vol. ii., p. 239.

one that you saw in the fourth watch of the night, and who is disgraced by the appellation of Lamia, was my daughter. So if you have the power, take her, or punish her yourself.' Mitránanda said: 'I will see once whether it is possible or impossible.' The king said, 'Be it so.' Then Mitránanda went by order of the king into the pavilion of Ratnamanjarí. She, seeing that he came by order of her father, showed him honour by offering him a seat, and so on. Then Mitránanda said to the princess: 'My good lady, let me tell you the state of affairs. My dear friend, Prince Amaradatta, saw your form sculptured in stone in a temple in the public gardens of the city of Páṭaliputra, and he has consequently fallen desperately in love with you, and if he does not obtain you he will die. I am his great friend, Mitránanda by name, and I have come here for you. For the sake of Amaradatta I have denounced you to the king as a Lamia. It was I that took away the bracelet from your left wrist during the night, and I made with my dagger a mark on your right thigh. Henceforth I will do whatever pleases you. Now you must do all that I tell you; if you do not consent, I will die in this very spot; and then Amaradatta will die in Páṭaliputra, so the title of Lamia will certainly attach to you. So do as you like.' When Ratnamanjarí heard this, she deliberated in her mind, and said to Mitránanda: 'Mitránanda, as your friend Prince Amaradatta is in love with a stone image of me, I must save him and you, even at the cost of my own life.' Mitránanda answered: 'If this is the case, then you must hiss when the king hands you over to me.' Having given her these instructions, Mitránanda returned into the king's court. The king said: 'Master of spells, can you subdue her or not?' He said: 'I can subdue that woman, but give me a horse. Before the sun rises I will take her to another country.' When he had said this, the king, being terrified, dragged her by the hair, and handed her over to Mitránanda, hissing all the time. Mitránanda also, muttering inarticulate spells, lifted Ratnamanjarí on to the horse, and departed from the city at sunset. As Ratnamanjarí was going along on the road, she said to Mitrá nanda: 'My lord, you ought not to ride on the same horse as your friend's wife.' He said: 'You are as a daughter to me, so why should we not ride on the same horse?' When she heard this, she said to herself: 'Happy is the man whose friend he is.' While she was engaged in these reflections, Mitránanda brought her into the public garden of Páṭaliputra. Just at this point, the two months being at an end, Amaradatta, through grief for his friend, had asked the merchant Ratnaságara for firewood.* Then Ratnaságara made ready the pyre, but the citizens said to Amaradatta: 'Wait somehow or other till this day comes to an end.' Then Amaradatta waited to please the people. Then the people said to Amaradatta: 'A horseman is approaching.' While all looked on with the utmost excitement, Mitránanda came up to Amaradatta. Then the two friends rejoiced greatly, and immediately the marriage took place in front of that very fire as a witness. The merchant Ratnaságara and the people of the city talked much of them to one another. Now, it happened that the king of that city died in the course of the night without leaving issue. Then the ministers had recourse to the five ordeals. The mighty elephant came into the garden outside the city. There the elephant sprinkled Prince Amaradatta and put him on its back. Then the horse neighed. The two chowries fanned the prince. An umbrella was held over his head. A divine voice was heard in the air: 'Long live King Amaradatta!' Then great rejoicings took place in the city. King Amaradatta entered the city in triumph, and arrived in the palace. Then the ministers and the feudatory princes and others anointed him king. Amaradatta made Mitránanda head of his cabinet, Ratnamanjarí was the jewel of his harem, and the merchant Ratnaságara was appointed royal merchant. So he ruled his realm. Once, after many days had passed, Mitránanda said to the king: 'King, that speech of the corpse presses on my mind, so grant me a favour; send me away to a distance.' As

* In order to burn himself.

Mitránanda was very importunate, Amaradatta at length sent him, guarded by his servants, towards Vasantapura.

> But as no news came of him, after some days the king
> Employed a man to inquire, but no intelligence came.

Then the king said to himself: 'What has become of my friend? If there were any seer in the neighbourhood, I would ask for information about my friend.' While the king was saying this to himself, a keeper of the garden and plantations came to him, and said: 'To-day a great hermit, possessing four kinds of knowledge, named the priest* Dharmaghosha, has arrived in the park.' When the king heard that, he was delighted, and went with Ratnamanjarí to adore him; and after bowing before him he received from his mouth religious instruction. At this moment an inhabitant of that town, a merchant, Açokadatta by name, bowed before the religious teacher, and said: 'Reverend sir, for what action is my daughter diseased in this birth? What is the cause of her sickness?' The holy man had her brought there, and cured her completely by casting one look at her. Then the merchant said: 'Revered sir, what action did this my daughter commit in a former birth?' The holy man said: 'In a former age there was a merchant named Bhútadeva in the city of Bhútasála. He had a wife named Kukshimatí. One day Kukshimatí saw the cat drinking the milk, and she spoke a wicked speech to her daughter-in-law, saying: "Are you possessed by the female demons, that you do not save the milk from the cat?" When that daughter-in-law heard that, she was immediately deluded by a female demon. Then the king and the rest of the people delivered her from the demon. So the wife of the merchant's son recovered her condition of health, but the mother-in-law, Kukshimatí, acquired the sobriquet of "Black-tongue." Then Kukshimatí, hearing the way in which she was reviled by the public, became inclined to

* *Súri*, a common title of Jaina teachers. Usually five kinds of knowledge are enumerated. See Dr. Hoernle's 'Uvásaga Dasáo,' p. 48, note.

renunciation. She took a vow and went to heaven. Falling from heaven, she became this daughter of yours. So, on account of the influence of her previous life, she has been possessed by the goddesses of the air. But just now, on beholding me, the goddesses of the air left her and fled.'

When he had said this the woman remembered her former birth, and beheld her previous life. A desire for renunciation sprang up in her. She asked to be allowed to take a vow; but the holy man would not sanction it. He said: 'The effects of indulgence still subsist in you.' So she observed the conduct prescribed for householders.

At this point Amaradatta asked the religious teacher what had happened to Mitránanda. Then the holy man said:

'Hear, O king! When Mitránanda left you, he went, surrounded by your brave warriors, towards the city of Vasantapura; and when they had advanced into a certain forest, a body of Bhillas made an attack on them. All the warriors fled, terrified at the attack, wishing to save their lives. Mitránanda, too, fled in a certain direction. When he had roamed about a considerable time in the wood, he reached a certain lake. Having drunk water from it, he slept under a banyan-tree. In the meanwhile a serpent came out from the hollow trunk of that tree, and bit Mitránanda; but at that very moment an ascetic came there, who restored him to life, when senseless from the effect of the poison. The hermit went to his own place, but Mitránanda, setting out to return to you, was on the way seized by bandits, who proceeded to sell him to some merchants who travelled in boats. Those merchants took Mitránanda to Persia. And bringing him back from Persia, with the intention of going to another country, they arrived at Ujjayiní. At that time the city of Ujjayiní was disturbed with fear of robbers. By order of the king, policemen were patrolling in every direction. Now, it happened that Mitránanda escaped from those members of the caravan, and was seen by the policemen entering Ujjayiní from the stream which formed a barrier to protect it. They cried out, "A thief!" and imprisoned him closely during the night. They then made him over to the head-policeman, who was their commander, and he, being angry, hung Mitránanda on that very same banyan-tree, so that he died, and as some herdsmen were playing, the ball entered his mouth.'

When King Amaradatta heard of the death of Mitránanda from the hermit, he lamented with a loud voice. Ratnamanjarí also cried. But the great hermit restored King Amaradatta to composure by exhortations tending to renunciation. He said: 'Do not sorrow, king; various is the transmigration of souls produced by works.' Then King Amaradatta said: 'Reverend sir, where has the soul of Mitránanda been again conceived?' The holy man discerned by the might of pure meditation the course of that soul, and said to the king: 'King, the soul of Mitránanda has been conceived in your own family, in your wife Ratnamanjarí, and shall be born as your son, Kamalagupta by name.' Then the king questioned the hermit about the previous life of Mitránanda. He said: 'Revered sir, what action did the soul of Mitránanda commit in a previous life, that it has suffered so much affliction in this life?' The holy man said: 'Hear, O king! In a former age there was in this very land of Bharata, in the city of Sáketa, a householder named Kshemankara. He had a wife named Satyaçrí and a servant named Chaṇḍasena, who was skilled in all kinds of work. One day the servant Chaṇḍasena was guarding a field. Now, it happened that he saw a pilgrim gathering corn in a field belonging to another man, near the field he was guarding. He cried out: "Masters, this is a thief; hang him on a branch of this tree." But the proprietor of the field, out of compassion, would not do that. His cruel speech produced great grief in the heart of the pilgrim. Chaṇḍasena came home in the evening. That action became attached to his soul. One day when Satyaçrí and her daughter-in-law were eating, a morsel stuck in the throat of the latter. When

Satyaçrí saw it, she cried out: "Ah! you must be a Rákshasí, to eat with such large mouthfuls." When the daughter-in-law heard this, she was grieved in her heart. One day Chaṇḍasena said to his master, named Kshemankara: "I am going to meet my relations." He, being angry, said: "May you not succeed in meeting your relations!" One day Kshemankara and Satyaçrí entertained a hermit with pure food. Chaṇḍasena also was standing by, and approving what they did. When the hermit had gone, a flash of lightning fell on all three of them. Then they all three went to Saudharma. When they fell from that heaven, the soul of Kshemankara was born as yourself, Amaradatta; the soul of Satyaçrí was born as Ratnamanjarí, and the soul of Chaṇḍasena was born as Mitránanda. Then Mitránanda, because he spoke an evil speech, was hanged on a branch of a banyan-tree. Because Satyaçrí in a former birth spake an evil speech in denouncing her daughter-in-law as a Rákshasí, she, in this birth as Ratnamanjarí, was disgraced by the imputation of being a Lamia. Because you in a former birth expressed a wish to your servant that he might not meet his relations, you have in this birth been separated from your relations.'

When they heard these circumstances of a former birth, they all took the vows of lay disciples. Amaradatta addressed another question to the holy hermit: 'Reverend sir, does a corpse speak?' The hermit said: 'The soul of the pilgrim after he had died became a demon; so, on account of his enmity to Mitránanda in a former birth, he entered into the mouth of the corpse and spoke to Mitránanda.' When they had heard this, they all went away to their own places. The king continued to rule his kingdom with Ratnamanjarí for his consort. One day Ratnamanjarí gave birth to a son. She gave him the name of Kamalagupta. Prince Kamalagupta was instructed in the Çástras, and in course of time he attained adolescence. One day King Amaradatta, having placed his son on his throne, went with Ratnamanjarí and took a vow before that very same spiritual teacher. After they have performed asceticism, they will in course of time attain salvation.

Wine, the pleasures of the senses, sin, sleep, and boasting, which is mentioned in the fifth place,
These are the five delusions which plunge the soul into the circuit of mundane existence.

Therefore, having heard the story of Amaradatta and Mitránanda, sin * is to be avoided. Here comes to an end the story of Amaradatta and Mitránanda, having reference to sin.

Munificence, chastity, asceticism, meditation—this piety is of four kinds;
They who observe it heartily, those souls are a vessel of merit.

By munificence creatures are tamed; by munificence even enmities come to an end;
By munificence is gained glory pure as the moon; there is no instrument superior to munificence.

A spotless family; a handsome shape, such as heart could wish, and free from disease;
Prosperity that enriches the whole world; an illustrious development of fortune;
Moreover, also, blameless learning, an extensive good reputation;
A multitude of attractive qualities; all these are obtained by munificence.

Even the siding with virtue produces success, as in the case of Lalitánga;
But the opposite conduct produces destruction, as in the case of his servant Sajjana.

STORY OF LALITÁNGA.

Now follows a story with regard to the virtue of munificence. In Jambudvípa, in this very land of Bharata, there was a town named Çrívása; in it lived a king of the name of Naraváhana; his head queen, who wore the diadem, was called Kamalá. Those two parents had born to them a son named Lalitánga, the delight of their eyes. He possessed all the auspicious marks, was clever in all the accomplishments, exceedingly learned, full of discernment, and appreciated merit. He, even when a raw boy, dwelt in the minds of the learned; he was devoted to his god, to his

* *Kasháya.* See the 'Sarva Darçana Sangraha' (Cowell and Gough's translation), p. 55.

spiritual teacher, to his parents, and then to all the members of his family. Moreover, he was exceedingly generous; when he saw a petitioner he was delighted.

> That lunar day seemed to have slipped away, and yet was in his mind like an extra month,
> That day was not counted, on which there was not the arrival of a petitioner.
> That prince had a servant named Sajjana, whom he treated as a friend;
> Sajjana* he was by name, but by character he was exceedingly wicked.

One day that Prince Lalitánga gave away to a beggar a very valuable ornament which his father had given him. Sajjana told the king of Lalitánga's vice of generosity. His report put the king in a rage. He summoned his son, and spoke to him at first with conciliatory words, but firmly, for a son is like a friend: for

> A father should pet his son for five years, for ten years he should beat him;
> But when the sixteenth year has arrived, he should treat his son as a friend.

He said: 'My son, have you not heard,

> 'A tree is burned from too much cold; famine comes from too much rain;
> From too much giving comes unseemliness; "too much" is nowhere approved.†

For this reason, my son, you must spend less.' The prince said:

> 'Father, even by great bestowing wealth does not come to destruction,
> As the water in a great well, though drawn up by the village.

Nevertheless, I will not do what is displeasing to the king. The command of a superior must be implicitly obeyed.' Having said this, the prince went home. The prince was now forbidden to indulge in excessive generosity. The petitioners said: 'Prince,

> 'How is this? Having been, O king, like a wishing-jewel on earth from thy munificence,
> How is it that thou hast now become like an ordinary stone?

---

* Sajjana means 'good man.'

† My MSS. read *nekshyate*, but Böhtlingk ('Indische Sprüche,' No. 2504) reads *neshyate*, which makes better sense.

If the moon shall withdraw her digit, the giver tribute, the cloud rain,
In these cases, how shall the world manage to subsist?
The ocean, intent only on accumulation, has sunk down to the abyss;
But, see, the cloud, the giver, roars above the firmament.
The seas leave their place, the mighty mountains move;
But even amid dissolving worlds great ones leave not their promised vow.'

The prince, having heard this, began again to give charity, and the king heard of it. The king forbade his entering the palace. The prince was grieved in his soul. He said to himself:

'When illness, defilement, poverty, dishonour, or the rainy season comes,
Except a foreign land, there is no happiness here for men of spirit.'

Having formed this resolution, he mounted his horse in the middle of the night, when people were not about, and set out in a certain direction. His friend Sajjana also went with him. As they were going along, they conversed as follows. The prince said: 'Sajjana, tell me some news.' He said: 'Prince, of virtue and vice, which is preferable?' The prince said: 'O fool,

'Women, children, herdsmen, ploughboys even, know this clearly,
That from virtue comes triumph, but by vice is brought about destruction.'

Sajjana said: 'I am a fool, no doubt; but with regard to virtue and vice, say what is virtue and what is vice.' The prince said:

'True speech, devotion to one's spiritual teacher, almsgiving according to one's power, compassion to the afflicted,
This is virtue that procures men objects of desire, and keeps off calamity.

The opposite of this is vice.' Sajjana said: 'Come, prince, virtue brings about destruction, and vice produces success; for you are now reduced to such a miserable condition, though you are virtuous. So how can virtue bring success? Therefore it is incumbent on you now to practise vice. Acquire wealth by some such an occupation as robbery.' The prince said: 'Sajjana, do not speak like that.

'Am I to obtain fortune by injustice? That illumination is like a lamp:
For a moment it lights up objects; but when it is at an end, there is nothing but darkness.

We are two people only in a forest: who shall be arbiter in our dispute? If, as we advance, any witnesses shall declare that vice produces success, then I, though a prince, will be your servant as long as you live.' Sajjana said: 'If my assertion is declared true, then I will take your horse, ornaments, and other possessions.' The prince said: 'So be it.' When they had made this agreement, they went to a forest hamlet. There they asked some decrepit old Pulindas: 'Ho! you Pulindas, does virtue or vice produce success?' As it happened, they also said that vice produced success. Sajjana took from the prince his horse, ornaments, and other possessions, and Prince Lalitánga went along on foot. The wicked Sajjana said: 'Prince, you have experienced in an obvious way the result of taking the side of virtue; now make vice your rule of life.' The prince said: 'I will not desert virtue even at the "crack of doom."' Accordingly they made an agreement that the prince's eyes were to be surrendered, if virtue were worsted in the dispute. As fate would have it, they reached first the very village they had left before, and those very same old Pulindas said that vice ensured success. When they had gone a considerable distance, Sajjana said to the prince: 'Fulfil your promise; give me your eyes.' The prince went under a banyan-tree, and pulled out his eyes with his own hands, and gave them to Sajjana, exclaiming: 'Virtue brings success!' The wicked Sajjana went off with the two eyes. While the prince was under that very banyan-tree, the sun set.

Many birds came screaming, as if crying out from sorrow
At the prince's misfortune, and settled down in their nest-dwellings.
In the meanwhile, being assembled together in that banyan-tree,
Some *bhárunda* birds of their own accord thus began to converse.

One said: 'Well, birds, what strange thing has anyone seen to-day?' Another answered: 'In the city of Champá there is a king named Jitaçatru. His daughter, Pushpávatí by name, as fate will have it, owing, that is to say, to the influence of her sins in a former birth, is without the use of her eyes, and blind, though old enough to be married. That is an affliction to the mind of her father, that pierces his life like an arrow. One day the king had a proclamation made throughout his city by beat of drum: "Whoever will restore the eyes of Pushpávatí, the daughter of Jitaçatru, by means of a herb or a spell, to him the king will give the half of his kingdom and his daughter besides."' A certain young bird asked the old bird: 'Father, is there any means by which her eyes may be restored afresh?' The old bird said:

'My child, I will tell you in the day, after looking round, and not at night;
Very cunning people wander about under the banyan-tree, like Vararuchi.*

For that reason do not ask now; at the time of dawn I will tell you of a means.' The young bird would not desist from its importunity, but asked very persistently, saying: 'I will not let you off without telling me.' The old bird said: 'A creeper embraces the root of this banyan-tree, and extends over it. If her eyes are sprinkled with the juice of that plant, they will be restored again immediately.' When the prince, who was under the banyan-tree, heard this speech of the bird, he first sprinkled that juice into the sockets of his own eyes. His eyes became clear as before. The prince said to himself: 'I will take the healing plant, and go to the city of Champá, and there make clear the eyes of the princess.' Then he took the virtuous herb, and crawled in among the feathers of a *bhárunḍa* bird, and lay there. At the hour of dawn all the birds went to the city of Champá. Lalitánga crept out of

* See my translation of the 'Kathá Sarit Ságara,' vol. i., p. 25, for the story of Vararuchi. In the note will be found a parallel. For other parallels see also note on p. 263, and Addenda and Corrigenda. In Kaden's 'Unter den Olivenbäumen' the witch says: 'I cannot tell you now, for the grass has eyes and the trees have ears.' I learn from an analysis of a MS. of the 'Kathá Prakáça' in the India Office, which Professor Eggeling has kindly lent me, that these lines are found in a story in that MS. entitled 'Bráhmaṇakathá.'

the bird's feathers, and entered the city.* Then he went to the palace, and entering it, he made the eyes of the princess quite clear.† The king gave him the half of his kingdom and the princess. Lalitánga married Pushpávatí in an auspicious moment. He ruled half of his father-in-law's kingdom. After some time had passed, that very Sajjana, roaming like a beggar from house to house for what he could get to eat, came to the gate of the prince's palace. The king saw him. He said: 'I have seen my great friend Sajjana.'

> Then the prince made him abandon his mean dress, bathe, and take food,
> And put on good clothes; and then he thus addressed him:
> 'To-day my kingdom has borne fruit, since in it you, my companion in misfortune, have arrived;
> Therefore enjoy all the happiness of it with a mind free from care.'

The prince gave Sajjana a seat of honour. One day Pushpávatí asked him in private: 'My lord, since yesterday you are on terms of great friendship with Sajjana. Who is this Sajjana?' The prince immediately told the whole story from the very beginning, commencing with the events that happened in another country. The princess said: 'My lord, this is not a good man [*sajjana*], but a bad man; you ought not to be friends with him. By all means he must be abandoned; considering this, give him up, king. Have you not heard this?

> 'He who associates with the excellent, converses with the wise,
> And makes friends with those who are free from covetousness, is never ruined.

To this is applicable the instance of the swan and the crow:

> 'Great king, I am a swan free from conceit in a clear lake;
> From addiction to the society of the vile comes death, without doubt.'

Though the prince was thus advised, he did not abandon Sajjana: for

> It is hard, as fate goes, to prevent even the great from associating with the vile;
> How can the camphor help having a love for the charcoal?

---

* Compare my translation of the 'Kathá Sarit Ságara,' vol. i., p. 221.

† In Ralston's 'Russian Folk-Tales,' the water of a magic well produces the same effect. See pp. 250 and 255.

One day King Jitaçatru, the father-in-law of Lalitánga, asked Sajjana in private: 'Who is this Prince Lalitánga? What is his origin?' Then Sajjana showed his character, for he said: 'King, I am a prince; he is the son of a potter.' When the king heard this, he was angry, and ordered his servants to kill Lalitánga. He said: 'You must destroy the man who comes by the gate leading into the main approach to the palace at the time of sunset.' So he sent a summons to Lalitánga at the time of sunset. Lalitánga took his sword and rose up to go. But Pushpávatí forbade him. She said:

> 'You must not trust this, if you are a man that understands these matters:
> Have you not read in policy, that a king can be no man's friend?

So, my lord, remain here yourself; send Sajjana on this errand.' Sajjana was sent, and as he was entering the gate of the palace avenue he was killed.* The princess saw that her father was angry, and she said to her husband: 'My lord, set your army in battle array, and march out.' He did so. Jitaçatru also was ready for the fray. But the nobles said to the king:

> 'The man who acts rashly is quickly deserted by happy fortunes:
> Hear, with reference to this, the example of King Jaya.

'This is as follows:

Story of the Parrot that brought the Fruit of Immortality.

'In a banyan-tree in a great wood on the Vindhya mountain there lived a pair of parrots. A young parrot was born. One day, when the parent birds had gone away into the forest, the young parrot went out of the nest. After it had gone a little distance, owing to its being so young, it fell on the ground. When wearied it was seen by a certain hermit. Out of compassion he gave it water to drink, took it to his own hermitage, and gave it the name of Çukanáça. The parrot's parents also came to that hermitage to look for

* Compare vol. i., p. 162, of my translation of the 'Kathá Sarit Ságara,' with the note.

their nestling. One day the parrot heard the abbot telling his pupils that in the middle of the sea there is an island, named Harisena; that in the north-east corner of that island there is a large fragrant mango-tree, bedewed with ambrosia; and that the fruit of that tree cures the body of deformity, disease, and old age. So the parrot flew up and went to that island to bring the fruit of the fragrant mango-tree. On its return, it fell in the middle of the sea, on account of the weight of the fruit, and was seen by the head of a maritime caravan, picked up, and restored to life. The merchant said to the parrot: "What is this fruit, and who are you?" The parrot told his story, and gave the fruit to Ságaradatta.* He brought another fruit and gave it to his parents. Ságaradatta presented the fruit to the King of Jayapura, and related the marvellous virtues attaching to it. The king, in order to benefit the whole world, sowed the seed of the fragrant mango-tree in an orchard. It triumphantly flowered and bore fruit, which ripened together with the wishes of the king. One day the poison of a serpent, that was held in the beak of a kite, dropped on a mango-fruit.† On account of the heat of the poison, the fruit ripened throughout, and becoming loosened from the tree, fell on the ground. The keeper of the garden brought the mango-fruit to the king. The king, remembering the maxim, "One should consecrate to religion what one values most," gave the fruit to his chaplain; and the chaplain immediately ate it up without washing it, and died. The king was in a rage, and exclaiming that the tree was a poison-tree, had it cut down. A host of men who longed for death, being maimed, diseased, blind, and lepers, ate the fruits of the tree, with the result that they all became sound of body. The king heard of that fact. He regretted what he had done all the rest of his life. So do you take care not to act rashly, having heard the story of the King of Jayapura.'

* In Grimm's seventeenth tale ('The White Snake') a crow gives a young man an apple from the Tree of Life.

† For a similar case see my translation of the 'Kathá Sarit Ságara,' vol. ii., p. 296.

At this juncture the chief nobles of King Naraváhana, who had come to fetch the prince, told his family and other particulars about him. Afterwards the parents of Lalitánga arrived. His father-in-law gave Prince Lalitánga his own kingdom, and, becoming a hermit, went to heaven. King Naraváhana brought his son to his own city, and persuaded him to forgive him his offence, saying: 'My dear boy, wealth is not diminished by almsgiving.' So the father gave his kingdom to Lalitánga, and took a vow, and after observing a holy conversation went to heaven. Lalitánga ruled his realm as king. Here ends the story of Lalitánga.

> Whoever being addicted to compassion towards living creatures gives up injuring others,
> To that man even calamity will become a feast, as in the case of Dámannaka.

Here follows the story of Dámannaka, concerning compassion to living creatures.

Story of Dámannaka, who was first born as a Fisherman, and then as the Son of a Merchant.

In this very land of Bharata is a city named Rájapura, in which city the troops of peacocks dance, when they hear the noise of the drums beaten in the temple of the Jina. In that city lived a respectable youth of the name of Sunanda, who was a fisherman. But he was by nature much inclined to show compassion to all living creatures. He had a great friend, a lay disciple named Jinadása. One day he went with Jinadása to his spiritual teacher. After bowing before the teacher, they both sat down, and the teacher gave them religious instruction with regard to compassion to living creatures. He said:

> 'Even one instance of compassion to living creatures produces ten million salutary results,
> And drives away infinite calamities and woes, and is the cause of heaven and salvation.'

Sunanda then made a solemn promise, saying: 'Reverend sir, henceforth I will not slay living creatures; I will not eat flesh.' Once on a time, after many days had elapsed, a famine took place. During that famine all people lived on the flesh of fish, as they could not obtain rice. Sunanda's wife said to him: 'You also must observe the same conduct as other people.' He said: 'I will have no more to do with deeds that are the cause of crime.' His wife said to him: 'O you fool! who has deluded you, so that you do not observe the customs of your race?' Thereupon some of his brothers-in-law met together, and dragged him by force to a great pool in the river, and made him throw his net into it. When Sunanda saw many fish caught in the net, wriggling helplessly, compassion arose in his heart. He let all the fish go, and returned home. In the same way Sunanda's brothers-in-law made him perform the same evil act for three successive days. He did not perform it with his inclination, as well as with his bodily organs. But from the striking of the fish against one another, the fin of one fish was broken. He said to his brothers-in-law: 'Alas! alas! I will not kill living creatures for the sake of my family: for

'When I am gone to hell, will that family deliver me
For the sake of which I now, fool that I am, slay crores of living creatures?
Since the body does not advance one step in the other world together with the soul,
Why do they inculcate the slaying of living creatures for its sake?'

After saying this, he took to fasting and died.

Now, in this very land of Bharata, in the city of Rájagṛiha, there was a king of the name of Naravarman; and in the same city there was a merchant of the name of Maṇikára, the possessor of twelve crores of gold coins. He had a wife named Sujasá. The soul of Sunanda was conceived in her. When her time was completed, a son was born, and the name of Dámannaka was given to him. Gradually he attained the age of eight years. One day, as fate would have it, the plague broke out in the house of the merchant:

He who gives food out of compassion, and gives men water to drink,
In his land the plague spreads, continually infecting crowds.

The king said: 'This is the plague. It will spread all over

the town.' So he ordered a wall to be built at the door of the merchant's house, and in a short time all the human beings in it, beginning with the father and mother of the family, died of the plague. But Dámannaka was spared by the plague, on account of the compassion that he had shown in a previous birth; but he could not get out of the house. However, in course of time, he got out by the passage made by the dogs, which came in to eat the dead bodies. Roaming about to beg alms, he entered the house of a merchant named Ságarapota. While he was standing at the door of the house, a couple of hermits came on their begging round. The elder of the two ascetics, when he saw Dámannaka, said:

> 'Hear my words: I infer from the marks on his body,
> This boy shall one day become a merchant, the master of this house.'

The merchant Ságarapota, being separated by a wall, heard this speech, and said to himself: 'Hermits do not say what is false even at the crack of doom, for

> 'Hermits who are free from attachment and hatred, who look impartially on jewels, straws, friends and enemies,
> Do not, like ordinary men, speak an inconsiderate speech.

So shall my family become extinct? Shall my son Samudradatta be destroyed, since, though my family is so numerous and flourishing, this beggar is to be lord in my house? However, what a hermit says cannot prove false.' The merchant was miserable. He said: 'Out on this drama of the universe! Shall this beggar become master of this wealth, which my father and grandfather and other ancestors so long cherished? So I will devise some scheme. What is the use of lamenting? I will think of a plan for killing him. If he is overlooked, he will be fatal like a disease.' Having thus deliberated with his own heart, he took a sweetmeat, and said to that Dámannaka: 'Come here, my darling, that I may give you a sweetmeat.' When Dámannaka heard this, he went with him. The merchant went to the quarter of the Chaṇḍálas. There was a chief of the Chaṇḍálas named Khangila. He called him aside and gave him money, and said to him: 'Come, do me this service, to kill this boy secretly; and when he is slain, you must bring me a token of it.' The Chaṇḍála agreed, and took Dámannaka a long way off from the city. The Chaṇḍála reflected in his mind: 'What crime can this poor wretch have committed, that Ságarapota tries to have him killed? So I will assuredly not kill him; my hands will not move for the purpose.' Then he drew his knife, that resembled the tongue of Yama, and cut off his little finger, and said to the child: 'If you remain in this city, I will kill you; if you leave the city and go elsewhere, I will let you off.' He wept, and said: 'I will do as you say.' So the Chaṇḍála spared him and went home. He showed the piece of his finger to Ságarapota, who was delighted.* Dámannaka, while roaming about in the wood, was seen by Ságarapota's herdsman, who asked him, 'Who are you?' He said: 'I am a son of a merchant, and my whole family has perished.' Then the herdsman took him to his house, and made him over to his wife, and said: 'The goddess of our clan has given this son to you, who have no son.' The wife of the herdsman was delighted. Owing to his modesty and other virtues, he became much beloved by the two women.† Then Dámannaka, growing up in that cattle-farm, reached adolescence. One day the merchant Ságarapota came to inspect the cattle-farm. He saw Dámannaka there, and asked: 'Who is this boy?' He said: 'He was roaming about alone in this wood without a master, so I adopted him as my son.' The merchant, seeing that his little finger was cut off, came to the conclusion that he was Dámannaka; then he said to himself: 'Can the speech of the hermit, that this boy is to be the lord of my external wealth, be falsified? Nevertheless, I must not cease to strive manfully.' Having thus reflected, Ságarapota said: 'Come, herdsman, I must go home.' He said: 'You have

* The order to kill a person, and bring back some part of the body as a token or voucher, is very common in European stories. In Gonzenbach's third story the old queen orders the cook to kill Maruzzedda's three children, and to bring their liver and heart. (Gonzenbach, 'Sicilianische Märchen,' p. 13.)

† There appears to be some omission here.

come to-day after a long absence, and even now you have not inspected the cattle-farm.' Ságarapota said: 'I have important business at home, so I must go this very instant.' The herdsman said: 'If there is any very urgent business, then this son of mine can take a letter there.' So Ságarapota wrote a letter, and put it into his hand, and sent him off. Dámannaka started on his journey. When he reached the garden of Rájagṛiha, he was tired, and he lay down in the temple of the god of love to refresh himself. Sleep fell upon him. In the meanwhile the daughter of that very merchant, Vishá by name, came there to worship the god of love. She saw Dámannaka with his broad eyes and broad chest; and while she was looking at him, her eye fell on her father's letter, so she took it from the end of his stick and read it. It ran as follows: 'Health and prosperity! Ságarapota from the cattle-farm lovingly embraces Samudradatta, and tells him what is to be done:

> 'Before he has time to wash his feet, you must immediately bestow on this man
> Visha (poison) and so make my heart free from the thorn of pain.'

She thought: 'No doubt my father has found here a bridegroom fit for me; as for the marriage having to be performed this very day, it means that to-day is an auspicious day, so the marriage must take place to-day. As for the order that Visha is to be given, in his eagerness he has written an *anusvára* instead of the long *á*, so I will put it right.' Having thus reflected, she took some collyrium from her eyes and made the letter *á* instead of a dot; and sealing the letter up again, she left it as it was, and went home.* After a short time Dámannaka reached the house. He gave the letter to Samudradatta. Samudradatta took the letter and read it and considered it. He said: 'My father's order is law to me,' so he collected all the necessary preparations for the marriage, and all the host of his rela-

* Compare Grimm's No. 29, in which the robbers alter the letter found in the pocket of the 'Glückskind.' The story is also found in Dasent's 'Norse Tales.' See my paper in the *Indian Antiquary* for July, 1881.

tions assembled. On that very day, as soon as an auspicious moment arrived, Dámannaka was married.

'The ceremony was begun in which people's bodies don splendid raiment, and gleam with the rays of jewels,
In which the bride and bridegroom despise sorrow,
In which feet are immersed at the door in the dense mud of saffron,
And in which women dance.'

In the meanwhile Ságarapota entered the city. The people, who met him in the road, said: 'You are lucky to obtain such a son-in-law.' Ságarapota said to himself: 'No doubt this rascal has married my daughter.' When he got home, he saw his daughter, and Dámannaka with his body adorned with the wedding bracelet. He thought: 'Ah! I proposed this matter one way, and destiny has disposed it another. Now this man has become master of all the persons in my house, for women bear rule in the house of householders, and over the women the son-in-law bears rule. Moreover, it has been said:

'Of triads, three are pleasing, blossom, lamp-black, and vermilion;
Three others are pleasing, milk, son-in-law, and cymbal.

I cannot bear to see this unbecoming sight; I shall more easily endure the widowhood of my daughter. Anyhow I will by all means kill him.' Having thus determined, he went to the quarter of the Chaṇḍálas, and said to Khangila: 'You did not obey my orders.' He said: 'On that occasion, when I saw that he was a child, pity arose in my bosom; show me him now that I may kill him.' Ságarapota said: 'If it is so, then I will send that Dámannaka to-day to worship the protecting divinity of the city; then you must kill him.' Then he came home. When he reached his home, he said: 'Have the bride and bridegroom observed the custom of our family or not?' They said: 'It has been observed.' Then he made preparations for the worship of the goddess of the city. Then the bride and bridegroom set out to worship the goddess. As they were going along they were seen by Samudradatta, who was in the market, and he asked them: 'Where are you going at such a time of twilight, when the sun has gone to rest and the darkness is spreading abroad?' Dámannaka said: 'We are going to worship the goddess of the city.' Samudradatta said: 'Then do you wait; I will go and worship the goddess.' So he went off with the necessaries for worship. But as Samudradatta entered the temple, he was killed by Khangila, who had entered previously. When Ságarapota had heard of the slaying, he came back to the house to look for Samudradatta, but he saw Dámannaka and his wife. When Ságarapota was informed of his son's death, his heart burst and he died. When the king heard the story, he made Dámannaka master in his house. One day the panegyrists chanted this:

> 'Misfortunes, as it were, flowing favourably, become triumphs to that man
> To whom the god of death, the revealer of joy, pain and calamity, is favourable.'

When he heard this, Dámannaka gave those three a thousand coins. The king hearing of this unusual gift, summoned Dámannaka, and asked him the reason of the gift. He told the king his former history. The king was pleased, and gave him the rank of royal merchant. He enjoyed great luxury, gave gifts, and built temples. One day he thought to himself: 'What action did I perform in a former birth that I have happiness in place of calamity?' While he was thinking thus the day dawned. In the morning the person, who was appointed to superintend religion, said to Dámannaka: 'The teacher Vimalabodha has arrived in the park.' Dámannaka was delighted, and went to worship him. After worshipping, he asked him about his former life. The hermit told him his former life, which has been related above. He said: 'As you caused calamity to fishes three times in a former life, so calamity came upon you three times in this life. As you broke the fin of one fish, so your little finger was cut off. It is owing to your compassion for living creatures that you have such prosperity.' When he heard this, he remembered his former birth, and took a vow, and went to heaven. The story of Dámannaka regarding compassion to living creatures is finished.

Even a severe penance undergone, even a life in the wood long endured,
Is useless here to a man destitute of respect for his teacher, like Kúlaválaka.

For instance, here follows the story of Kúlaválaka:

STORY OF KÚLAVÁLAKA, THE HERMIT, WHO PROVED UNFAITHFUL TO HIS VOWS.

In this very land of Bharata there is a city named Rájagṛiha. In it ruled a king named Çreṇika.* His seven humours were purified by the seven categories † proceeding from the mouth of the Jina. He had a son named Abhaya, born from his wife Nandá, and a prince named Açokachandra, born from his wife Chillaná, and other sons, Halla, Vihalla, and so on, also sons of Chillaná, and by other queens many princes, Prince Kálaga and others. He had also other children. Çreṇika was ruling his kingdom. One day the holy Mahávíra encamped there. The king went to worship him. After worshipping him, he sat down. At the end of the sermon Prince Abhaya asked the master: 'Reverend sir, who will be the last royal sage after this?' The holy man declared: 'In our religion ‡ the last royal saint is King Udáyí; after him the crowned kings will not take a vow.' Then Prince Abhaya, fearing that his taking a vow would be impeded, refused to accept the throne. Çreṇika said: 'You must not take a vow without saying good-bye to me. You must not depart unless I give you leave.' Prince Abhaya promised accordingly. Once on a time, when a great stress of cold had fallen on the country, the king went with Queen Chillaná to worship Mahávíra. When they were on their way back, after worshipping him, Queen Chillaná saw a great hermit standing in the statuesque posture, enduring the torture of cold. The queen said to herself: 'How will this great hermit live through the night in this stress of cold without a blanket?' With this thought in her mind, the queen went to sleep at

* Called also Bimbisára, Bhambhasára and Bibbhisára (Bühler, 'Die Indische Secte der Jaina,' pp. 20 and 21).

† I take *dhátu* as equivalent to *tattva*. See Cowell and Gough's 'Sarva Darçana Sangraha,' p. 53.

‡ *Tirthe*.

night in her bed. In the course of the night her hand somehow slipped out from under the blanket. That hand being cold, Queen Chillaná woke up. She said: 'How will he get through the night?' The king heard this speech, and said to himself: 'Surely the queen must have made an assignation with someone, as she says this over and over again.' The king fell into a passion. In the morning he said to Prince Abhaya: 'Burn all the harem'; and having given him these instructions, he went himself to the Jina. After bowing before him, he said: 'Reverend sir, is Queen Chillaná the wife of one or of many?' The master asserted: 'Queen Chillaná is devoted to one husband only, and is of good character; but the meaning of her saying, "How will he get through the night?" is as follows: At sunset she saw a hermit enduring the trial of cold. At night, when it was very cold, the queen's hand came outside the blanket, and that made her remember the hermit, and wonder how he was getting on.' The king's doubt was removed, and he went back to the palace full of remorse. In the meanwhile Prince Abhaya set on fire an empty elephant-stable, and went off to worship the Jina. On the way the king met him. He said: 'Prince Abhaya, have you set the harem on fire?' He answered: 'Certainly.' The king said: 'Why did you not enter it?' Prince Abhaya answered: 'My father, how could I enter it without permission?' The king said: 'I permit you.' Prince Abhaya said: 'If this is my father's order, never mind entering the material fire. I will enter self-restraint, the fire that consumes passion.' Then Prince Abhaya, together with his mother, took a vow with great ceremony. Then, after some time, the king made up his mind that he would give the kingdom to Koṇika;* so he gave to the two princes, Halla and Vihalla, the elephant Sechanaka. He gave to Queen Chillaná the necklace Devadatta, and also a pair of garments of woven silk and a couple of bracelets. One day Koṇika consulted with the ten princes, Prince

* Hofrath Bühler calls him Kúṇika, and tells us that he was also called Ajátaçatru. He appears to have been also called Açokachandra.

Kála, and others, and threw King Çrenika into prison. He gave him a hundred lashes every forenoon, and a hundred every afternoon, and ordered that he should have nothing to eat or drink. Then Queen Chillaná concealed beans in her hair, and with great difficulty took them in for him to eat; Chandrahásá also managed to take wine in her hair, and when her hair was washed a hundred times, all the water became wine. Owing to the strength given him by the wine, the king was able to endure the whippings.* One day there was born to that Koṇika a son, of the name of Udaya, by his wife Padmávatí. On one occasion Koṇika was eating with the child in his lap. The child's urine fell into the vessel of rice. Koṇika did not put him off his lap for fear of disturbing him, but ate the rice mixed with urine. He said to his mother, who was near him: 'Mother, did anybody ever love his son so much?' His mother said: 'You monstrous criminal, listen! When I was pregnant with you, I had a longing to eat your father's flesh.† The king satisfied my longing. When you were born, I abandoned you in an enclosure of *açoka*-trees, saying that you were a villain. When the king heard it, he himself went to the enclosure and brought you back; so you were named Açokachandra. Then a dog tore your finger. It became a whitlow. So he gave you the name of Koṇika. When the swelling on your finger ripened, you suffered a good deal of pain from it. Your father held that finger in his mouth, though streaming with matter; so you did not cry. To this extent did he love you.' When Koṇika heard this, he was full of remorse. He said: 'A sorry return I have made to my father.' So he immediately went off in person with an iron club to break the fetters. In the meanwhile the guards said to the king: 'Koṇika is coming in a very impatient mood, with an iron club in his

* This story is found in the 'Amitáyur-dhyána-sútra,' pp. 161 and 162 of vol. xlix. of the 'Sacred Books of the East.' The queen Vaidehí supports Bimbisára in a very similar way.

† This is mentioned in the 'Thusajátaka.' (Fausböll, vol. iii., p. 338.) The Buddhists give the name of Ajátaçatru to the king whom the Jainas call Koṇika, or Kúṇika.

hand; it is not known what his object is.' The king said to himself: 'He will put me to death by some painful mode of execution;' so he took *tálapuṭa* poison. When Koṇika arrived there, King Çrenika was dead. He became an inhabitant of hell, destined to live in the first hell for eighty-four thousand years. In this very land of Bharata he shall be the first Tírthankara, named Mahápadma. Then Koṇika was afflicted at the loss of his father, and repeated this verse:

'Gardens, houses, regions having enjoyed as if laughing,
Though the places are beheld, the men are not beheld like the regions.'

Though admonished by his nobles, he would not bathe or take food. Then, being unable to endure his sorrow for his father, he left Rájagṛiha, and founded the new city of Champá. This Koṇika made the seat of his rule. Then the princes Halla and Vihalla, mounted on the elephant Sechanaka, adorned with the silk garments, the beautiful bracelets and necklace, roamed about every day in the city of Champá. One day Padmávatí, the wife of Koṇika, seeing the splendid appearance that they made, said to the king: 'King, to you the kingdom is only a burden; but the princes Halla and Vihalla have all the enjoyment of it. They roam about the city amusing themselves, mounted on the elephant Sechanaka. Therefore demand from them those precious things, of which Sechanaka is the chief.' The king said: 'I am ashamed to demand the precious things given to them by my father.' The queen said: 'Give them other precious things instead of these.' Then the king asked the princes for Sechanaka and the other precious things. They said: 'You are king and lord of all we have; take the precious things.' Having said this, the princes went home. The two deliberated, and came to the conclusion that the king would take their possessions by force; so they mounted the elephant Sechanaka, and went off by night to the city of Vaiçálí to King Cheṭaka. King Koṇika, when he heard what had happened, sent an ambassador to King Cheṭaka. The ambassador said: 'Send Halla and Vihalla quickly.' King Cheṭaka said: 'There is no difference between them and yourself in my mind. Halla and Vihalla and all of you are alike in my estimation, as being the sons of my daughter. How can I give up these that have sought refuge with me? No one else gives up those that fly to him for refuge, especially if they be the sons of his daughter.' When King Koṇika heard this, he flew in a passion, and sent the ambassador a second time with this message: 'Deliver up the princes; if you do not deliver them up, make ready for battle.' Cheṭaka said:

'Let my fortunes go to ruin, let my whole family go to destruction,
Let my head be cut off, let calamity also prevail on all sides;
But virtuous men do not recede from a thing that they have promised,
Dispersing the darkness of delusion with the illumination of the sun of discernment.'

Having thus deliberated, Cheṭaka agreed to fight. Koṇika, for his part, having made all the necessary preparation for war, came to Vaiçálí. The war began. But Cheṭaka had this advantage, that he could shoot one arrow every day at a warrior equal to himself, and by the power of the deity it was not ineffectual. Then in ten days the ten younger brothers of Koṇika, Prince Kála, and others were killed. Then Koṇika's mind was distracted with fear, and he said to himself: 'No doubt I shall be killed on the eleventh day, so it is not expedient to fight.' So the king retired, and performed the asceticism of the eighth day. Then, according to previous agreement, the lord of Saudharma and the lord Chamara * came to Koṇika, and said to him: 'King, what can we do to please you?' The king said: 'Destroy Cheṭaka.' They said: 'How can we destroy Cheṭaka, who is supremely orthodox? But we will protect your life when you are fighting.' The king said: 'So be it.' Then King Koṇika fought with Cheṭaka. And by the help of the lord Chamara, Koṇika kept dispersing the host of his adversary by means of combats with the *rathamuçala* and the *çilákaṇṭaka*,† and came near Cheṭaka. Then King

* For the magnificence of the Asura prince Chamara, see Weber's 'Bhagavatí,' p. 210. 'By the lord of Saudharma' is meant Çakra.

† See Dr. Hoernle's 'Uvásaga Dasáo,' appendix iii., p. 59, for a description of these formidable engines. The *rathamuçala* appears to have been a scythed chariot; the *maháçilákaṇṭaka* appears to have been a ballista which threw large stones.

Cheṭaka discharged an arrow at Koṇika. The arrow struck on a stone, and by virtue of Indra's power diverged in its course. King Cheṭaka said: 'Has the stream of my merit diminished, that this never-failing arrow has diverged in its course? Then it is not expedient to fight any more.' So he entered the city. King Koṇika, for his part, remained blockading the city. The city had lofty ramparts, and therefore no one could take it by escalade. Every night the Princes Halla and Vihalla, mounted on the elephant Sechanaka, penetrated into the camp of the besiegers, and killed many of their soldiers. Then King Koṇika asked his ministers: 'Is there any stratagem by which these two princes may be killed?' The ministers said: 'If the elephant Sechanaka could be killed, then these two, without being killed, would be as good as dead.' Then a stratagem was devised for killing the elephant Sechanaka. A trench was made in the path by which the elephant used to come, full of firebrands of acacia-wood, and it was covered above with a quantity of grass. Then Halla and Vihalla came at night mounted on the elephant. The elephant reached the border of the ditch, but would not advance, though troubled (at having to stop). Then the Princes Halla and Vihalla, being enraged, said to the elephant; 'O you wicked elephant, you have been fed by us, and it is thanks to you that Cheṭaka is now reduced to such a condition; now in the time of distress you will not advance.' When the elephant heard this, he put the princes down from his back, and, falling into the trench full of firebrands, died and went to hell. The princes were afflicted at the death of the elephant, and being disposed to renunciation, they were taken to Mahávíra by the goddess that executes the orders of the Jina. There they were both admitted to a vow by the hand of the teacher. Then one day, as Koṇika was absorbed in thought, he heard a voice in the air utter these words:

'If the hermit Kúlaválaka shall love the *hetæra* Mágadhiká,
Then King Açokachandra shall take the city of Vaiçálí.'

When the king heard this, he said: 'Who is this hermit

Kúlaválaka?' Then a certain minister, who knew the facts, told the story of Kúlaválaka. He said:

PREVIOUS HISTORY OF KÚLAVÁLAKA.

'King, in this very land of Bharata there is a teacher named Sangamasúri, who is surrounded by many pupils. One of his pupils was ill conducted, being addicted to expatiating on the beauty and charms of women. He delighted in beholding them. The teacher admonished him, saying: "Great-souled one, it is not fitting for hermits to look at women; as it is said in the Scriptures:

'"'As even a small jungle-fire consumes a whole forest of bamboos,
So even the name of young women drives away severe penance.'"

Though the pupil was admonished in this way, he did not learn wisdom, but nursed a special hatred against his teacher. One day the teacher ascended the top of Girnár. When they had worshipped the lord Nemi and were coming down, that wicked pupil said in his heart: "This is an opportunity for destroying my teacher, so I will kill him, otherwise he will smite me with severe speeches." So he let loose a huge stone behind his teacher. He saw it coming along with many checks, and going out of the path he escaped to a distance. The hermit said to his pupil: "O you wicked one, defiler of the bed of your teacher, enemy of your teacher, what have you done? Some people do not forget a benefit once conferred; I have for a long time been conferring benefits on you by imparting to you learning and other things." Then the teacher said: "Since you bear an enmity against me with reference to women, your asceticism shall be destroyed by a woman." When the teacher had said this, he went to his monastery.* That wicked pupil, for his part, went to the forest, thinking that he would falsify the word of his teacher. He performed asceticism on the bank of a mountain torrent. Then the rainy season came on, and the river began to flow with a full volume of water. Then the goddess of the water,

* Skṛit, *gachchha.*

pleased with the severe asceticism of that great hermit, said to herself: "I must take care that the river does not sweep away this great-hearted man with its stream." So the river began to flow close to the other bank. That fact was bruited abroad by the people who lived in that country, and so he has acquired the name of Kúlaválaka. Whatever caravan arrives in the neighbourhood at the end of the monthly fast, or the fortnightly fast, goes there, and the members of it break their fast in that very place.'

Then Koṇika, hearing this, sent for Mágadhiká, a *hetæra*, and said to her: 'My good woman, bring here the ascetic Kúlaválaka.' She said: 'I will do so.' She disguised herself as a Jaina female disciple, and went there with a caravan. She bowed before the ascetic Kúlaválaka, and said to him respectfully: 'Reverend sir, hearing that you were here, I came here to pay my respects to you.' Then she praised him as follows:

'To-day is a successful day for me, since I have seen you, a moving sanctuary;
Now show me favour, great and excellent hermit, by receiving my alms;
Receive my alms, for such worthy objects, as you are, are obtained by the power of merit;
Does a rain of gold take place in the courtyard of one devoid of merit?'

When Kúlaválaka had been propitiated by her respect, that showed itself in this way, he went to her place to receive alms, and she gave him sweetmeats. After he had eaten the sweetmeats, he was attacked with dysentery, and was so tortured by it that he could not even rise up. Then Mágadhiká said to the hermit: 'Alas! alas! I have brought you into a state of suffering; now I wish to cure you, so permit me to treat you with pure remedies: should you break your vow in any way, you can confess it afterwards; for

'In all cases an ascetic, who is trying to save his soul by abstinence,
Is delivered from transgression, but the fact is, cessation from the strict rule is in itself purifying.'

Being thus admonished by her with appropriate precepts stated in religious text-books, that high-souled man consented to allow her to attend on him, as an exceptional case. Then Mágadhiká attended on him. For some days she treated him with medicines and things of the kind. Then the hermit attained a healthy condition of body. Thereupon one day that Mágadhiká, displaying all her charms, having adorned her body with all her ornaments, with an arch smile spoke thus to the hermit: 'What is the use of this difficult penance? Cultivate me, the only auspicious treasury of happiness; abandon the seal of your vow; leave the forest; repair to the city.' When Kúlavá-laka heard such words from her, he abandoned the virtue of self-control, and gave up his vow. Then Mágadhiká returned with him, delighted in her mind, to King Koṇika. She said to him: 'King, this is my lover, a hermit of the name of Kúlaválaka; let whatever you wish to have done by him be done.' The king said to Kúlaválaka: 'Great-souled one, think of some stratagem for taking the city of Vaiçálí.' The great-souled one accepted the commission. He assumed the dress of a wandering mendicant, that carries three bamboo staves, and entered the city. He saw the *stúpa* of the holy hermit, the lord Suvrata, in the middle of the city, and he said to himself, 'Surely it is due to the power of this *stúpa* that the city is not taken;* so I will take steps to make the people dig it up.' The people said to him: 'Ho, wandering mendicant, will the siege of the city ever cease?' The hermit said: 'If you dig up this *stúpa*, the siege will cease, and if not, it will not cease.' Then he went into the besieging army, and made this arrangement with King Koṇika, that when the people removed the *stúpa*, he was to march away with his army. The king agreed to it. The hermit again entered the city. The people said to him: 'Wandering mendicant, what assurance have we in this matter?' He answered: 'While the *stúpa* is being dug up, the besieging army will march away; this is the assurance.' The people began to dig up the *stúpa*. As fast as they tore it up, the army retired.

* Compare Jacobi's introduction to his edition of the 'Pariçishṭa Parvan,' p. 58.

When the people saw this proof of the truth of the mendicant's saying, they began to root up the *stúpa* with double zeal. Then, the *stúpa* having been rooted up, Koṇika wheeled round and took the city. At this moment King Cheṭaka fell into a well with an image of the Jina in his hand. As he was falling he was seized by King Dharaṇa,* and taken to his own city. There he fasted for a month in great exultation, and went to heaven.

Thus Kúlaválaka, being devoid of regard for his teacher, lost his asceticism. Therefore men should be devoted to their teachers. The story of Kúlaválaka, having regard to the displeasing of a teacher, is finished.

Now follows the story of Kanakaratha, having reference to munificence.

STORY OF KANAKARATHA.

In this very land of Bharata, on the mountain Vaitáḍhya, is a city named Kanakapura. In it there lived a king named Kanakaratha. In him abode these virtues: he was munificent, simple, the essence of courtesy, handsome, and able to assume what shape he pleased. By means of his power of changing his shape he attained all the objects he desired. One night he was roaming about his own city incognito, and there happened to be a play going on in a temple. In it a song was being sung, and in the song the singer uttered the following verse:

> 'Swans are everywhere white, peacocks everywhere have their feathers painted with various hues;
> Everywhere are birth and death, everywhere does the enjoyer enjoy.'

When the Vidyádhara heard this verse, he reflected in his mind: 'The meaning of these lines is clear: in this world swans are everywhere white, peacocks have everywhere variegated feathers, everywhere are death and birth; but this is not clear, that everywhere do enjoyers enjoy. This is wrong; for a king who leaves his own country does not meet with respect in other lands. A man enjoys the love of his wife in his own home, but not elsewhere. This is

* King of the *Nágakumáras*. See Weber's 'Bhagavatí,' p. 211.

most indubitably false. For instance, I possess all kinds of enjoyments; if I find the same in a foreign land, I will acknowledge that this speech is true.' Having gone through these reflections, he summoned his minister, and after deliberating with him, he went to the city of King Támrachúḍa, a hundred *yojanas* off. When the king entered that city, he thought: 'A handsome man, wearing splendid clothes, meets with respect everywhere.' For this reason he took the form of a deformed man, with both his eyes streaming, with his nose gone, and his two lips fallen away. To cut the story short, he was excessively repulsive, impossible to look at. Such he became. At this moment King Támrachúḍa, seated in a seven-storied palace, was looking at the beauty of the city. Near him, for the purpose of doing him honour, were seated the nobles, the chief feudatories, the secretaries, the paymasters, and the other courtiers. Then the king, puffed up with the importance of his own kingdom, said: 'You courtiers, by whose favour do you enjoy such a fortune of rule?' They said to the king, with servile complaisance: 'King, all this springs from your favour.' Then the princess, whose name was Madanamanjarí, when she heard those feudatories and other courtiers say this, laughed a little, and then remained silent.* The king asked his daughter the reason of her laughing, saying: 'My darling, what is this?' His daughter answered: 'My father, these servants of yours said what is not true; for that reason I laughed.' The king said: 'My dear, what is untrue?' She answered: 'Their assertion that their happiness springs from your favour; that is untrue.' The king asked his daughter: 'Then, my dear, what is true?' She said: 'Every man fares according to his own actions.' When the king heard this speech of his daughter in the audience-hall, he flew into a passion, and calling his

* Madanamanjarí reminds one, to a certain extent, of Cordelia. See also Kaden, 'Unter den Olivenbäumen.' In the story headed 'Wasser und Salz,' a daughter tells her father the king that she loves him like water and salt, and he orders her to be slain. When she is happily married to a prince, he acknowledges that she was in the right.

ministers, said this to them: 'Come, come! bring some poor leper, afflicted with disease, and very wretched, as a fit bridegroom for my daughter, in order that this Madanamanjarí may be given to him, so that she may reap the fruit of her own actions.' When they heard this speech of the king's, they all searched all over the city for such a bridegroom. At this moment her mother, hearing from people what had happened, came into the audience-hall, and said to Madanamanjarí: 'My dear child, what have you said to your father?' The daughter said: 'I did not say what was false, since all people reap the reward of their own actions.' Her mother said: 'So far, no irreparable harm has been done; obey the command of the king.' The daughter said: 'Even if the world comes to an end, I will not say what is false.' Then those servants of the king, roaming about in the city, saw, in a place where four roads meet, that very being, who had assumed the form of a leper. They said to one another: 'This is exactly the sort of man the king ordered to be brought; no one more wretched than he has been born, so let us go to the king with him.' Having thus deliberated, they said to him: 'Leper, rise up; the king summons you!' Then that leper said: 'I was before mocked by fate. It is not becoming on your part to mock me further. Is there no other bridegroom fit for the princess?' The king's servants said: 'Come, rise up; we are merely carrying out the king's orders; but about this matter our master knows—we do not know.' When they had said this, they all dragged him up, and took him to the king. Then the ministers took their hands off the leper, and said to the king: 'Your majesty, this man has been brought by your orders.' Then the king gave his daughter to that leper. Then the leper said to the king: 'My lord, it is not proper to give your daughter to a sick man, whose family you do not know. Moreover, it is not fitting for me to marry her. Is it becoming for a crow to marry a female swan?' Though the leper expressed his unwillingness in these and similar words, the king made him marry his daughter, and dismissed him. Madanamanjarí bowed before the feet of her father and mother, and, with her lotus-like face full of joy, went out of the palace. While Madanamanjarí was walking along with her husband, the leper fell down in the main street, and remained lying there.* The leper said to his wife: 'Princess, I cannot move a step from this place.' Then Madanamanjarí said: 'My lord, do not be unhappy; get upon my back, in order that I may carry you where you wish to go.' The leper, perceiving her disposition, said: 'We will remain here to-day; to-morrow we will do what is fitting.' At this moment a great multitude of men went to the king's palace, and said to the king: 'Grant, your majesty, that we may build a straw hut for your son-in-law, and give it to him.' The king permitted it. Then the crowd built the couple a hut, and made it over to them; and in it the leper lived with his wife. In the meanwhile that leper thought in his heart: 'I wonder whether this wife of mine is attached to me or not; so I will test her affection or aversion.' Then he began to speak: 'Princess, hear this one speech of mine with attentive heart; from associating with me you will in a short time become leprous, since these diseases are contagious—herpes, consumption, leprosy, jaundice, ophthalmia: these five diseases are propagated by contagion. Owing to leprosy, your hair, which is as black as a swarm of bees or lampblack, will perish; your lotus-like face will lose its bloom; your two eyes, which are like a couple of petals of full-blown blue water-lilies, will close up. Ah! slender one, your lip, which resembles a ripe *bimba*-fruit, will not retain its hue. To speak briefly, your body will be destroyed in every way by association with me, as a mango-fruit is spoiled by the neighbourhood of a poisonous tree. So, seek the protection of your mother and her brothers; why should you perish for my sake?' When the leper had said this, he remained silent. Then Madanamanjarí said: 'My lord, why do you utter such an im-

* The tests to which the leper subjects his wife remind one of Grimm's story No. 52, 'König Drosselbart.'

proper speech? Women born in a good family do not do such things, even when the world is coming to an end. Have you not heard this, husband? To excellent women husbands are deities: for

> 'Let my body fade away, let my eyes stream, let my youth disappear,
> Let my life even go, nevertheless, my lord, I will wait upon thee;
> Thou art my lord, thou art my friend, my relation, ornament, and refuge,
> Thou art my life, my dearest—what need of much speech in this matter?

My lord, before me such words, appropriate only to vile persons, must not be spoken.' When that Vidyádhara knew that his wife really loved him, he summoned by a thought the goddess that produces various forms. He said: 'Lady, thou goddess that producest various forms, make me now a palace of pure gold.' Then the goddess produced the palace in half a second. Of what kind was it? Its floor gleamed, inlaid with jewels of five colours; its walls shone, composed of pure crystal; in that palace there were a thousand statues of precious stone, set upon pedestals of gold; moreover,

> It was forty stories high; it glittered with a hundred pinnacles and balls;
> With its lofty bulk it obstructed the onward advance of the chariot-horses of the sun.

The leper beholds himself exalted on a golden throne in the centre of it, resembling a prince of gods. When the people saw that palace, they were astonished; they said: 'Is this a *vimána* of the gods come down from heaven, since it has never been seen by us before, nor read of in books? Surely this palace is very astounding!' Then King Támrachúḍa heard of the palace. Thereupon the king went to see the palace, with a heart full of eager curiosity. When the king, accompanied by his retinue, ascended the palace, he could not find the way on account of the nature of the crystal walls, as it was all full of dazzling brightness. Then, with great difficulty, the king at last found the path. In the highest story of that palace he saw a Vidyádhara sitting on a throne of heavenly beauty, and wearing heavenly ornaments. When he saw him such as has been described, astonishment arose in his mind. At that moment the minister of that Vidyádhara, named Buddhiságara, arrived, attended by the Vidyádhara warriors. Buddhiságara bowed before the king and sat down, and all the Vidyádhara warriors sat down in order of dignity. Eight lovely women, all heavenly nymphs, waved chowries. At this moment a Vidyádhara play was begun to be acted. All the people inhabiting the city, when they saw it, were astonished. Támrachúḍa also was astonished. He said with amazement: 'First a leper, then possessed of such beauty! Who is this? Is it Indra? or the god of love? or Náráyaṇa? or Baladeva? or the Yaksha named Dhanada?' While Támrachúḍa and all the people were making these surmises, a Vidyádhara warrior recited this verse:

> 'Hail, lord of the Vaitáḍya mountain! Hail, thou that by great science hast conquered thy enemies!
> Hail, thou that art also kind to thy friends and dependants! Hail, King Kanakaratha!'

When the people heard this verse, they said: 'Of a truth this is a prince of the Vidyádharas, who has come here, having assumed, for some reason, the form of a leper; so this Princess Madanamanjarí is fortunate, and must have accumulated merit, since she has gained as her husband this lord of the Vidyádharas. Then King Kanakaratha rose up, and himself caused a throne to be given to King Támrachúḍa. At this moment the queen Dháriṇí, the mother of Madanamanjarí, came there. Then Madanamanjarí bowed before her father, King Támrachúḍa, and said to him: 'Father, you gave me to a leper of mean form; but owing to the might of my merit, he has become like a celestial prince.

> 'Let him go to a foreign land, let him wander about in the forest, let him be whelmed in the sea;
> But even in his house a man from merit obtains successions of blessings.

So, father, was your speech true, or was my speech true?' The king said: 'Your speech was true, without doubt, my daughter: for so long a time have I been deceived by my wrong notion. Henceforth I admit that everyone's lot is determined by his own actions.' Then King Támrachúḍa said to the Vidyádhara: 'My lord, with what curiosity was it that you came here, having assumed such a shape?' Then the Vidyádhara told him the whole story from the beginning to the end. The king was delighted when he heard it. Then the Vidyádhara said to the king: 'King, permit me to return to my own city.' The king answered: 'You must not go until you and your retinue have feasted in my house.' The Vidyádhara accepted the king's proposal. Then the king regaled that prince of the Vidyádharas with heavenly baths, food, clothes, ornaments, perfumes and other things, and said to his daughter: 'My dear child, let me see you again at some other time.' When he had said this, he dismissed them to their city. Then the Vidyádhara produced a heavenly chariot. He mounted it, and set out with his wife, and so went to his city. There much rejoicing at his return took place. Then he made a triumphal entry into the city with great pomp. Kanakaratha reached his palace, and in the society of Madanamanjarí enjoyed the pleasures of the Vidyádharas. Subsequently, one day the keeper of the public park came with his palms joined, and said to King Kanakaratha: 'King, you are fortunate; for to-day the saint Dharmaghosha, surrounded by many disciples, has arrived in the delightful park.' When he heard that from the keeper of the public park, he was pleased, and gave him a reward. Then he went with great pomp to worship the sage, accompanied by Madanamanjarí. He reached the park, and having there adored the spiritual teacher, he listened to his sermon. The teacher said: 'O Vidyádhara, the state of a man is hard to obtain. Now that you have obtained it, you must make an effort in the matter of religion. For enjoyments, glory, blessedness, fortune, beauty, salvation, all these things are obtained by merit. Therefore, king, knowing this, you must exert yourself in the way of religion in order to obtain happiness that will bear fruit.' When the king heard this, he asked about his former life. He said: 'Reverend sir, what merit did I perform in a former life, that in this life enjoyments come to me everywhere?' The teacher said: 'Listen; in a former age there was in Sáligráma a householder named Dhanadeva. He had a wife named Yaçodeví. One day a hermit came to your house to eat, after a month's fast. You and your wife Yaçodeví restored him with milk and rice. Owing to the merit of that action you have been born as a prince of Vidyádharas, after your death; Yaçodeví, also, after her death, has been born in this birth as Madanamanjarí, your wife.' When this had been said, both of them remembered their former birth. They saw their former life in a swoon. At the end of the swoon they thought: 'Does even a small gift given to a worthy recipient produce so much fruit?' Then they pronounced the twelve vows.* After they had bowed before the teacher, they went to their own place. Kanakaratha, helped by his wife, kept giving gifts to fit recipients. When the end of life approached, they placed their son on the throne, and, adopting a vow of abstinence from food, they both went to heaven. Here ends the story of Kanakaratha, having reference to the bestowal of charity on a fitting recipient.

Báhubali† and Maríchi accumulated pride, and the lord Sthúlabhadra; and Sádhu, who sojourned in the lion's cave, and was arrogant; Siddhasena the poet, Cháṇakya and Koṇika also, the King Duryodhana, and Rávaṇa, and the Sage, reverenced under the name of Ságarachandra, and (Sanatkumára) the fourth universal emperor, on account of his beauty. For religion is not possible in arrogance.‡

* The five lesser and the seven disciplinary vows.—Dr. Hoernle's 'Uvásaga Dasáo,' appendix iii., p. 34.

† Before this, the MS. which I call C inserts *Kávyam* (a poem). What follows is in verse, but some lines are defective.

‡ Átmárám Muni has been good enough to furnish me with a note on this passage. The story of Báhubali will be found in the text. Maríchi was the son of Bharata, and took the vows under Ṛishabhadeva. He became puffed up because he heard that he would be born as the Tírthankara Mahávíra. Consequently, he was punished

### Story of King Bharata and his Brother, King Báhubali, and of the War that took place between them.

In the town of Viníté King Ṛishabhadeva had two wives, Sumangalá and Sunandá. From the Queen Sumangalá were born the twins Bharata and Bambhí; from the Queen Sunandá were born Báhubali and Sundarí. When King Ṛishabhadeva had taken a vow, he gave a kingdom to Prince Bharata, and distributed another territory among his ninety-eight sons, and then he attained absolute knowledge. Then King Bharata,* having spent sixty thousand years in subduing the lords of the holy place called Mágadha in the East of India, of that called Varadáma in the South, and of that called Prabhása in the West, and having established his sway in the region of the Indus, and having taken the roads of the dark cave to the North, and of the Khaṇḍaprapáta cave to the South, returned to the city of Vinítá. As he had conquered the earth, and his ninety-eight brothers had abandoned their kingdoms, and been admitted to vows before his father, Bharata returned after sixty thousand years to Vinítá. His discus would not enter the armoury.

by having to endure many low births. Sthúlabhadra was puffed up with his knowledge, and Bhadrabáhu forbade him to read four Púrvas. Sádhu was the elder brother of Sthúlabhadra. He fasted for four months in a lion's cave. Siddhasena was the son of Vikramáditya's *purohita*. He told his superior that he was ashamed to repeat the Jaina texts before learned men, as they were written in Prákrit, and asked permission to translate them into Sanskrit. For this he was punished by having a twelve years' penance imposed on him, and by being ordered to convert to the Jaina faith eighteen kings. Among these eighteen he converted Vikramáditya. Siddhasena was a great poet and a great preacher. Ságarachandra was a pupil of a pupil of Kálikácharya. When Kálikácharya came to his village, he did not recognise him, and treated him with contempt.' Kálikácharya humbled his pride in a religious disputation, and then Ságarachandra performed a severe penance. The fourth emperor, according to the Jainas, was Sanatkumára. He was proud of his personal appearance. His story is related in this work. It will be found also in Jacobi's 'Erzählungen' in Maháráshtrí.

* Here the following words are found in A and C: 'Mágadha-varadáma-prabhása-Sindhukhamḍa-ppaváya-timisa-guhá saddhim vása sahassa uyaviyaṃ ágao Bharaho.' Nearly the same words are found in Jacobi's 'Ausgewahlte Erzählungen,' p. 26. I have followed, to the best of my power, a Hindi paraphrase furnished to me by Atmárám Muni.

Then he determined to make war on Báhubali, in Takshaçilá. He sent to him an ambassador named Suvega. The ambassador went to the court of Báhubali. Báhubali said :* 'Is there victorious triumph among the subjects in the kingdom of my elder brother, the inhabitants of the city of Vinítá, who were once cherished by my adored father, whom he fostered by bestowing on them a multitude of accomplishments? Are the chiefs of the city and the country, the horses, the elephants, the generals, and the soldiers well?' When the king had asked this question he ceased, and Suvega answered without perturbation. The ambassador said :† 'Since the king has conquered the kings of men, and even fate would be powerless to harm him, could any one do any harm to any one of the horses, troops, and generals in that city that lies around his palace? That elder brother, the emperor, is to be respected by you, on account both of his elder birth and of his valour. If you wish for long life and rule, then abandon, O Báhubali, your pride.' When he had said this, he ceased, and Báhubali said :‡ 'Ambassador, what you have said is becoming; you are exceedingly eloquent; there is no one like you, that would dare to say this in my presence. As you are executing your master's errand, you have no fear for your life.' Then he took him by the back of the neck and sent him about his business. The ambassador went and told exactly what had taken place to King Bharata, saying: 'My lord, Báhubali, rendered arrogant by his might, says thus: "Ambassador, go to your master, and say to him: 'Do you forget that day on which you were tossed about like a ball? Why are you proud of having conquered Gangá and Sindhu, a couple of females, and the Náhala warriors?'"' When King Bharata heard this, he proudly ordered his drum to be sounded for the advance. When the armies met, there was a great fight. At this point, Anilavega, the young

* The speech that follows is in verse in the original.
† The following speech also is in verse.
‡ This speech also is in verse.

Vidyádhara, who was in an underground house, heard the drum of battle and came out. That brave warrior, adorned in heavenly style, bowed before Báhubali, and first challenged the enemy. He carried on the combat with weapons in various ways; the army was terrified, and Bharata himself rose up.

Then all fought there, elephants with elephants,
Horses with horses, charioteers with charioteers, soldiers with soldiers.

Bharata was deprived of his weapons by Anilavega with his weapons. Then at the end of a year Bharata sent forth the discus. Anilavega with his fist fought a splendid fight against the discus. The discus fight lasted twenty-one days; then, on the twenty-first day, Bharata cut off with the discus the head of the brave warrior Anilavega, who was senseless from thirst. Then Báhubali, seeing much loss of life, sent an ambassador to Bharata to say: 'The battle and enmity is between us two; why do we allow so many soldiers to be killed?' Bharata agreed, and engaged in five kinds of fighting; first fighting with eyes,* next with speech, then also with arms, fists, and clubs, and in all of them Bharata was defeated. Bharata was, in fact, beaten by Báhubali in all the five combats. Being angry, he sent forth the discus, but the discus had no power against his own family. It revolved round his head, and returned to its place. Báhubali said to himself: 'Oh, the stream of the ever-developing universe, subject to pleasures of sense and attachment!' Then he tore out his hair and took a vow. Bharata, seeing Báhubali absorbed in meditation, did obeisance to him, and thus spake: 'I reverence that warrior, the son of Sunandá, who has conquered those eyes, victorious over the three worlds, by which I, Bharata, the conqueror of the six divisions of the world, have certainly been conquered.' Having praised him in these words, he instituted his son in the kingdom, and then the emperor returned to his own place. Báhubali remained on

* Compare the 134th story in Grimm, 'Die sechs Diener.' One of these can break in pieces whatever he looks at. '*Der guckte die Feinde ein bisschen scharf an, da sprangen sie auseinander wie Glas.*

that spot for a year, in a statuesque posture, out of pride. saying to himself, 'I will not go near my revered father, and make a bow to my younger brothers.' So the creepers, wreathing round the boughs of the trees on the bank, clung to his neck, and crowned his head with their canopy, and the blades of *kuça*-grass grew between his feet, and he became in appearance like an ant-hill. Then Ṛishabhadeva, finding this out by his knowledge, sent his two daughters, Bambhí and Sundarí, to admonish him. They said to the hermit, 'Brother, descend from the mighty elephant of pride.' Then the hermit, having been taught wisdom, breaking loose from his bonds, lifted up his foot. At that moment, as if by previous agreement, absolute knowledge sprang up in him. He went to his father and sat down among the company of *kevalins*. Therefore pride must not be indulged. Here ends the story of Báhubali, having reference to pride.

STORY OF NALA AND DAVADANTÍ.

In this land of Bharata there is a country called Koçala, and a city of the Koçalas. In it there was a king of the name of Nishada, sprung from the race of Ikshváku. He had a queen named Sundarí, and two sons, Nala and Kúvara. At this time, in the country of Vidarbha, there was a city named Kuṇḍinapura. In it was a king, by name Bhímaratha. He had a wife Pushpadantí. As they were living together in loving union, they had a daughter born to them. On her forehead was a natural mark like the orb of the sun.* Because, when her mother was pregnant with her, she saw in a dream an elephant being burned in a forest fire, therefore the child was called Davadantí. She grew every day like a digit of the moon in the white fortnight. In due time she was sent to a teacher of accomplishments, to learn knowledge, and she gradually became clever in all learning. One day, the goddess that executes the commands of the Jina, being pleased with her

* Compare No. xx. in Miss Stokes's "Indian Fairy Tales,' and the parallels adduced in the notes. A very striking one will be found in Grimm's ninth story.

great merit, gave her a golden image of the illustrious lord Çánti,* and said to her: 'My daughter, this image of the adorable lord Çánti must be worshipped by you three times a day.' She, for her part, did so. In time she grew up. The king when he saw her of ripe age, said to himself: 'This girl is of matchless beauty; to whom must I give her? Either there is no bridegroom fit for her, or, if there is one fit for her, I do not know of him. So I must appoint a Svayamvara, in order that my daughter may select a bridegroom according to her own wish.' Then he sent an ambassador, and summoned the kings and the princes, and they came, surrounded by elephants, horses, chariots, and footmen. Nala also came there. King Bhímaratha welcomed them all in splendid dwellings. Then he had made a Svayamvara-pavilion, adorned with pillars of gold. In it he placed golden thrones, and on those the kings and the princes sate. In the meanwhile, by order of her father, Davadantí arrived, adorned with the mark that shot forth a blaze of glory, with calm face, graceful with shapely bosom, herself gracing the Svayamvara-pavilion. When the kings saw her, the faces of all of them were full of astonishment. Then, by order of the king, the warder of the women's apartments, Bhadrá by name, began to tell the princess the families of the kings. She said: 'Princess Davadantí, this is the lord of Káçí (Benares) of great strength of arm, Bala by name; if you wish to see the river Gangá with its tossing waves, choose him.' Davadantí said: 'Bhadrá, the people of Benares are addicted to the bad habit of cheating their neighbours, so my mind does not take pleasure in him. Go on further.' Then she went on further, and said again: 'Princess, this is the lord of Kunkuṇa, named Siṃha; choose him, and in the hot season enjoy yourself agreeably in the plantain-groves.' Then Davadantí said: 'Bhadrá, the people of Kunkuṇa get angry without reason, so I cannot please him on every occasion; mention another king.' She went forward, and said again: 'Princess, this is the King Mahendra, an

* The sixteenth Tírthankara of the present age.

inhabitant of the region of Káçmíra; if you desire to indulge in the saffron game,* choose him.' Davadantí said: 'Do you not know that my body shrinks from a quantity of snow?' Then she went on, and proceeded to say: 'Princess, this is the lord of Kauçámbí, the King Jayakoça; so choose him.' Davadantí said: 'Kapinjalá,† this is a very beautiful garland that they have made for me.' The warder said to herself: 'Her not answering me about the king amounts to a refusal.' Then she went further on, and spoke again: 'Throw the garland of selection on the neck of King Jaya, the lord of Kalinga, by the Ráhu of whose sword the moons of his enemies have been swallowed.'‡ Davadantí said: 'My respects to him who is as old as my father!' Then Bhadrá went forward, and said: 'Does this lord of Gauḍa, who is like the sun in the heaven, the roaring of whose numerous troops of elephants cleaves the world,§ please you?' Davadantí said: 'Mother, the colour of the man is black and horrible like that of the elephants, so pass on quickly.' Then Bhadrá went on, and said again: 'Princess, this is the lord of Ujjayiní, the king named Padmanábha; if you wish to amuse yourself among the trees growing on the banks of the Siprá, choose him.' Davadantí said: 'Alas! I am wearied out with the trouble of walking round this enclosure of the Svayamvara-pavilion. So I will go further on.' Then Bhadrá went further on, and said: 'Princess, here is King Nala, the son of Nishada, equal in beauty to the god of love.' Davadantí thought, 'Oh, his matchless beauty! Oh, his wonderful grace!' Then she threw the garland of selection on the neck of Nala. Then there arose a cry among the people: 'Bravo! bravo! Davadantí has chosen well!' Thereupon King Krishṇa drew his sword, and began to reproach Nala, saying: 'Nala, it is not possible that you should marry Davadantí. This Davadantí has

* *Kunkuma-krídá.*

† I suppose *kapinjalá* must be a term of affection here: 'Partridge.'

‡ An allusion to the idea that an eclipse of the moon is caused by the swallowing of that luminary by Ráhu.

§ Literally, 'the egg of Brahmá.'

acted in an unseemly fashion in choosing you; therefore give her up, or prepare to fight.' Nala answered: 'Vilest of men, are you in any way injured in not having been chosen by Davadantí? So, as you have left the path of virtue, you must be disciplined by me.' So Nala drew his sword, and the fire of wrath blazed up in him. Then the troops of both of them prepared for battle. Davadantí said to herself: 'Alas! I am unfortunate, since this calamity has arisen for my sake; so, if I am devoted to the divine Arhat, let Nala be victorious, O goddess, that dost execute the orders of the Jina, or let the battle cease!' When she had said this, she took a pitcher full of water, and threw three jets of water. When King Krishṇa felt that water touch his body, he lost his fierceness. Then King Krishṇa, being freed from anger, said to himself: 'Alas! I have done what is unbecoming; this is not an ordinary man, so it is fitting that I should propitiate him;' then he inclined himself before Nala, and obtained his pardon. Nala conversed with King Krishṇa, and then dismissed him. Then King Bhímaratha, observing the might of Nala, was astonished, and celebrated his marriage with great pomp; he gave Prince Nala elephants, horses, jewels, ornaments, dresses, and other gifts. Having thus remained there some days after his marriage, Nala set out again for his own city. When Davadantí was starting with her husband, her mother spoke thus to her:

'My daughter, say what is pleasant, act humbly, avoid reproach of others;
As long as you are in the body, do not desert your husband, even in calamity;
Even when you attain prosperity, do not indulge a thought of pride, even in a dream;
Preserve also your chastity stainless, even at the cost of your life.'

Davadantí welcomed this instruction from her mother, and set out, after bowing before her parents. Nala put her in the chariot, and took her in his lap; and then, as Nala marched along, obscuring the circle of the heaven with the dust of the earth flung up by his horses and soldiers, the sun set in the intermediate space, and the bosom of the sky was filled with a mass of darkness. It was impossible to distinguish water, dry land, trees, mountains, and hollows. Nevertheless, Nala, being eager to reach his city, did not desist from his advance. Then the darkness went to its lair, and the army proceeded on its course without an obstacle. One day, as Nala and Davadantí were advancing, they came in sight of a hermit in the statuesque posture, the whole of whose body was being devoured by bees. Nala and Davadantí delivered him from the bees, and refreshed him with pure* food. After taking respectful leave of the hermit, Nala reached the environs of the city of Koçalá in a few unimpeded journeys. Nala said to Davadantí: 'Queen, this is my city, named Koçalá, in a region adorned with temples of the Jina.' She said: 'I am fortunate; having obtained Nala for a husband, I will continually worship the gods.' Then, on an auspicious day, Nala entered his city, in which vast wealth was displayed on platforms of many kinds, and on every house a dancing flag kissed the sky with its border, which filled the atmosphere with the sound of various drums, which was densely crowded with bands of dancing girls, and at every step he received a special welcome. And then Nala, accompanied by Davadantí, bowed before his father and mother. Then Prince Nala at one time amused himself with Davadantí by sporting in the water; at another time he enjoyed the delights of swinging; at another time he himself interweaved perfumed flowers, and so made for her an ornamental braid of elaborate construction; at another time he amused himself with dice; at another time he played on the tabor, beating it himself, and made Davadantí dance to the music in private. Thus inseparable from Davadantí, he passed the time in ever fresh enjoyments. One day King Nishada placed Nala in his own office, and made Kúvara crown prince, and took a vow; then Nala ruled the realm, being, like fire, irresistible in the expansion of his splendour. One day he asked his ministers: 'Do I rule the territory acquired by my father, or

* I have translated *práçuka* by pure.

a larger one?' The ministers said: 'You have reduced under your power half of India, with the exception of three districts; but two hundred *yojanas* from this place is the city of Takshaçilá: in it there is a king, named Kadamba, who does not attend to your orders. He has been long overlooked by you like an insignificant disease, and has become difficult to deal with. So first send an ambassador to find out his inclinations.' Then an ambassador was sent, and he went immediately to Takshaçilá, and said to Kadamba: 'Nala, the fire that burns up the wood of his enemies, thus commands: "Do homage to me, and then rule your own kingdom; but if you will not do so, you will meet defeat at the hands of this king."' When King Kadamba heard this speech of the ambassador, not knowing his own weakness, he bit his lips, and said to the ambassador: 'Ambassador, is your master a child, or mad, or epileptic, that he does not know that I am the Garuḍa that swallows up all enemies like snakes? Or has he no ministers capable of distinguishing between good and bad qualities, that they have not restrained Nala from such unbecoming babble? So depart, ambassador! If your master is exceedingly tired of life, let him prepare for combat and approach quickly; I am now prepared for battle.' Then the ambassador returned and told Nala what Kadamba had said. Then the eyes of Nala became red with rage, and he set out with a force of all four arms, and in course of time reached Takshaçilá; then Nala invested the city of Takshaçilá. Kadamba could not endure that, so he prepared for battle and marched out. The two armies began a battle. It doubled the brilliancy of the sun's rays with the flashing of many weapons; it obstructed the circle of the earth; it gleamed with points of flame springing from clashing sword-blades; it presented to view a multitude of headless trunks dancing, gazed on by gods, Siddhas, and Yakshas; while heads of warriors appeared like lotuses on the streams of blood that flowed along. Nala said to Kadamba: 'What is the use of killing these poor worms of foot-soldiers? Let you and me fight.' Then the two began to engage in wrestling and other combats. Whatever kind of contest Kadamba challenged Nala to, he was beaten in by Nala. Then Kadamba fled, and took to a life of mortification, and remained in the statuesque posture. While in that posture, he was thus addressed by Nala: 'I am vanquished by thee by means of this holy conduct, so rule thy own kingdom.' But Kadamba would not take the kingdom, having abandoned longing for such things. And then Nala, pleased with the goodness of Kadamba, placed his son, who was named Jayaçakti, on the throne. Then the kings anointed Nala king of half India. Then Nala returned to Koçalá, and there he spent his time in various amusements with Davadantí.* Kúvara, the firebrand of his own family, being desirous of the kingdom, kept seeking a stratagem against Nala. One day, by the power of fate, Nala contracted the vice of gambling; then Kúvara played with Nala, thinking to himself: 'I will take his kingdom from him.' And a long time passed, during which victory first fell to one and then to the other, as the hand alternately strikes the two faces of a drum. One day, as fate would have it, Nala could not beat Kúvara; the die he wished for would not fall to Nala. Then the cruel Kúvara again slew Nala's pieces;† then Kúvara won from Nala cities, villages, fields, and market-towns, and so on, until Nala, being deprived of his wealth, was like a lake being deprived of water in the hot season; the people were despondent. Kúvara was delighted at having his wish granted by the blind power of gambling; the people devoted to Nala lamented; and Davadantí came, hearing that lamentation. She said: 'King, do me a favour. I entreat you, abandon this bad habit of gambling. Truly these dice are, like enemies, clever to bring you calamity. Give, if you like, this kingdom to your younger brother Kúvara with your own hand, but do not gain for yourself disgrace. This kingdom has been won by many warlike efforts, and the

* Here the MSS. have Damadantí.

† The game appears to have resembled backgammon.

idea that it should be lost by play vexes my heart like wax found somewhere else than in the ear.' Though Davadantí said this to Nala, he would not cease playing; then Davadantí sent the ministers. Though they appealed to him in many ways, Nala could not be induced by them to stop playing. When a man is seized by a derangement of the three humours, no medicine or other remedy has any effect on him. Then Nala lost all his kingdom; he lost Davadantí and all his other wives, and he lost every ornament on his person. Then Kúvara said: 'Leave my kingdom; do not remain in it. This realm, which your father gave you, has been given in turn to me by the dice.' Then Nala, with the garments that he had on as his only property, left his kingdom and went away. Davadantí was going with him, but Kúvara forbade her, saying: 'Fawn-eyed one, do not depart. You have been won by me in gambling; adorn my harem.' Then the ministers said to Kúvara: 'Davadantí will not even touch the shadow of a strange man, so do not put her in your harem, because the wife of an elder brother must be looked upon as a mother; so, if you do it by force, the chaste one with her curse will reduce you to dust in a moment: for nothing is difficult for chaste women. Moreover, you need not give Nala cities or villages, but you must give him a chariot, with a charioteer, and provisions for the journey.' So Kúvara, afraid of the ministers, let Davadantí go. He gave his brother a chariot, with provisions and a charioteer. Nala said: 'What is the use of a chariot to me, who have thrown away in sport the prosperity acquired by the conquest of half India?' The counsellors said to Nala: 'We were ready to follow you, but Kúvara forbids it, though we have long been your servants. Moreover, we serve him who is king in this family; this is our hereditary usage. Now your wife Davadantí is your minister. But how will she travel on foot with her feet soft as a lotus, with her body tender as a *çirísha* flower, on the road which is made difficult by grains of sand heated by the rays of the sun? So take, prince, this chariot; mount it with

Davadantí.' Being thus entreated by the counsellors, Nala mounted the chariot, and set out with Davadantí. When the women of the city saw Davadantí with one garment on, as if she were going to bathe, they wept. Then Nala, going along the street, saw a pillar five hundred cubits high. Forgetting the grief produced by the loss of his kingdom, he easily pulled it up in sport as if it were a banana-stem, and again restored it to its place. When the citizens saw this, they said: 'Alas! though Nala is possessed of such remarkable strength, he is deprived of his kingdom by the dispensation of fate. Long ago, when Nala was playing with Kúvara in the city gardens, a hermit, that knew the future, arrived there. When he saw Nala, he said: "This Nala shall be the ruler of the southern half of India, and he shall move a pillar of five hundred cubits' height standing in the town." These two things have come to pass; but we have seen with our own eyes that, while Nala is alive, another king has been established in Koçalá. That does not agree with the prediction. However, it is certain that the prediction of a man of unlimited knowledge must prove true. Kúvara shall not enjoy the kingdom. Nala shall be king here.' Such conversation did Nala hear among the people, while, mounted on the chariot with Davadantí, he was leaving the city. As he went out, he said to Davadantí: 'Where shall we go?' She answered: 'King, go to the city of Kuṇḍina; favour my father by becoming a guest there.' Then by Nala's order the charioteer drove the chariot and horses in the direction of the city of Kuṇḍina. In course of time Nala reached a forest. It was one where the troops of travellers were terrified by the spots of the growling tigers, and where the deer were devoured by them with loud roars. It was alarming on account of the serpents, dangerous from their venom, that roamed about, and the multitudes of savage beasts that were seen. In that wood some Bhillas, holding in their hands bows, arrows, and darts, stopped Nala. He got out of the chariot, and went to meet them. But Davadantí held his hand, and said: 'My lord, how can you, being like a lion, attack these creatures, who are like jackals? How can you use against these your sword, which is the pleasure-house of the fortune of the conquest of half India? Are you not ashamed?' Then Davadantí uttered shouts, which the greatness of her chastity rendered terrible, and the Bhillas fled in every direction, alarmed by those cries, like deer terrified by the roaring of a lion. Nala and Davadantí followed on the track of the Bhillas, and went a long distance. In the meanwhile another party of Bhillas seized the chariot. When fate is adverse, what can the valour of a hero accomplish? Nala went along in the forest, holding Davadantí's hand with his, calling to mind the happy day of their marriage. Davadantí's soft, lotus-like feet were wounded by the points of the *darbḥa*-grass, and so, with drops of blood falling from them, she marked the forest as if with cochineal. Formerly Nala had bound her head with the silk turban as his queen consort, but now he bound her feet with pieces of his garment. Then, as she was worn out with travelling on foot, Nala made her sit in his lap, and fanned her with the border of his own robe, and brought her water to drink in cup-like lotus-leaves. Then Davadantí said to him: 'My lord, how far have we to go now?' Nala answered: 'Queen, this forest extends for a hundred *yojanas*, and as yet we have only got over five *yojanas*; so keep up your courage.' When they had finished this conversation, the sun set. Then Nala made an excellent bed with soft leaves, and said to Davadantí: 'Queen, sleep here. You need not be afraid of any danger; I am keeping guard.' When Nala had said this, he threw half his own garment on the bed. Then Davadantí worshipped the gods, and called to mind the five chiefs of religion,* and went to sleep. When she was asleep, Nala said to himself: 'Those men, who make their father-in-law their refuge, are not included in the list of men; so in my present condition I will not enter the house of Davadantí's

* Probably these five are Yugádíça, Çánti, Nemi, Párçva, and Víra. (Weber, 'Über das Çatrunjaya Máhátmyam,' p. 15.) See also Fleet's 'Corpus Inscriptionum Indicarum,' vol. iii., p. 66.

father. I will make my heart as hard as adamant, and desert Davadantí, though she is dear to me; and then, like a beggar, intent only on the relief of my own wants, I will roam about in another land. Owing to the might of Davadantí's virtue, no harm will befall her; for to chaste women virtue is a complete panoply.'* Then with his dagger he cut off half his own garment, and wrote on the border of Davadantí's robe the following letters with his own blood:

> 'On the right side of the banyan-tree goes the path to Vidarbha;
> But on the left side to Koçalá, if your inclination is set thither.'†

Then, with suppressed weeping, so that he could not be heard, Nala proceeded, like a thief, to walk away with noiseless foot, leaving Davadantí asleep, looking at her with neck turned back. After he had gone a little way, he said to himself again: 'Now that the girl is thus left asleep in the wood unprotected, some tiger or lion will devour her. Then what will become of me? For this reason, I will guard her until the sun rises; in the morning let her go where she likes.' Then Nala returned by the very same path by which he went, and when he saw her sleeping on the ground, covered with one garment only, he said to himself: 'Alas! Davadantí, covered with only one garment, is sleeping alone in the uninhabited wood. Alas for Nala's ladies that never see the sun! It is through the fault of my actions that Davadantí is reduced to such a condition. What am I to do? That I, miserable wretch, do not blush, when I see my wife rolling on the ground, proves that I am truly shameless, and made of adamant; or, rather, I am proved to be so by the fact that I left her in the forest. But my heart cannot bear to leave this faithful wife and go away; let me live or die with her! No! rather let me alone be a vessel of woe in the forest, teeming with a thousand dangers; but she, if she carries out my instructions written on her garment, will reach the abode of her own family, and live in comfort. May this be her

* Compare Milton's 'Comus,' 420, 421.

† The second line is partly obliterated in A, and there are evidently large omissions in C.

lot!' Having made up his mind to this course, he spent the night there, and went away with rapid step, just as Davadantí was on the point of waking. Now, just at this point, at the very end of night, Davadantí had a dream. She thought that she climbed up on a fragrant mango-tree, charming with flowers and fruit, and ate its mellow fruit. And then a wild elephant suddenly rooted up the fragrant mango-tree, and she fell supportless on the earth. At that moment Davadantí woke up. Not seeing Nala, she began to look all round the horizon, like a doe that has strayed from its herd. She exclaimed: 'Alas! an exceedingly wicked thing has been done, in that I have been left unprotected by my best beloved in an uninhabited wood. But no doubt he has gone to some lake to fetch water for me to wash my face in the morning. Or some Vidyádharí, in love with his matchless beauty, must have carried him off for her pleasure.

'The mountains are the same, the trees, the forest, and the landscape,
Only I do not see Nala the lotus-eyed.'

Her mind was distracted by much doubt of this kind, and terrified at not beholding Nala, though she looked in every direction, she began to consider the meaning of her dream. 'The fragrant mango-tree, abounding in flowers and fruit, was King Nala; the tasting by me of the fruits referred to the joys of empire. The rooting up of the tree by a wild elephant indicated Nala's loss of his throne by the appointment of destiny; as for my falling from this fragrant mango-tree, that indicated my loss of Nala; so according to this dream it will be hard for me to see Nala.' Then Davadantí began to lament aloud unrestrainedly, for tender-hearted women have no self-control when misfortune befalls them. She said: 'O my husband! how came you to leave me? Did I burden you? Why, even a serpent is burdened by its skin! Goddesses of the wood, I entreat you, show me my beloved; or show me the path purified by his lotus-like feet. Break open, O Earth, like a ripe cucumber, that by that aperture I may enter Hades and obtain rest.' Thus lamenting, and bedewing the forest-trees with streams of tears, not being able to find rest without Nala anywhere, either on land or on water, at last she saw the letters on the border of her robe, and she began to read them with expanding countenance. She said: 'Truly I am deserted by my beloved, but only in body, not in mind; otherwise, how could I have been favoured with instructions? So if I fulfil the command of my husband as that of a spiritual superior, the world here will be pure for me. So, I will go to the house of my father; as for the house of my husband, such an abode, in the absence of a husband, is a place of reproach for women.' Having thus determined, she went by the path to the right of the banyan-tree, looking at Nala's characters, as if they were Nala himself at her side. Owing to the might of her spotless chastity, no harmful things had power to molest her. The lion, which, through wrath, had its spring prepared, displaying its crooked teeth, was not able to attack Davadantí. Even the herd of elephants that deafened the whole horizon with the bees that followed their scent, that had their trunks extended like poles, though angry, fled far away, owing to the might of Davadantí's chastity. The forest fire, that with the blowing of its smoke defiled the whole horizon, and with its vast size touched the heaven, did not come near her or scorch her, but went away to a distance. The serpents, extending their broad hoods, and discharging, with hissing sound, jets of poison, disturbed with increasing anger, were not able to strike her. Then Davadantí, when her limbs were exhausted with perspiration produced by the fatigue of the journey, when blood was streaming from the soles of her feet pierced with thorns, when her body was defiled with dust, saw a caravan approaching. She thought: 'Heavens! it must be owing to the development of my merit that I have beheld this blessed caravan, which will be the means of taking me out of this forest.' At the very moment that she felt a little consoled, a number of bandits, terrible with various weapons, enclosed the caravan on all sides. The travellers were terrified; Davadantí cried out: 'Do not be afraid! do not be afraid!' Then she addressed the robbers: 'Oh, you villains! do not plunder this caravan which I am protecting; otherwise you will fall into calamity.' Nevertheless, the thieves did not desist. Then she uttered shouts, terrible on account of her virtue; and all those brigands fled from them, as if they were the twanging of the strings of bows. Then the people of the caravan said: 'This is some sylvan goddess that has come, attracted by our merits, and by her cries of triumph has delivered the caravan.' The head of the caravan adored her as a mother, and said to her: 'Goddess, who are you? How came you to be roaming in the wood?' Then Davadantí, weeping, told him her whole story. He said: 'As the wife of the great King Nala, you are an object of reverence to me, and by delivering me from the robbers you have benefited me. So purify my dwelling-place.' Having said this, he took Davadantí into his own dwelling-place. He worshipped her as a divinity. In the meanwhile the rainy season arrived. There was rain for three nights without intermission. Davadantí was in comfort; but when the rain ceased, Davadantí left the caravan, and again went off alone. And as she was going along, she saw a Rákshasa, with yellow hair, body black as a swarm of bees, and hand terrible with a dagger. Then the Rákshasa said: 'I have fasted for seven nights, and now food has come to me.' Davadantí said: 'My good sir, every soul that is born must certainly die; does the unsuccessful fear death?* I am afflicted with many sorrows, and I ask for death, that I may be delivered from my pain. You will easily devour me, as I am consumed with sorrow on account of my separation from Nala. So devour me. Why do you delay? I give you this body of mine: without death, how can I bid farewell to my woes?' Then the Rákshasa was pleased with her courage. He said: 'My good lady, I am pleased with you; what kindness can I do you?' She answered: 'If you are pleased with me, then tell me, when shall I be reunited with my husband?' The Rákshasa

* I am unable to ascertain the correct reading here.

knew by his magic power,* and answered: 'When twelve years have been accomplished from the day of your banishment, while you are in the house of your father, Nala will, of himself, come to you.' He went on to say: 'Why endure this toil of travelling? if you give the word, I will take you to your father's house in the twinkling of an eye.' She answered: 'I am satisfied with what you say about my reunion with Nala: I will not go with a strange man. Go to your own place.' Then he became invisible, after exhibiting a divine body gleaming with a mass of splendour. Davadantí, having heard that Nala's absence in a foreign land would last for twelve years, took certain vows. She said: 'I will not use red garments, betel, ornaments, unguents, nor cooked food, until Nala is reunited to me.' Then, being devoted to the performance of severe asceticism, and even when she broke her fast, subsisting on fruits without seeds, thinking on that image of the lord Çánti enshrined in her heart, she remained in a mountain cavern. The leader of the caravan, not seeing her in the caravan, being anxious in mind, looking for her everywhere, came to the mountain cave. When she had finished her meditation, she spoke to the head of the caravan. Hearing their conversation, some hermits arrived there, and stood with motionless ears like deer. In the meanwhile the cloud began to rain with large drops. When they were alarmed, she said: 'My good men, fear not.' She made a trench round them on all sides, and proclaimed her chastity, saying: 'If my chastity is unimpaired, let the cloud rain outside this trench!' Thereupon no rain fell in the space within the trench, as if it had been a house covered by a thatched roof; while outside even the stones were carried away by the violence of the deluge. When the ascetics saw that, they were astonished in their minds, and thought: 'Surely no woman has such beauty and such power, therefore she must be some goddess.' The head of the caravan said: 'Queen, what are you meditating on, or why do you remain without fear?' She answered: 'I am meditating

* The Sanskrit word is *vibhanga*.

on the divine Arhat, and owing to his power I have no fear.' She then declared at length the real truth of the doctrine of the divine teacher, and made the leader of the caravan accept the Jaina faith. The hermits also, having now drunk the milk of true religion, reprobated their own religion as sour gruel, and adopted the Jaina faith. The leader of the caravan caused a city to be built there, and because five hundred ascetics had been converted, he named that city Tápasapura. There he had a temple of the Jina made, and an image of the holy lord Çánti set up in it, and all spent their time in devout attention to the Jaina religion. One night, at twelve o'clock, Davadantí saw an illumination on the summit of the mountain. She saw gods ascending and descending. Their cries of triumph woke the inhabitants of the town. Davadantí ascended the mountain with them; there the gods had conferred the distinction of a *kevalin** on the hermit Siṃhakeçarin. After worshipping that hermit, they all sat down in front of him. Now, at that time Yaçobhadra, the spiritual guide of that hermit, came there. He, too, bowed before the *kevalin*, and sat down in front of him. The *kevalin* delivered a sermon on religion. At this juncture a god came there, illuminating the circle of the sky. He bowed before the *kevalin*, and said to Davadantí: 'My good lady, in this very wood of ascetics I was a pupil of the abbot; my name was Karpara, and I was a maintainer of the five sacred fires; but the ascetics were angry with me, so I went to another place, nursing anger in my heart against them. One night, as I was going along my path, blind with anger, I fell into a mountain chasm; my teeth struck against a point of crag and were broken; I remained where I fell for seven nights, overpowered by the pain caused by the breaking of my teeth; the other ascetics troubled themselves about me no more than if I had been a bad dream, much less did they think of rescuing me. On the contrary, the ascetics were especially delighted, as I had left the grove of ascetics,

* A possessor of unlimited knowledge.

even as a serpent leaves a house. Then I died with my anger still more violently kindled against the hermits, and became a serpent in that very forest of ascetics. Once on a time, puffing out my hood, I rushed to bite you;* but when you saw me, you recited the charm of the five chiefs of religion; the moment that charm reached my ears, my advance was checked, and I again entered my hole. One day I heard you teaching religion to the ascetics, to the effect that whoever, actuated by anger, pride, delusion, and greed, kills a living creature, suffers terrible agonies in a future birth. Then I said to myself: "Alas! what will become of me, since I live by destroying life? Moreover, I have seen these ascetics somewhere before." While I was thus intently reflecting, there arose in me recollection of my former birth. I reprobated with horror my former evil deeds, and had recourse to starvation. I then died, and was born as a god in Saudharma, Kusumaprabha by name; and as it is owing to hearing your religious discourse that I have become a god, I have come here looking upon you as my benefactor. So I am your son in the faith.' He then said to the ascetics: 'Pardon my former anger against you.' He observed the vow of a layman which he had formerly made. He dragged out that body of a serpent from a mountain ravine, and suspended it on a tree, and said: 'Whoever shall indulge in anger, he, like Karpara, shall become a serpent in a subsequent birth.' Then the abbot, being alarmed in mind, said to the *kevalin*: 'Admit me to a vow, reverend sir.' Then the *kevalin* answered: 'This spiritual teacher Yaçobhadra will admit you to a vow.' The abbot said again: 'Reverend sir, how did you take a vow?' The *kevalin* said: 'I am the son of Kúvara, in the city of Koçalá, and Keçarin, the king of the city of Sangá, gave me his own daughter, Bandhumatí by name. By order of my father I went there and married that maiden. When I returned with her I saw on the way a teacher named Jayabhadra, who had arrived. I adored him with the utmost devotion, and I heard from his mouth

* I change the *darçanárthaṃ* of the MSS. into *daçanárthaṃ*.

a sermon full of nectar to the ears. At the end of the sermon I asked a question: "Reverend sir, how much time have I to live?" Then the teacher thought intently, and said: "You have, my child, a life of exactly five days before you." Then, knowing that death was near, I said: "Reverend sir, I have but a short period to live; what shall I do now?" The teacher said: "My child, do not be afflicted; take a vow: for this vow observed for only a single day is the cause of heaven and of emancipation." Then I took a vow, and by the order of the teacher I came here, and having burnt up the fuel of actions by the fire of pure contemplation, I have attained unlimited knowledge.' Having said this, and having obstructed the impulse to action,* and destroyed the deeds that promote repeated birth, Simhakeçarin obtained salvation. The gods performed the funeral rites of his body. The abbot was admitted to a vow by the saint Yaçobhadra. Davadantí said: 'Reverend sir, admit me also to a vow.' The saint said: 'My good woman, you have still to enjoy worldly pleasures with Nala, so you ought not to take a vow.' The next morning the saint Yaçobhadra descended from the mountain, and arrived in Tápasapura. In this state of devotion to religion, Davadantí remained seven years in the mountain cavern, with limbs unwashed. One day she suddenly heard this: 'Davadantí, I saw your husband Nala to-day in a certain place.' When she heard this, she ran in the direction of the voice, and after going a long distance she fell down in the forest. Not seeing Nala, she began to weep, saying: 'Alas! where shall I go? What shall I do?' And then Davadantí was beheld by a Rákshasí, who extended her mouth, and exclaimed: 'I will devour you!' but owing to the might of her chastity, the Rákshasí could not devour Davadantí. Then the Rakshasí disappeared like someone seen in a dream. Going on further, she saw a river with no water in it. Being afflicted with thirst, she produced water by a blow of her heel, through the power of her chastity. Then, having drunk

* *Yoga.* For the meaning of this word in Jaina philosophy see Cowell and Gough's translation of the 'Sarva Darçana Sangraha,' p. 53.

water there, she again went on. Being fatigued, she rested under a banyan-tree, and was seen by the members of a caravan. They said: 'Good lady, who are you? You appear like a goddess.' She answered: 'I am a human being; having strayed from my caravan, I am wandering about in this wood. Show me the way to Tápasapura.' They said: 'We came here to fetch water. As the sun is near the mountain of setting, we cannot show you the way. But if you will come with us, we will take you with the caravan to some place of refuge.'* Then Davadantí went with them to the caravan. The leader of the caravan saw her, and asked her: 'Who are you?' She said: 'I am a merchant's daughter, who, while asleep in the forest, was deserted by my husband, and I came here with your men as if with relations.' The leader of the caravan said: 'I shall go to Achalapura; so, my child, you had better come there too: I will transport you like a flower with the utmost care.' Then he made her get up into the best waggon. The leader of the caravan set out on his journey. He halted in a mountain thicket perfumed with the clouds of fragrant dust that issued from the expanded blossoms of the trees. At night Davadantí heard some member of the caravan reciting the formula of adoration of the five chief saints of the Jaina religion. She said to Dhanadeva, the head of the caravan: 'He who is reciting the formula of adoration must be a lay disciple, a religious man; therefore I wish to behold him.' The head of the caravan was as kind to her as a father, so he took her there. She saw the lay disciple, and found that he was worshipping a likeness of a Jina drawn on cloth, which was black as the leaf of a *tamála*-tree. Davadantí also worshipped the likeness, and welcomed and honoured the lay disciple. She asked him: 'Of what Tírthankara is this a likeness?' He answered: 'I am a merchant dwelling in the city of Kánchí. One day a holy man named Jnánayukta came there. I bowed before him, and asked: "When shall I attain salvation?" He

* This passage appears to be corrupt, and I cannot conjecture the right reading.

answered: "After you have fallen from the world of gods, you will become a king in the city of Mithilá, of the name of Prasannachandra, and after you have been admitted to a vow by the lord Malli, the nineteenth Tírthankara, you will attain perfection." From that time forward I have been devoted to the lord Malli; for this reason I worship his likeness.' He then said to Davadantí: 'Who are you, my good lady?' She told him her whole story. The lay disciple, who was of the same faith as herself, said: 'This leader of the caravan, Dhanadeva, stands to you in the position of a father, therefore you must not be afflicted.' The next morning, at dawn, the leader of the caravan reached Achalapura. The caravan left Davadantí there, and went elsewhere. Then Davadantí, being thirsty, entered the city tank to drink water. All the women of the city there looked upon her as a water-nymph. While she was drinking water, an iguana laid hold of her left foot, since in affliction fresh affliction ever comes. Then Davadantí repeated the formula of adoration, and it compelled the iguana to let go her foot. When she had drunk and come out of the tank, she sat down near it in a melancholy frame of mind. At that time there was a king named Ṛituparṇa in Achalapura; he had a queen named Chandrayaças; her maids saw Davadantí, and were struck with her beauty; so in their amazement they went and told Chandrayaças. She had Davadantí summoned into her presence, and said to her: 'My good lady, who are you?' She answered: 'I am the daughter of a merchant, and I have been abandoned in the forest.' Chandrayaças said: 'You are my daughter, and your name shall be Chandravatí. So remain in comfort in my house.'

Now, after this, Davadantí was in the habit every day of giving gifts to poor and unprotected men in the neighbour hood of the town. One day, when she was in the alms house, she saw a thief being taken along by the police, tied with peacock bonds;* then Davadantí asked: 'What has he stolen?' They answered: 'He has stolen a casket

* This is a literal translation.

belonging to Chandravatí; therefore he is to be put to death.' The thief seized his fingers with his teeth, and said to Davadantí: 'Princess, deliver me; I take refuge with you.' Then Davadantí proclaimed her chastity, and by the might of her chastity the thief's bonds were broken, and the policemen were driven to a distance. When the king heard of this occurrence, he came there. The king said to Davadantí: 'My dear child, how did you come to do this unbecoming deed? You ought not to rescue a robber.' Davadantí said: 'I did so because my heart was overpowered by pity. Pardon this offence of mine.' Then the king set the thief at liberty. The thief every day came to worship Davadantí as his mother. One day she said to him: 'Who are you, and whence do you come?' The thief said: 'How is it that you do not recognise me? I was Pingala, the slave of the caravan leader Vasanta, who lived in Tápasapura. One day, being addicted to gambling and other vices, I dug a hole into the house of the caravan leader, and took away the choicest part of his wealth. As I was going along with it, some robbers took it away from me. So I came here to Achalapura. I became a servant of King Ṛituparṇa. One day, seeing Chandravatí's jewel-case, my heart was fluttered; when I got an opportunity, I stole it. When the king's constables found that out, they pinioned me; as I was being led off to slaughter, you saw me, and rescued me. But after you left Tápasapura, the caravan leader Vasanta remained a sevennight without taking food. Then, at the end of seven days, the saint Yaçobhadra admonished him, and made him take food. One day the caravan leader Vasanta went to Koçalá, to visit Kúvara, with a large present. Then Kúvara, being pleased, gave him the headship of the town of Tápasapura. Then Vasanta returned to his house as Çriçekhara, filling the air with the noise of his drums. There he reigns over Tápasapura.' Then Davadantí said to him: 'My dear child, take a vow.' He said: 'Mother, I will do whatever you tell me.' Then Pingala took a vow.

In the meanwhile, one day King Bhímaratha heard that

Nala, being addicted to play, had lost his kingdom, and had entered a great forest with Davadantí; but it was not known whether he was alive anywhere or dead. When Pushpadantí heard that, she wept, deluging her heart with a copious flood of tears. Then King Bhímaratha sent off a young Bráhman, named Harimitra, who was clever in his lord's affairs, to look for them. As he was wandering about, he came, in course of time, to Achalapura, and went to see King Ṛituparṇa. Chandrayaças asked him: 'Is my sister Pushpadantí well?' The Bráhman said: 'Pushpadantí continues in good health, but she is grievously afflicted in her mind at hearing that Nala and Davadantí have lost their throne.' Chandrayaças said: 'Bráhman, why do you talk like this?' Then the Bráhman Harimitra told the whole story of Nala and Davadantí from the beginning. When Chandrayaças heard it, she wept very copiously. When they saw her weeping, all the courtiers wept also. When the Bráhman saw that every one was full of grief, being afflicted with hunger, he went to the almshouse, and entered to get something to eat; there he saw Davadantí superintending the distribution of alms and he was delighted. He rose up and bowed before Davadantí, and said: 'Queen, what is this miserable condition that has befallen you? It is a happy thing that I have seen you yet alive.' Then he forgot the pangs of hunger, and went to Chandrayaças, and said to her: 'Queen, you are fortunate; Davadantí is in your almshouse.' When Queen Chandrayaças heard that, she came there, and, seeing Davadantí, folded her in a close embrace. Chandrayaças said: 'Shame on me! shame on me! for not recognising you in this condition! But, my dear child, how could you deceive me by disguising yourself? Alas! did you leave Nala, or did Nala leave you? If you could bring yourself to leave your husband, even when he had fallen into evil courses, then surely the sun must rise in the west. Alas! Nala, are you not ashamed of abandoning this treasury of virtues? Why, Nala, did you show this want of discernment? My darling, I sympathize with your sorrows; pardon my fault in not recognising you. Moreover, what has become of the mark on your brow from which so much brilliancy shot forth?' Then Chandrayaças rubbed Davadantí's forehead with the moisture of her mouth, and the mark on her brow stood out in all its brilliancy, like the sun emerging from clouds, like a lump of gold withdrawn from the fire. Then Chandrayaças gave Davadantí a bath with her own hands, and clothed her in splendid garments, and brought her to the king. The two, Chandrayaças and Davadantí, sat down with the King. Now, it happened that exactly at this time the sun set. The circle of the sky was filled with darkness, as a vessel with lampblack. But nevertheless the darkness did not penetrate into the palace. Then the king said: 'Surely the sun has set, and there is no lamp in this palace; so why is there illumination here?' Then Davadantí pointed out the mark on her forehead to Queen Chandrayaças. Then the king, out of curiosity, covered the mark with his hand, and the king's palace became as full of darkness as a mountain cave. The king, withdrawing his hand, asked Davadantí the story of her losing the throne, and of her other troubles. Then Davadantí, weeping, with downcast face, told the whole story of their losing the throne and subsequent troubles. The king wiped her eyes with his own outer garment, and said: 'My dear child, do not weep. Fortune prevails even against gods and Asuras.' At this moment an immortal, bright as the rays of the sun, entered the palace, and, joining his hands in an attitude of supplication, said to Davadantí: 'I, being a thief, by name Pingala, went by your order, and took upon me the observance of vows, and, roaming about, went to Tápasapura. There I remained in the cemetery in the statuesque posture, being burned with the fire of the funeral-pyres, meditating on religion, remembering the formula of the five chiefs of the faith, reprobating my former sins; and so I died and became a god. As by limited knowledge I perceived my former life, I came here to visit you, since you benefited me by saving my life, and inducing me to adopt the life of a wandering hermit. So may you long be happy!' Then the god returned to his own place, after raining down seven crores of gold. Then King Ṛituparṇa, seeing with his own eyes the fruit of good actions that the god had reaped, adopted the Jaina faith. Then, after some days, King Ṛituparṇa was thus addressed by the Bráhman: 'King, dismiss Davadantí to the house of her father.' Chandrayaças said: 'Be it so.' Then Davadantí, having been dismissed by King Ṛituparṇa, set out, surrounded by a force of all four arms. When King Bhímaratha heard that Davadantí was coming, being bound by the cords of affection, he went out to meet her, accompanied by Pushpadantí. Then Davadantí, beholding her parents afar off, got out of her carriage and fell at their feet. Their tears fell so copiously, on thus meeting after so long a separation, that mud was produced on the surface of the earth all round. Davadantí, embracing her mother as Yamuná embraces Gangá, clung to her neck, and lamented for a long time without restraint. Then, wiping their lotus-like faces, they told one another all their joy and grief. Then Pushpadantí took Davadantí on her lap, and said: 'My dear child, if indeed I have seen you alive, my merit must be awake and active. If you remain in our house, you will easily meet with your husband.' Then King Bhímaratha, being pleased, gave Harimitra five hundred villages; then they entered the city in triumph. They worshipped the gods and spiritual teachers earnestly for seven days. On the eighth day King Bhímaratha said to Davadantí: 'My dear child, I will take steps to have you reunited with Nala.'

Now, after Nala left Davadantí, he wandered about in the forest, and saw smoke arising from a thicket. Then, after a time, it became terrible with flame, and then there burst forth a forest conflagration, spreading and making a crackling noise among the burning canes; awful with the cries of various wild beasts, destroying the trees. Then Nala heard a cry: 'Rescue me, thou circle of the sun to the lotuses of the Ikshváku race.' Then Nala, entirely dominated by disinterested compassion, went in the direction of the cry, and saw a great snake exclaiming: 'Rescue! rescue!' He said to himself: 'How does this serpent know my name or family? Or how comes it that a serpent speaks with a human voice?' While in amazement at these strange things, Nala threw his upper garment to draw the snake towards him. When the garment reached the bottom of the pit, the snake coiled his body round it, and Nala drew it up out of the pit like a rope. When Nala was trying to put the snake in a place free from grass, it bit his hand. He flung the snake down on the ground, and said: 'You have shown gratitude and done a noble action in thus benefiting me your benefactor. Certainly, this is true, that whoever gives your race milk to drink, is bitten by them.' When Nala had said this, he proceeded to go away, but the poison of the serpent in a moment made him hunchbacked, yellow-haired, like a Piçácha, with attenuated hands and feet like a camel, and with protuberant belly like Ganeça. Such did Nala become.* When Nala saw that all his limbs were thus of repulsive appearance, he said to himself: 'With this shape my life is worthless, so I will take a vow that will do me good in the next world.' While Nala was engaged in these thoughts, the god abandoned the form of a serpent, and manifested himself, and said: 'King, abandon your despondency; I am your father, Nishada by name. On that occasion, when I resigned the throne to you, I took a vow, and dying was born in the world of gods presided over by Brahmá, as a god. I knew this condition that you are in by my limited knowledge. So I assumed by my delusive power the form of a serpent, and have made your body, as you have fallen into an unhappy state, thus deformed. You must look upon that like the drinking of a bitter medicine. Since you have reduced all kings to the position of servants, this deformity has become

* As the metamorphosis of King Nala was really a benefit, we may compare this incident with one in a Servian story referred to by Preller in his 'Griechische Mythologie,' vol. ii., p. 475. A shepherd saves the life of a snake in a forest fire. In return for this, the snake's father gives him endless treasures, and teaches him the language of birds.

necessary. Owing to it they will not attack you, as it will not be possible to recognise you. But do not entertain at present the desire of taking a vow. You have still to enjoy the whole earth. I myself will announce to you the proper time for religious observance. Now receive this *vilva*-fruit and this jewel-case; you must keep both most carefully; but when you desire to regain your own form, you must break open this *vilva*-fruit, and in it you will find garments fit for gods; you must also open this casket, and there you will see a chain and other ornaments; by putting on those garments and those ornaments you will recover your own shape.' Then Nala asked the god what had happened to Davadantí. The god related her whole story, laying special stress upon her chastity. The god said to Nala: 'Why do you roam about in the wood in this way? I will take you wherever you want to go.' Nala said: 'Take me to Suṃsumárapura.' Then the god took him to Suṃsumárapura in a moment, and putting him down there, went to his own place. Nala, for his part, worshipped the lord Nemi in a Jaina temple in the garden of that city, and went to the gate of Suṃsumárapura. And at this moment a mad elephant broke loose. It had torn up the post to which it was fastened; it made the howdah on its back tremble in the wind of its movement, and dragged down with its trunk the birds that hovered over it. So it roamed along, tearing to pieces the plantation of trees. Then King Dadhiparṇa ascended the walls of the city, and exclaimed: 'Whoever subdues that elephant, I will give him all his desire.' The hunchbacked Nala said: 'Where is that elephant, that I may subdue it?' While Nala was saying this, the elephant came to that place, roaring like a cloud. The hunchback ran towards it. Nala, being skilful in avoiding the blows of the elephant's trunk, ran in front of it, behind it, and at the side of it, until he had tired the elephant out. Then the hunchback jumped up like Garuḍa, and climbed up on its shoulder. He sat in the front part of the howdah, let down his legs on its back, and slapped it with his hand on the temples. Then the people uttered a cry of triumph. The king gave him a golden chain; and Nala, having subdued the elephant, conducted it to the post to which it had to be tied. Then he got down from the elephant, and took a seat, without bowing to Dadhiparṇa. King Dadhiparṇa said: 'Hunchback, you that are so clever in managing elephants, do you know any other art?' Nala said: 'If you wish to see a delicious sun-cooked dish, I will make one.' Then the king gave delicious ingredients to the hunchback. He put the dish in the rays of the sun, and calling to mind the sun-charm, prepared a heavenly delicious dish. The king and his attendants ate that delicious dish, which was as exquisite as if given by the wishing-tree. Then King Dadhiparṇa said: 'Oh, the admirable cooking of this delicious dish! Oh, the sweetness of the flavour! Oh, the wonderful tenderness! Oh, how attractive it is to all the senses! Nala knows how to cook a delicious dish of this kind. I was long accustomed to it while I was in the service of Nala. So can you, hunchback, be Nala? But such a deformed person cannot be supposed to be Nala. Moreover, how could one separated by two hundred *yojanas* come here? Moreover, how could that lord of half India travel alone?' Then the king, being pleased, gave the hunchback dresses and ornaments, a hundred thousand rupees, and five hundred villages. The hunchback took all the rest, but he would not take the villages. The king said to the hunchback: 'Let me give you something else.' The hunchback said: 'If this is your wish, then prohibit hunting and the use of intoxicating drinks in your dominions.' The king did so out of his great regard for his advice. One day King Dadhiparṇa asked the hunchback: 'Who are you, and whence do you come?' The hunchback said: 'I am the cook of King Nala in the city of Koçalá, and my name is Huṇḍika. I learned accomplishments from that Nala. Nala lost his kingdom at play to Kúvara. He reached a forest with Davadantí, and perished in that very forest. For this reason I have come to you; but I would not remain with that Kúvara, who does not appreciate merit, and is treacherous and deceitful.' Then King Dadhiparṇa, hearing the news of the death of Nala, was so grieved that his grief cannot be described. One day King Dadhiparṇa sent an ambassador for some reason or other to the father of Davadantí. King Bhímaratha received him kindly. One day, on some occasion or other, the ambassador happened to say to King Bhímaratha: 'My master has Nala's cook. He has been taught by Nala how to make a delicious dish cooked in the sun.' Then Davadantí, hearing of it, said to her father: 'Father, send a spy, and find out what kind of a man this cook is. There is no one in the world, except Nala, that knows how to make a delicious dish cooked in the sun. Perhaps it may be Nala in disguise.' Then King Bhímaratha sent a Bráhman named Kuçala, skilful in his master's affairs, to find out the appearance of Dadhiparṇa's cook. The Bráhman Kuçala went to the city of Suṃsumára. Moreover, his zeal was doubled by good omens. When he saw the hunchback, he was depressed and despondent, and thought: 'What a difference between Nala of godlike beauty and this hunchback! There is as much difference between them as between Meru and a mustard-seed.' Then the messenger, having reflected a little in his mind, sang a *dodhaka* song:

> 'Surely Nala was a singularly heartless, cruel villain, and no mistake,
> Since he left at night the chaste Davadantí asleep in the forest.'

Then the hunchback, hearing the song sung again and again, remembered Davadantí, and lamented with a shower of tears. Kuçala said: 'Hunchback, why do you weep?' The hunchback answered: 'I weep on hearing your song, full of pathetic sentiment.' Then the hunchback asked Kuçala the meaning of the song. Then Kuçala told the whole story, from the gambling of Nala until Davadantí's entry into the city of Kuṇḍina. Kuçala went on to say: 'Hunchback, the ambassador of King Dadhiparṇa told King Bhímaratha that you could prepare a delicious sun-cooked dish. Now, Nala also was able to prepare this dish; and reflecting on this, Davadantí persuaded her father to send me here to look at you. When I saw you, I said to myself: "There is a vast difference between an exceedingly ugly hunchback and Nala, who was handsome in all his limbs and lineaments. Who would compare the crane, that destroys the families of fish, with the moon that delights men?" When I was coming near this place where you are, I met with a multitude of favourable omens, but they have proved fruitless, since you are not Nala.' Then the hunchback, being overpowered with affection for Davadantí, took the Bráhman to his house: for

> Even a crow, coming from the place where a beloved person lives,
> Produces pleasure, much more a man sent by the beloved.

The hunchback said: 'How can I welcome you, Bráhman, by way of showing my gratitude for making me hear a song about the chaste Davadantí and the great hero Nala?' When he said this, he made preparations for giving him food and other refreshments. Then he gave to the Bráhman all the ornaments that Dadhiparṇa had given him. Then Kuçala reached the city of Kuṇḍina in safety. He told King Bhímaratha the whole story of the hunchback, beginning with his taming of the mad elephant, Davadantí said: 'Father, surely that must be Nala himself, and he must have become deformed owing to some bad food or some evil action in a previous state of existence, for such cleverness in managing elephants, and skill in preparing food by means of the sun, and such a magnificent gift—all these are characteristic of no person except Nala. So bring that hunchback here by means of some device, that I may test him myself.' King Bhímaratha said: 'My dear child, if the hunchback comes quickly on hearing of a pretended *svayaṃvara*, we may be sure that he is Nala. Then he will be discovered by his driving rapidly the chariot and horses. I will name a near day. If the hunchback comes to the *svayaṃvara* quickly, no doubt he is Nala. Even an ordinary man would not endure the disgrace of his wife, much less Nala, that king of men.' Then Bhímaratha sent a messenger to Dadhiparṇa. He announced the *svayaṃvara* of Davadantí on the fifth day of the white fortnight of Chaitra.

Dadhiparṇa thought: 'Davadantí is a lady that I should love; but she lives in a very distant country. The fifth day is to-morrow. I cannot go there in the time. What am I to do?' So Dadhiparṇa was tortured by anxiety, like a fish in a small piece of water. The hunchback said to himself: 'Davadantí is exceedingly chaste, she will never desire a second husband; besides, if she were to have a fancy that way, who would take her while I am alive? So I will take Dadhiparṇa to that *svayaṃvara* in six watches; for I shall go there with him as being attached to his person.' Then the hunchback said to Dadhiparṇa: 'Why are you so afflicted? Tell me the cause; for one cannot cure a patient that does not tell his disease.' The king said: 'Hunchback, Nala has made his auspicious entry into the city of the gods, and Davadantí will make her *svayaṃvara* a second time to-morrow morning. I long to obtain Davadantí; but Vidarbha is far off, and there is an interval of six watches only. The messenger has taken many days to come; how, then, can I go there in so short a time? Thinking over this, I can obtain no peace of mind.' The hunchback said: 'Do not be unhappy, king; give me a chariot with thoroughbred horses, and I will take you to the city of Kuṇḍina by to-morrow morning.' The king said to himself: 'This is not an ordinary man; this is some Vidyádhara or some god.' So he gave him a chariot with thoroughbred horses. Then Nala made ready the chariot, and said to Dadhiparṇa: 'King, mount the chariot.' Then the king, his betel-box-bearer, his umbrella-bearer, and his two chowrie-bearers, five men in all, ascended that chariot, and the hunchback was the sixth. He fastened up that *vilva*-fruit and that casket in his clothes on his loins; he invoked the gods and the spiritual teachers, and urged on the horses. Then the four-horsed chariot, being driven on by Nala, who knew the dispositions of horses, began to move quickly. Thereupon the garment of Dadhiparṇa, being blown away by the wind raised by the motion of the chariot, fell on the ground. Dadhiparṇa told the hunchback. The hunchback laughed, and said: 'King, where is your garment? The chariot has come twenty-five *yojanas* since the garment fell.' Then Dadhiparṇa was astonished; but seeing in front of him a *vibhítaka*-tree, he said to the hunchback: 'Mark, hunchback, I know the number of fruits on this *vibhítaka*-tree without counting them.' The hunchback said: 'Then show the marvel.' The king said: 'I will not show it now, as there would be delay; I will show it to you on the way back.' The hunchback said: 'King, do not be afraid, there will be no loss of time with me as your charioteer. With one blow of my fist I will lay all the fruits in front of you.' The king answered: 'Bring all the fruits down and behold a marvel. There are eighteen thousand fruits.' Then the hunchback brought them down with a blow of his fist. Dadhiparṇa counted them, and there turned out to be exactly as many as he had said. Then the hunchback, being entreated, gave Dadhiparṇa the art of understanding the dispositions of horses, and himself received from him the art of numbering fruits. The next morning the chariot approached the city of Kuṇḍina. The lotus of Dadhiparṇa's face was expanded with joy. In the meanwhile, Davadantí saw a dream at the end of night.* She told it to her father. She said: 'I saw the revered goddess of happiness. She carried me through the sky to the garden of Koçalá; then, by the command of the goddess, I climbed up a fragrant mango-tree, which was full of fruit and flowers. The goddess put a splendid fruit into my hand. A bird, which had before gone up to guard it, fell down.' Bhímaratha said: 'My daughter, you have seen a most favourable dream. The goddess of happiness is your accumulated merit in active operation. The garden of Koçalá is the kingdom of Koçalá. The climbing up the fragrant mango-tree is the chain of events leading to a meeting between you and Nala. The falling down of the bird, that had previously ascended, is the deposition of Kúvara. As for your seeing the dream in the morning, that means that

* For the belief that dreams seen at this time are sure to prove true, see my translation of the 'Kathá Sarit Ságara,' vol. i., p. 441; and vol. ii., p. 482.

you will be re-united to Nala to-day.' At that very moment Dadhiparṇa reached the gate of the city. A man, named Mangala,* came and announced his arrival to Bhímaratha. Bhímaratha embraced the king as a friend, and gave him a splendid lodging. After Bhímaratha had made Dadhiparṇa take food and other refreshments, he asked him: 'Have you a cook who can cook in the sun? Show him to me.' Then Dadhiparṇa ordered the hunchback to prepare a delicious dish. The hunchback immediately prepared it. At the request of Dadhiparṇa, Bhímaratha and all his retinue ate of that delicious dish. Then Davadantí, in order to try the taste of it, had a pot full of the food brought, and took some of it.† The moment she tasted the flavour, she said: 'Undoubtedly this hunchback is Nala himself. Long ago, a spiritual teacher, possessing supernatural knowledge, said to me: "No one in India, except Nala, knows the art of making a delicious dish cooked in the sun." So this must certainly be Nala. As for his being at present a hunchback, there must be some special reason for that. One test of Nala is the delicious dish; but there is another also. If I am touched merely by the finger of Nala, all the hairs of my body stand on end. So let the hunchback touch me with his hand. If this test also proves successful, then, undoubtedly, this hunchback is Nala himself.' Then she asked the hunchback: 'Hunchback, are you Nala?' He said: 'What similarity can there be between the broad-breasted Nala and me, a hunchback, only fit to give pain to the eyes of men?' Nevertheless, being earnestly entreated, he touched the breast of Davadantí with his finger, and the mere touch of his finger gave her such pleasure that the hairs stood on end all over her body, and it became like a *karkoṭaka*-plant. She said: 'On that occasion you left me asleep; now, my husband, ouy have been seen by

* Fortunate or auspicious.

† In the story of Shams ul din and his son, Hasan Badr ul dín is discovered by his skill in cooking (Lane's 'Arabian Nights,' vol. i., p. 266). Bhíma disguises himself as a cook in the Viráṭaparvan of the Mahábhárata. De Gubernatis ('Zoological Mythology,' vol. i., p. 158) remarks that service in the kitchen is especially dear to the young hero.

me, where will you go?' While saying this, she took Nala into the house, and asked him to display his real form. So he took the garments and ornaments out of the *vilva*-fruit and the casket, and put them on, and so assumed his own form. When Davadantí saw him, she was delighted, and embraced him closely, as a creeper does a tree. Bhímaratha, perceiving it, placed Nala on his own throne, and said to him: 'You are my lord; tell me what I am to do.' Saying this, he sat down before him, with his hands joined in an attitude of supplication. Dadhiparṇa said to Nala: 'You are my sovereign, pardon what I did to you that was unbecoming towards a sovereign, since it was done in ignorançe.' King Ṛituparṇa, having been summoned by Davadantí, came with Chandrayaçças; and Vasanta, who under the name of Çríçekhara had become lord of Tápasapura, was also summoned. King Bhímaratha showed them all honour. One day, when they were all sitting down in the audience-hall of Bhíma, a god arrived. He joined his hands in an attitude of supplication, and said to Davadantí: 'I am the abbot of the ascetics who was converted by you, and dying I became by the might of the Jaina religion a god in Saudharma.'

For this reason, having rained down seven crores of gold, he returned to his own place. Bhímaratha, Ṛituparṇa, Vasanta, and the other kings, met together, and anointed Nala as sovereign. Then Nala gave them the order, and then, accompanied by them, surrounded with all their forces, with his wild elephants roaring, filling the heaven with the dust raised from the earth by the hoofs of his horses, terrifying the ears of all his enemies by the creaking of his chariot-wheels, Nala arrived in the neighbourhood of the city of Ayodhyá. When Kúvara heard that Nala was coming, his body was swallowed by great distress. Nala sent this message to Kúvara by an ambassador: 'Fight with me; let your fortune become mine, or let my fortune become yours.' Then Kúvara, being afraid to fight, began again to gamble; and Nala, being superior in merit, stripped him of all that he had. After this, Nala restored him to his former position of crown prince, because, though he was cruel, he was his younger brother. Then, having recovered his kingdom, Nala, together with Davadantí, worshipped eagerly at all the sacred shrines in Ayodhyá. The kings offered various presents, and bowed before the lotus of his foot, and Nala held the sovereignty of half India for many thousands of years. One day the god Nishada came from heaven, and said to Nala, who was full of projects for engaging in the pleasures of the world: 'You are not a man, since you do not defend your treasure of discernment, which is being pillaged by such robbers as passion and its crew. I promised you long ago that I would tell you the time to become a hermit; so now adopt self-restraint.' When the god had said this, he went to his own place. At this moment a religious teacher, named Jinabhadra, who possessed supernatural knowledge, arrived there. Then Nala went to worship him with Davadantí. When the king had worshipped him, and heard the religious instruction he had to give, he asked: 'Reverend sir, what good deed did we two perform in a former life that we acquired such a splendid sovereignty, and, after losing it, recovered it again?' The sage said: 'In this very Jambudvípa, in the land of Bharata, near the mountain Ashṭápada, there is a city named Sangara. In it there was a king named Mammaṇa, and he had a wife named Víramatí. One day the king, having gone out to hunt, saw a hermit coming with a caravan. He thought that the hermit would impede his hunting, and was an evil omen to him; so he took him out of the caravan, and, making him turn back, brought him to his palace. They mocked the hermit for twelve hours; then the two asked him these questions: "Whence do you come, and where are you going?" The hermit said: "I have come from Rohitapura with a caravan, to worship the images of the Jinas on the Ashṭápada mountain." When they heard this speech of the hermit, their anger melted away. Then the hermit, knowing their good disposition, preached to them religion, the principal characteristic of which is mercy to all living things. Then they made some progress in religion. They refreshed the hermit with food and drink. After they had kept the hermit some time, and had heard from him the truths of religion, and had entreated his forgiveness, they sent him away, and he went to Ashṭápada. Thus, having been converted by association with a saint, they diligently observed the vow of lay disciples. One day the goddess, that attends upon the Jina, took Víramatí to the Ashṭápada mountain to confirm her faith. There Víramatí saw the images of the Arhats, each of life size, made of various jewels, splendidly constructed by gods and Asuras, and was highly delighted. After she had worshipped these images, she returned to her own city. And Víramatí, believing that she had worshipped a great object of devotion, performed twenty-four *Áchámla* mortifications,* one for each of the Jinas. She had made suitable forehead-marks for each of the twenty-four images of Jinas, composed of gold, set off by jewels placed upon them. On a subsequent day Víramatí went with her retinue to the Ashṭápada mountain, and worshipped the Jinas by bathing and anointing them, and other pious acts, and then she fixed with great devotion those marks on the foreheads of the images of the Jinas. Víramatí gave suitable gifts to those that came to the holy place, wandering hermits and others, and completed her vow of mortification, and, considering that her human birth had fulfilled its object, that her wealth had produced fruit, and that her life was truly successful, she returned to her own city. Thus some considerable time passed over this couple, while they were engaged in the religious observances of the Jaina faith. They died when their allotted period of life came to an end, and were born as a god and a goddess in Saudharma. Then the soul of Mammaṇa was born in this very land of Bharata, in a country named Rahulí, in the city of Potana, as the son of Dhammillása, a cowherd, and Reṇuká his wife. After his birth he was called Dhanya. The soul of Víramatí fell

* *Áchámla* means the eating of dry food simply moistened or boiled in water. See Dr. Hoernle's paper in the *Indian Antiquary* for August, 1890, note 31.

from the world of the gods and became Dhúsarí, the wife of Dhanya. Dhanya used to go outside the city and pasture his oxen.

'Then, the rainy season having arrived, and the clouds pouring down showers, Dhanya went to the forest to pasture his oxen, holding an umbrella over his head. There he saw a hermit, thin from severe self-mortification, standing motionless in the statuesque posture. Then Dhanya held with great devotion the umbrella over the head of the hermit, on account of the rain that the cloud was pouring down. Then Dhanya prostrated himself before the hermit, and said: "Whence have you come here?" The hermit said: "Worthy sir, I have come from the land of Pándu, and I am bound for Lanká; I am going to worship the spiritual teachers there. But I have been detained by the cloud that has been raining for a sevennight." Dhanya said: "My lord, the ground is unfit for walking on account of the mud, so get up on this bullock of mine, and come to my house in the city." The hermit said: "Worthy sir, it is not fitting for hermits to make use of any means of conveyance;" so the hermit walked to the city with Dhanya. There Dhanya took the hermit to his house, and made him break his fast by giving him milk. Dhanya and Dhúsarí took the vows of lay disciples in the presence of the hermit. He remained during the rainy season in that city of Potana, and afterwards went elsewhere. Dhanya and Dhúsarí for a long time observed the vows of lay disciples, and then took upon themselves regular vows, and having observed these regular vows for seven years, they both died, and in their fourth birth were born as twins in the Himálayan region. Then they lived a religious life, and eventually died, and were born in their fifth birth in the world of gods called Saudharma. Dhanya became a god called Kshíradiṇḍíra. Dhúsarí was born as his wife in the same world of gods, and went by the name of the goddess Kshíradiṇḍírá. Then the soul of Dhanya fell from the world of gods, and was born as yourself, Nala. The soul of Dhúsarí fell from the world of gods, and was born as this your wife, Davadantí. Because in a former life you gave a gift to a hermit, and became a lay disciple, by way of fruit of that merit, divinity and kingship have fallen to your lot. And this Davadantí also became your wife owing to the power of that religious observance. Because, Davadantí, in a former life you worshipped the twenty-four Jinas on the Ashṭápada mountain, and gave them forehead-marks made of jewels—owing, I say, to the influence of that pious act, you were born with a natural mark on your forehead resembling the disc of the sun. Because in a former birth you two separated the hermit for twelve hours from his caravan, therefore you have both been deprived of your kingdom for twelve years.' When Nala had heard this, being inclined to renunciation, he placed on his throne his son named Pushpala, and, accompanied by Davadantí, he took the vows in the presence of the teacher. Then he began to read the books of the sacred canon and to endure severe ordeals. Then, one day, Nala was so influenced by his previous actions that he wished to return to the married state. Thereupon he was abandoned by his spiritual teacher. The god Nishada came and admonished him. Being unable to keep his vow, Nala starved himself. Davadantí also had recourse to starvation. Nala died and became Kuvera; Davadantí died and became his wife. They have obtained the position of low deities because they inflicted some pain. Both of them will consume their actions, and will in due course attain salvation. Here ends the story of Nala concerning gambling.*

---

1. The story of Dhanada, having reference to the worship of him who is free from passion. 2. The story of Devapála, having reference to the worship of the gods. 3. The story of the two *ṛishis* in Kuṇálá, having reference to anger. 4. The story of the hermit Saṃvara, having reference to anger. 5. The story of the merchant Açoka, having reference to covetousness. 6. The story of Puṇḍaríka and Kuṇḍaríka

* What follows is found in the Sanskrit College MS. only. The list of stories appears to be incorrect.

and Yaçobhadrá, having reference to timely speech. 7. The story of Madanarekhá, having reference to the vow of chastity. 8. The story of Nágadatta, having reference to the eight-day ceremony. 9. The story of Sanatkumára, having reference to asceticism. 10. The story of Amarachandra, having reference to meditation. 11. The story of the parrots, having reference to worship by means of whole grain. 12. The story of Madanávalí, having reference to worship by means of perfumes. 13. The story of the ploughman, having reference to worship by means of a food-offering. 14. The story of Dípaçikha, having reference to worship by means of candles. 15. The story of Dhanya, having reference to giving. 16. The story of Árámaçobhá, having reference to worship. 17. The story of Ṛishidattá, having reference to chastity. 18. The story of Metárya, having reference to compassion to living creatures. 19. The story of Ratnaçikha, having reference to the formula of adoration. 20. The story of Amarachandra and Mitránanda, having reference to sin. 21. The story of King Amarasena. 22. The story of Lalitánga. 23. The story of Dámannaka, having reference to compassion to living creatures. 24. The story of Kúlaválaka, having reference to outraging a spiritual teacher. 25. The story of Kanakaratha, having reference to giving to a worthy object. 26. The story of Báhubali, having reference to pride. 27. The story of King Nala, having reference to gambling.

HERE ENDS THE KATHÁKOÇA.

# NOTES BY PROFESSOR LEUMANN.

THE following notes have been sent me by Professor Leumann, whose familiarity with Jain literature is well known. They form a most useful addition to my translation, and will, I think, greatly increase its value. Professor Leumann wishes me to express his thanks to Professor Bendall for the loan of his MS. of the 'Kathákoça.' He adds: 'I have used it before for making extracts, which now form MS. L 94 (Cf. 'Zeitschrift der Deutschen Morgenländischen Gesellschaft,' vol. xlvii., p. 310).' [My additions to Professor Leumann's notes, which consist principally of extracts from the MS. which I call C, are enclosed in square brackets.]

P. 1*. This is the traditional introduction to Jain tales, both Çvetámbara and Digambara.

P. 2, ll. 3, f. Bendall's MS. seems to have *nijárámamálikayá-upáyani-kṛitta-pushpa-catu(ḥ)sarikaḥ*, which seems to mean: he took[1] a *pushpa-catuḥsarika*, *i.e.*, a fourfold flower-garland, which had been plucked by the woman attending his own garden[2] as an offering for obtaining a particular boon from the deity. *Catuḥsarika* is a word like *trisaraka*—threefold necklace, or string; in Prákṛit, *tisara* (see 'Aupapátika Glossary,' p. 123*c*). *Upáyana*, if the reading be right, is an offering to deities for obtaining a son, or some other wish. The reference given in the note is, at any rate, out of place, because the gardener's wife can have only flowers. [C reads here: *Nijárámamálikayá-upáyani-kṛitaḥ pushpacatusarikaḥ*.—C. H. T.]

P. 2, ll. 12, f. This passage is to be changed, according to the preceding one. Here the reading *pushpa-catuḥsara-pújá* leaves no doubt, and confirms the above translation. The Yaksha means, apparently, to say: 'Give me a *pushpacatuḥsara*, that I may be able to present it to the Jina for obtaining the merit from such offering.' Accordingly, *Dhanada* answers: 'I cannot give such flowers[3] to anyone except the Jina.' This is certainly the meaning, and therefore the passage in print (p. 2, l. 15, f.) should be changed; at least, Bendall's MS. has not here the word *puṇya*, 'the benefit of.' And so, also, the Yaksha's words would read in English: 'Dhanada, give me the benefit obtainable by worshipping the Jina with a *pushpacatuḥsara*.' Dhanada can certainly not transfer his merit (*puṇya*);

[1] This is not expressed in the above reading, but must be supplied, apparently. [Professor Leumann's footnotes are numbered consecutively.]

[2] *Nijárámapálikayá* is apparently meant. But, as the MS. C has the same reading, it is better to translate: out of a garland of his own garden he made a *pushpa-catuḥsarika* (for presenting it) as an *upáyana* (to the deity).

[3] *Kusumasya . . . dánaṃ*; there is no '*puṇya*' here.

he can only offer flowers to the Yaksha for enabling him to obtain the same merit. But even this he wished not to do, as his creed is not to worship anyone except the Jina.

So the request of the Yaksha is only a trial to see whether Dhanada is really faithful to the Jina or not. And this is the general character of the Yakshas in the Jain legends, viz., to try the creed, and then to reward it.

P. 3, ll. 4-7. These lines should be put in small type, as the original is a verse in the Áryá metre.

P. 3, l. 17, 'drops of rain.' Bendall's MS. has *lavai vijjulá gapapo.*[4] The second word is the same as *vijjulayá* (*vidyul-latá*), and the first must be the third singular of a verb, which, however, is not known elsewhere. Or should Sanskrit *lapati* or *plavati* be meant?

P. 3, ll. 25-28. Also here the original is in metre; in Bendall's MS. it is a defective *çloka*, which possibly can be restored with the help of the other MSS.

> *Aho bhágyam ! (aho) . . . ! aho me puṇya-saṃgamaḥ*
> *Aho me karma-sámagrí-kaṭare karma-lághavaṃ !*

In the last line of the çloka there must be a misreading, but the sense is clear: 'Oh, how light are my actions in the midst of the huge totality of actions!' viz.: 'I am no longer suffering from the weight of actions causing numerous re-births.' The first seems to point to *kaṭake* for *kaṭare*.

[C repeats *aho bhágyam*, which completes the first line; it also reads *kaṭare*.—C. H. T.]

P. 3 ‡. On the other hand, Buddhist texts use frequently the expression *devo varshati* (cf., *e.g.*, the 'Sumágadhávadána,' §§ 43, 44).

P. 6 *. Nothing is wanting except 'she answered,' which must be supplied before *yat*. The translation of p. 6, l. 1, f. would then be: 'Queen, what is that?' [She answered :] 'Because I saw this *kápálika*, [therefore] I remembered my former life.'

P. 6, ll. 13, ff. The following story is taken from the Ávaçyaka tales. It is found in the different commentaries on 'Ávaçyaka-niryukti,' x. 35, 4. The opening verse is (according to the comments) spoken by the two hermits named Karaḍa and Ukkaraḍa in the following way :

Karaḍa said : *Varisa deva*[5] *Kuṇáláe*
Ukkaraḍa said : *Dasa divasáṇi panca ya*
Karaḍa said : *Muṭṭhi-mettáhiṃ dháráhiṃ*
Ukkaraḍa said : *Jahá rattiṃ tahá divaṃ.*

The same distribution is made in the 'Kathákoça.' Accordingly, the opening line of the verse should read as follows:

'Rain, cloud, on Kuṇála' 'for full fifteen days.'

According to the 'Ávaçyaka' commentaries, the tale is based on *some historical event which took place thirteen years before Mahávíra* reached the *kevalajnána*.

P. 7 †. It would be as well to insert the omitted passage,[6] and to

[4] For *gayaṇe* in the sky. [Here C has :

> *Gajjanti ghaná nachchanti sihigaṇá lavaiṃ vijjulá gayaṇe*
> *Kúlaṃkasá ya kalusaṃ vahanti varasanti váridhará.*—C. H. T.]

[5] So against what was said on p. 3 ‡.

[6] First comes a Çárdúlavikríḍita stanza, which deserves notice. Then Bendall's MS. has *tathá hi : dhammo maráṇa kunto*, which is a wrong pratíka

give an exact reference where to find the 'twenty-sixth story.' The last phrase, 'Here follows the story of Açokadatta,' is certainly in its place here, as other stories are introduced in a similar way. Also Bendall's MS. has got it.

P. 7, ll. 10, ff. The same story, without the tales inserted in it, is found in the comments on 'Ávaçyaka-niry.,' viii., 162, 13. The man here, instead of trying suicide, simply becomes a Jaina monk, and, on reaching Northern Mathurá, makes his friend do the same.

The two intercalated stories both describe how somebody tried to kill his younger brother for a treasure common to both. A similar incident is found at the beginning of a Daçavaikálika tale ('Zeitschrift der D. Morg. Gesellschaft,' xlvi., 603).

P. 11 *. Literally, 'I am a cheat,' or some similar expression. Bendall's MS. has *ahaṃ varáṃsitaḥ*. [So my MSS.—C. H. T.]

P. 13 †. This often-quoted çloka is = 'Uttarádhyayana-sútra,' xiii. 16 (see 'Wiener Zeitschrift für die Kunde des Morg.,' vol. vi., p. 24).

Pp. 13-18. The story of Prince Yaçobhadra is drawn from the commentaries on 'Ávaçyaka-niry.,' xvii. 15-17. The last of the three verses (xvii. 17) is quoted in the sequel (p. 17, ll. 5-10). In p. 16 * *váditaṃ* (in Prákrit *váiyam*) is, indeed, the correct reading (though *vimditaṃ* is given by Bendall's MS.).

P. 14, ll. 12-16. This passage, which is very faulty in Bendall's MS., seems to be a verse—at any rate, it is coined after some very old sayings found both in Jain and Buddhist literature, and terminating with the refrain: *Jáyaṃ saraṇato bhayaṃ*. See Weber's 'Samyaktvakaumudí' ('Sitzungsberichte der Berliner Akad.,' 1889, p. 756, note), and Oldenburg's 'Játakas' (*Journal Royal As. Soc.*, 1893, p. 349, f.). The 'Kathákoça' passage should be given for the sake of comparison. [It runs thus in C: *Rájni vadati: he rájan, amrite visham utpannaṃ súryád andhakáraṃ chandramasaḥ angáravṛishṭiḥ yato rakshas tato bhayaṃ jalád agniḥ utthitaḥ yadi sunetro naraḥ unmárgaṃ yáti tat dṛishṭivikalasya ko doshaḥ?*—C. H. T.]

P. 15 *. *Gitártha* literally denotes one who has sung (*i.e.*, learnt), not only the *sútra* (*i.e.*, the text), but also the *artha* (*i.e.*, the commentary); it is, therefore, a term for a monk fully versed in the necessary texts.

---

of some Áryá drawn apparently from some Niryukti or Bháshya. Then a new tale is referred to *Vinítáyáṃ nagaryáṃ çrí Ṛishabhadeva-priyá* 2 *Sumangalá-Sunandá*.

Now follows a *gáthá* ('Ávaçyaka-niry.,' ii., 124), numbered 3; finally a prose phrase.

[The twenty-sixth story is that of 'Báhubali,' beginning on p. 192. I proceed to copy out the omitted passage as it stands in C:

*Mánaṃ Báhubalir Maríchir achayat çrí Sthúlabhadraḥ prabhuḥ*
*Sádhuḥ Siṃhaguhásthitau* (*sic*) *matimadaḥ çrí Siddhasenaḥkaviḥ*
*Cháṇakyaḥ kila Koṇikaḥ kshitipati Duryodhano Rávaṇaḥ*
*Súriḥ Ságarachandra ityabhimataç chakrí chaturtho'pi cha* 1.

*Tathá hi dhammo maeṇa kunto* ° 1. *Vinítáyáṃ nagaryáṃ Çrí Ṛishabhadeva-priyá* 2 *Sumaṃgalá Sunaṃdá. deví Sumaṃgaláe Bharaho Bambhí ya mihuṇayaṃ jáyaṃ, Deví ya Sunaṃdáe Báhubalí Suṃdarí cheva* 3. *çrí Ṛishabhadeve vratam ápanne çrí Bharateçvarasya rájye datte ashṭanavatiputráṇáṃ vibhajya rájye datte svámí kevalajnánam avápa. Vanchanávishaye Açokadatta-katháṇakaṃ kathyate.*—C. H. T.]

P. 17, l. 17. Before 'went' insert 'obtained the universal knowledge [*kevalajnána*] and.'

P. 18*. The story which, by Jacobi, has been drawn[7] from Devendra's commentary on 'Uttarádhyayana-sútra,' ix., occurs also in the commentary on 'Ávaçyaka-niryukti,' xvii. 45 (='Uttarádhy.-niryukti,' verse 318).

P. 18, ll. 32-34. The original seems to have a çloka line (or an Áryá line?):

*Bhadre'sau rájá tava guṇánurakto, manmukhát idaṃ vadati.*

This is the reading of Bendall's MS., which apparently requires emendation. [C inserts *tváṃ* before *vadati*. For *idaṃ*, my text has *evaṃ*.—C. H. T.]

P. 20*. The passage is: *bhartur antyárádhanáṃ kárayámása*. We should expect *bhartáram*, 'She made her husband fulfil his final reconciliation with all.'

P. 21*. *The eighteen sins* are mentioned, *e.g.*, in 'Aupapátika Sútra,' § 56, p. 61, f.

P. 21 †. Bendall's MS. reads *tyaktaṃ* for *naktaṃ*, which is equally wrong.

P. 23 †. The four kinds of knowledge, *i.e.*, the five without the highest of them, which is the *kevalajnána*.

P. 26, ll. 21-23. This passage should be printed as a verse. It is a çloka in the Sanskrit text.

P. 28*. The last Páda is the same as in the verse translated on p. 5, ll. 16-18.

P. 29. It seems that the author has here made free use of some recollections from the story of Udáyaṇa (Jacobi, 'Ausgewählte Ezählungen,' p. 29). This story of Udáyaṇa is also among the Ávaçyaka tales (on 'Ávaçy.-niry.,' viii. 52). Jacobi has borrowed it[7] from Devendra's commentary on 'Uttarádhy.' xviii. 48.

P. 29 ‡. The word *na* before *mahat-pramáṇá ḍhakkáḥ* is certainly a mistake. Bendall's MS. has it. It is therefore a bad reading, which already belonged to the common source of our MSS., like the one mentioned in p. 16*.

P. 30, l. 10. 'An eight days' course of self-mortification.' This renders *Ashṭáhniká tapaḥ*, which should be translated by 'the *Ashṭáhniká* penance.' *Ashṭáhniká* is a religious festival of the Jains, described in the Berlin MS. or. fol. 1693. See also Rájendra Mitra's 'Notices,' vol. ix., p. 8, f.

P. 30, l. 30. 'The eight-day ceremony.' This again renders *Ashṭáhniká tapaḥ*.

P. 31*. The story is taken[7] from Devendra's commentary on 'Uttarádhyayana,' xviii. 37.

P. 34 †. Bendall's MS. has: *Tasyáḥ svasáṃ ca Sandhyáyáṃ pariṇinye*. If the form *svasáṃ* is found in the other MSS., it is worth noting. [It is found in C and in my text.—C. H. T.]

P. 36, l. 1. 'A perfectly-instructed monk.' This well represents *gitártha* (p. 15*).

P. 36*. The passage in Hoernle's book treats of the *eleven* standards of a *layman*, for which the best reference would be Samaváyánga xi. Here, however, a *monk's* standard is mentioned. The

[7] I point out this reference, as by its help the reader may find an easy Sanskrit version of the same tale in the Indian edition of the 'Uttarádhyayana.'

*ekallavihára pratimá*, 'solitary stay[8] *i.e.*, apart from fellow-monks,' is often mentioned; it belongs, however, not to the regular *twelve* monks' standards, as may be seen from the list of them in Samaváyánga xii.

P. 36 ‡. Read 'of the eighth meal.' If the day were meant, we should have *ashṭamí*, not *ashṭama* (*sc.*, *bhakta*).

P. 36, ll. 6-8. The enumeration of diseases is a çloka in the Sanskrit text.

P. 36 §. *Annaruchi* (or *bhaktacchanda*) is 'morbid appetite.'

P. 38 †. Bendall's MS. has the right reading *kumára-bhuktiḥ pradattá.*

P. 42 ‡. The sign ought to stand before the phrase, not after it, for the explanatory note stands immediately after the two *gáthás.*

P. 45 *. Read 'diagrams' instead of 'amulets.'

P. 50 *. See also the story in the comments on 'Viçeshávaçyakabháshya,' i. 862.

P. 59 * †. Also elsewhere the masculine gender is used with female Kevalins, or Tírthakaras (like Malli, see p. 214, ll. 4 and 6).

P. 64 and p. 69. Bendall's MS. has Svetămviká both times. If this is confirmed by the other MSS., it should be restored as a wrong variation for the older Svetaviká, or Svetabiká, often occurring in Jain legends (*Seyaviyá* is Prákṛit). [C has *Svetămbiká.*—C. H. T.]

P. 64 *. The passage is an Áryá, which may be restored from the different MSS.:

> *Cangaṃ angaṃ suddhá buddhí avalakkhaydi akkháiṃ*
> *Savvuttamaṃ paḍuttaṃ jiṇinda-dívaya-payáṇa-phalaṃ.*

This seems to be about the wording which may be derived from Bendall's MS., but it is liable to correction. At any rate, several words in the translation seem to be superfluous.

[C has:

> *Cange aṃgaṃ suddhá buddhí avalakkhaáiṃ akkháiṃ*
> *Savvuttamaṃ pahuttaṃ jiṇanda dívayi payaṇa phalaṃ.*

It is clear that a gloss is inserted in A, but I cannot compare it, as it is in Calcutta.—C. H. T.]

P. 70, ll. 22, f. The first query is wanting in Bendall's MS. (perhaps also in others). The whole address of the king should be given. It will become clear, I think, that on p. 78 * nothing is wanting. Bendall's MS. has: *Kena karmaṇá vasúphala-pramukháni panca 2 vastúni pratidivasaṃ dhopanikáyáṃ sampadyante? táni prashṭáni bhaṇitvá átmaná upabhunjámi, anyasya kasyápi na dadámi etat sarvaṃ mamágre saṃdiça svámin.* [Professor Leumann marks as wrong the second syllable in *vasúphaláni* and the first syllable in *prashṭáni.* I proceed to copy out C: *Rájá prastávaṃ prápya pṛishṭo Jinaḥ: svámin kena puṇyena mayá evaṃvidhaṃ rájyaṃ práptaṃ anyachcha kena karmaṇá vasuphala pramukháni panca 2 vastúni pratidivasaṃ dhoyanikáyáṃ sampadyaṃte? táni bhaṇitvá átmaná na upabhunjámi anyasya kasyápi na dadámi etat sarvaṃ mamágre saṃdiça svámin.* I find the omitted *prashṭáni* in my text, I therefore conclude that it is in A.—C. H. T.]

P. 71, l. 18. Read 'also' instead of 'but.' The Sanskrit has *Droṇako'pi.* Only Dhanapati and Dhaneçvara were cheats.

P. 74, l. 17. Also Bendall's MS. has here 'Kámala' (instead of

[8] 'Roaming' is incorrect.

Kámapála); it may be a short form of the name, or a mistake of the original MS.

P. 76 †. *Daṃtasya*, also in Bendall's MS. Again a common mistake of all the four MSS. The line ought to have been printed as a verse.

P. 76, l. 32. After 'who,' insert 'lived in Çankhapura and.' The Sanskrit text has *Çankhapuravásini*.[9] The maiden is here throughout called 'Mairá,' while her name was 'Maillá' in the former story (p. 71, l. 30).

P. 77. Omit the last phrase in the bottom line, and read at the top of p. 78 as follows: 'Also those two (friends) had come (with their wives to listen to the lord) on his arrival[10] (in the garden of Gajapura). The Jina showed them to King Kurucandra, (saying) that all five . . .'

P. 78 *. By the preceding correction everything is in order. The curious dependence of the king on his four fellow-creatures is explained by their collective offering made to a hermit in a former life.

Pp. 78, f. The introduction to the story of Dhanya is found in an Ávaçyaka tale.

P. 85, ll. 17-20. This is a çloka in the Sanskrit text. It ought to be printed accordingly.

P. 116, ll. 18 and 21. Read *Chandrayaçá*. This form is clearly indicated at the second passage, *Chandrayaçá-samípe*. It is certainly not good Sanskrit, but common in works drawn from Prákṛit sources. See also the Prákṛitic form 'Sujasá' (p. 169, l. 32).

P. 116, ll. 15, 17, 19, 26, 34. Read *Gangádatta* and *Gangásená* throughout.

P. 116 †. 'You' is quite right, as Gangasená is simply the former existence of Ṛishidattá, and therefore the same person.

P. 117 *. Read 'of the lord of the Íçána' (Kalpa). The Íçána (Kalpa) is the second Kalpa. Other Kalpas are named in other parts of the 'Katháкoça.'

P. 117, l. 14. Read *Bhadrayaça* for °*ças*.

Pp. 117-123. The story of Metárya is borrowed from the Ávaçyaka tales; it is found in the comments on Ávaçyaka-niry., viii. 182, 2. A Sanskrit version will also be found in Merutunga's 'Mahápurushacharita,' iv. (Weber's Catalogue, ii., p. 1026, l. 32), and elsewhere.

P. 122 †. Correct this according to the note on p. 36 *.

P. 123 *. Bendall's MS. has *pácara*, like the MS. B.

P. 123 †. Add: It should be printed as a verse, for it is an Áryá in the original.

P. 132 †. Bendall's MS. has: *Manjúshá-dvárâṇi maiṇasáritáni*.

P. 135 †. Bendall's MS. has: *Ekákinyau ávám bibhyataḥ atas tvayá tvaritaṃ iti kathayitvá gato rákshasaḥ*. The other MSS. will probably help to restore the correct reading. [C has *ágaṃtavyaṃ* after *tvaritaṃ*, so has my text. Both have *bibhyataḥ*.—C. H. T.]

P. 140, ll. 4, f. Read: 'A man ought to go to whichever place, or to carry out whatever design; excelling then by merits, he will obtain joys like . . .' Compare the similar Gáthá on p. 189, ll. 33-36. This is the exact rendering. At any rate, the first line seems to have:

*Vaccatu jattha vi tattha vi jaṃ vá taṃ vá karetu vavasáyaṃ.*

[C has: *Vaccau jattha vi tattha vi jaṃ vá taṃ vá kareviu vavasáyaṃ*
*Punnáhio ya pávai suhâiṃ Víranga ráo vva.*]

---

[9] Read also 'Çankhapura' for 'Çankapura' on p. 71, l. 29.

[10] *Samavasaraṇe.*

P. 140 *. Read 'tried' (*Kasijjamáṇa*=Sanskrit *kashyamáṇa*).

P. 142, l. 9. Read 'have become happy' (*saphalí-játa*) instead of 'gave her her desire.'

P. 142 *. Read 'Sagara.' This is also the reading of Bendall's MS., and it ought to have been adopted in the text.

P. 142, l. 18. Read 'Raviteja.' This is the form appropriate to a text of this kind. See also 'Bhadrayaça' above (on p. 117, l. 14).

P. 143 *. The taming of the elephant is intentionally omitted, because it has been related before (p. 141, ll. 15 ff.). Continue: 'Then, as it happened, Chandraprabhá . . .'

P. 143, l. 15. For 'Even so; say no more. My,' read: 'Indeed, but.' *Naparaṃ* means 'but.' The conversation between the Vidyádharí and the groom is intended to point out that Ratnaçikha, the hero, cannot be simply fetched by a groom. Therefore the meaning of the first query of the Vidyádharí is: 'Has he stolen the elephant?' There is irony and anger at the same time in this query.

P. 143, ll. 22, 29, 32, and p. 144, l. 6. Read 'Vasuteja' for 'Vasutejas,' and compare the note on p. 142, l. 18. See also the name 'Sujasa' (p. 145, l. 24), which is entirely Prákṛitic.

Pp. 146, f. The introduction to the story about Amṛitadatta and Mitránanda occurs in an Ávaçyaka tale.

P. 148, ll. 2, f. The sport of a demon. Bendall's MS. has: *Paraṃ tu eshá'ṃtara-kríḍá*. [C has: *Vyaṃtara-kríḍá*.—C. H. T.]

P. 149 *. In Bendall's MS. the passage reads: *Tato'ham api upáyenántaráyaṃ hanishyámi, mitra Mitránaṃdam áha Mitránaṃdenoktaṃ: mitra tato 'yaṃ deçaḥ* . . . [So, too, C.]

P. 156 *. See note on p. 23 †.

P. 160 *. *Kasháya* is more exactly 'passion.' There are four *kasháyas*: *Krodha*, anger; *mána*, conceit; *máyá*, deceit; *lobha*, desire.

Pp. 160-168. The story of Lalitánga is found among the Ávaçyaka tales. See also Hemacandra's 'Pariçishṭaparvan,' iii. 214-275.

P. 161, ll. 8-11. This is no verse.

P. 161 †. Bendall's MS. has *nekshate*, which is also wrong.

P. 171 †. It is quite natural that with the herdsman's wife also Ságarapota's wife became fond of the boy. In Bendall's MS. the syllable *va* is wanting. (It has: *Striyor atí vallabho babhúva*.)

Pp. 175, ff. The story of Kúlavála is one of the Uttarádhyayana tradition; it is found in the 'Comments on Uttarádhy.,' i. 2. Jacobi published Devendra's version in the 'Zeitschrift der Deutschen Morgenl. Gesellsch.,' vol. xxxiv., p. 291, in the note. The story occurs likewise in the 'Commentaries on Ávaçyaka-niry.,' chap. ix., 65, 6. The 'Kathákoça' has taken in much matter besides, which occurs also in canonical books. The introduction (pp. 175, f.) is found in an Ávaçyaka tale; what follows (pp. 176-180) is found in the Bhagavatí, as well as elsewhere (for instance, in the 'Comments on Ávaçyaka-niryukti,' xvii. 11). The whole is most interesting, as it is based entirely on *historical facts*. The Bhagavatí passage comprises, after a short introduction of an entirely different topic, the whole of vii. 9. It is no regular narrative, but a dogmatic disquisition on the base of those historical premises.

P. 177 †. The same episode is told in the 'Nirayávaliyá-sutta,' edited by Warren, in the 'Transactions of the Academy in Amsterdam, 1879.' This text (which forms the eighth *upánga* of the Jains) contains besides many other incidents out of the lives of Çreṇika and Koṇika.

See also Jacobi's remarks in the 'Zeitschr. der D. Morg. Ges., vol. xxxiv., pp. 183-188.

P. 179 *. This incident (with Saudharma and Camara) particularly rests on the above Bhagavatí passage.

P. 191, l. 22. Here Bendall's MS. closes (*supátra-dána-vishaye Kanakaratha-kathánakam̧. iti çríKathákoçaḩ sampúrṇaḩ çubham̧ bhúyát*). What follows is certainly an Appendix, made to supply the shortened passage on p. 7 †. All MSS. have the necessary reference, and the story *fits in well there*, as it illustrates the second *kasháya* (see note on p. 160 *). The first *kasháya* (*kopa*) is illustrated on p. 6, l. 18, to p. 7, l. 9. The third *kasháya* (*máyá*), 'cheating' (*vancaná*), is illustrated on p. 7, l. 10, to p. 11, l. 34. The fourth *kasháya* (*lobha*), 'avarice,' is illustrated on p. 12, l. 1, to p. 13, l. 31. From this it becomes clear that, after p. 7, l. 9, a story illustrating *mána* ('pride') is absolutely wanted. It may be that the author purposely put in its place the introductory verses only, and added the tale at the end, as it was perhaps not to hand in time.

P. 191 †. *Kávyam̧* here means a Çárdúlavikríḍita stanza. This meaning is common in modern anthologies and in tale-collections which contain verses in different metres. The stanza should be restored, as has been pointed out above (on p. 7 †). Bendall's MS. leaves only one word uncertain. It has:

> *Mánam̧ Báhubalir Maricir acayat çríSthúlabhadraḩ prabhuḩ*
> *Sádhuḩ sim̧haguhá-sthito mati-madaḩ Sçrí iddhasenaḩ kaviḩ*
> *Cáṇakyaḩ [kala kauṇaktḩ] kshitipatir Duryodhano Rávaṇaḩ*
> *Súriḩ Ságaracandra ity abhimataç cakrí caturtho' pi ca.*

[The uncertain words appear from C to be *kila koṇikaḩ.*] All the tales here referred to, except those of Siddhasena, Duryodhana, and Rávaṇa, are found among the Ávaçyaka tales. The first forms also the long introductory tale in Çubhaçílagaṇi's 'Kathákoça,' which after it is also called 'BharahesaraBáhubali-vṛitti.' This work of Çubhaçílagaṇi would be well worth translating; there are good MSS. of it available in Berlin,[11] Strasburg,[12] and Poona—the Berlin copy has even got a *ṭabá*, which would certainly prove very useful. The arrangement of Çubhaçíla's 'Kathákoça' is very similar to that of the present one. There are in the whole thirteen Prákrit Áryás, which chiefly enumerate heroes and heroines of the faith, and which are successively commented on by the respective tales. This is the reason why the whole is also called a *vṛitti* ('commentary'). In the tales many verses are interspersed, as in the story of Lalitánga (pp. 160-168). The language is good Sanskrit, and therefore rather different from the idiom of the present 'Kathákoça.' Átmárám Muni's note regarding *Sádhuḩ sim̧haguhásthitaḩ* requires emendation. *Sádhu* is not a proper name, and the man is not a brother of Sthúlabhadra. The respective tale is printed by Jacobi in Prákrit from Devendra's Uttarádhyayana commentary (Hemacandra's 'Pariçishṭa parvan,' Appendices, p. 9, l. 4, to p. 12, l. 5), and in Sanskrit (Hemacandra's 'Pariçishṭaparvan,' viii. 109-169). As has been said before, the tale is also among the Ávaçyaka tales.

[11] It is one of the recently acquired manuscripts not yet mentioned in Weber's Catalogue; its signature is MS. or. folio 1880 (dated Sam̧vat, 1833, *phálguna su di 5 Çukravára*).

[12] The Strasburg copy is mentioned (along with MS. L 94, in the 'Zeitschrift der Deutschen Morg. Ges.,' vol. xlvii., p. 310. Its date is, Sam̧vat, 1737, *varshe caitra ba di daçamí raviváare*.

Also Sthúlabhadra's story is printed both ways by Jacobi in his edition of the Pariçishṭaparvan. And so is Cáṇakya's. A Prákṛit version of the tale about Kálikácárya (in prose and verse) is printed and translated by Jacobi in the 'Zeitschrift der Deutschen Morg. Ges.' vol. xxxiv., pp. 247-318. Two metrical versions in Prákṛit are published with a glossary in the same journal (vol. xxxvii., pp. 493-520) by Leumann.

P. 191, ll. 29, f. These two lines are apparently not in the Sanskrit text. At any rate, only what precedes ought to be in smaller type.

P. 192*. The passage is an Áryá = Ávaçyakaniryukti iii. 128[1]. Read:

*Mágaha-Varadáma-Pabhása-Sindhu-Khaṇḍappavdya-Timisaguhá*
*Saṭṭhiṃ vása-sahasse oyaviuṃ ágao Bharaho.*

Jacobi's passage has been corrected by Leumann in the 'Wiener Zeitschrift für die Kunde des Morgenlandes,' vi., p. 44, note. There it has been pointed out that the whole story has been treated as well in the comments on Ávaçyaka-niryukti iii. 128[1], as in the seventh Upánga of the canon.

P. 193 * † ‡. Smaller type should have been used to indicate verses in the original.

Pp. 195-231. It is not surprising that the tale of Nala and Davadantí is added only as a second and last Appendix (wanting altogether with the first Appendix in Bendall's MS.). The story has been noticed by Jain novelists only in quite modern times. It was probably an innovation that the author of our Katháкoça, or the writer that supplemented it (if the author has not done so himself), added the story to the general stock of Jain tales. It is printed from the 'Kathákoça' in the 'Ṣáhityaparicaya,' part ii., pp. 52-93, Calcutta, 1881, published by Nílamaṇi Mukhopádhyáya Nyáyálankára. I owe the 'Sáhityaparicaya' to the extreme kindness of Dr. Reinhold Rost, who gave me the two little books (part i. and part ii.) during my last stay in London (in 1892). The same little volume prints also (on pp. 37-51) from the 'Kathákoça' the story of Lalitánga. As the editor has added some valuable notes[13] at the bottom of the pages, the translator of the 'Kathákoça' might have spared some trouble by referring to it. [I am glad to acknowledge here that I have derived much advantage from this book, though perhaps I have not made as good use of it as I ought to have done.—C. H. T.] Sometimes, however, difficult or incorrect readings are changed by Nílamaṇi; so for *atiḥ kutrápi neshyate* (see above on page 161†) he prints *nátiḥ kutrápi çobhate*, and for *vaṭe Vararucir yathá* he puts (see translation, p. 164*) *vaṭe yakshádayo yathá*.

P. 195, l. 20. Read *Nishadha* for Nishada.

Pp. 196, 197. These two pages are much shortened in the edition.

P. 198. The second verse on this page is omitted in the edition.

[P. 201. Add to second footnote: 'It was, no doubt, Pachísí.' See 'Daça Kumára Charita,' ed. Bühler, p. 47, l. 21.—C. H. T.]

[13] He goes, however, astray sometimes when he tries to explain particular Jain terms; so his note on *avadhijnána* (at the bottom of p. 78) is wrong, and displays, as a Jain would say, some *vibhanga-jnána* (see note on p. 209*). Also the rendering of the word *avadhijnána* by 'limited knowledge,' which has been adhered to throughout the present translation, cannot be accounted for. It ought to be 'limit-knowledge' at least, but this would not do, as limit is not exactly the same as *avadhi*. As the case stands, it is better to say Avadhi-knowledge, and to refer the reader to the different passages where the word occurs, so that he may see in which application it is used.

P. 205 †. The reading of the edition is entirely different, and at the same time unmetrical.

P. 207, l. 34 ('At'), up to p. 208, l. 9 ('caravan'), viz., the whole passage treating of the bandits, is left out in the edition.

P. 208 *. The edition has *akṛitárthasya mrityur bhayáya nálam*, for the unlucky, death is not enough to cause fear. [C has *akṛitárthasya mrityunayaṃ.*]

P. 209 *. Read, 'by a wrong conception.' This is the sense of *vibhanga-jnána.* The Rákshasa is indeed mistaken. Nílamaṇi has changed the word, as he did not understand it; he prints *vibhutva-balena jnátvá.*

P. 209, l. 24 ('In the'), up to l. 33 ('that'). This fanciful incident is discarded by Nílamaṇi.

P. 210, l. 12 ('One'), up to p. 212, l. 22 ('Tápasapura'), and p. 212, l. 28 ('saying'), up to p. 213, l. 11 ('caravan'). Both passages are omitted by Nílamaṇi on account of their Jain tendencies. To connect the following phrase he inserts *atrántare kenacit* before *sárthaváhena.*

P. 213, ll. 14, f. The little phrase 'and . . . relations' is of course omitted by Nílamaṇi in accordance with the preceding omissions.

P. 213, l. 20, to p. 214, l. 11. All omitted by Nílamaṇi as not being of interest for anyone but a Jain.

P. 214, l. 14 ('Then'), up to l. 22 ('time'). This incident is again omitted by Nílamaṇi.

P. 214, ll. 24, 26, 29, and pp. 216-218. Read Chandrayaçá throughout for Chandrayaças; cf. Nílamaṇi's note on p. 72 of his edition, and the note above on p. 116, ll. 18, 21.

P. 214, l. 34 ('One day'), up to p. 215, l. 37. Omitted in the edition. The whole incident is most interesting, not for its contents, but for its origin; for it is clearly made up of the two little stories related in the commentaries on 'Âvaçyaka Niryukti,' ix., 139, 4 and 5. Most of the later Jaina tales, which seem to be original, are certainly of the same making, though generally this cannot be so strictly proved as in the present case.

P. 216, ll. 37, f. Instead of 'did you show this want of discernment?' the edition has *etat te kulocitaṃ?* [The translation should be, 'Is this becoming to your family?'—C. H. T.]

P. 217, ll. 2-7 (up to 'fire'), and ll. 11-20 (up to 'cave' and 'withdrawing his hand'). All wanting in the edition; as this double incident is very silly, one is inclined to think that Nílamaṇi had access to some better MSS., not so overloaded with ridiculous episodes. Of course it may as well be that his taste has led him to discard the present passage.

P. 217, l. 27, to p. 218, l. 5 (up to 'faith'). Wanting in the edition.

P. 218, ll. 14-16. This most silly exaggeration is also in the print. So, probably, also the other passage on which we passed our verdict (viz., p. 217, ll. 2-7; ll. 11-20) belonged to the original version. All this, however, shows that the story of Nala and Davadantí differs in style a great deal from the rest of the work; and this is another proof for its being a separate production, which has come in from some independent source not generally explored by Jain collectors. Also the simile (p. 218, ll. 17, f.), 'as Yamuná embraces Gangá,' and similar passages, betray an entirely different origin. Also the *dodhaka* on p. 222 points to the same fact, as the other tales have all Gáthás instead.

P. 219, l. 26. Read Nishadha for Nishada.

P. 222. The *dodhaka* is turned into Sanskrit by Nílamaṇi, and accordingly he calls the words (though they are entirely unmetrical) a *gíta*. Apparently he disliked the Prákṛit, and even more the vernaculars; that is certainly the reason why he has selected just two tales, of Lalitánga and of Nala, which do not contain any *gáthás*.

P. 223, ll. 4, f. 'That destroys the families of fish.' This seems to render some word like *matsyakulántaka*. Nílamaṇi has a curious misreading, *matsya-kuṭumbaka*, which he in vain tries to explain in a note on p. 95. [The words are in C: *kutra dalita matsya-kuṭumbako vakaḥ?*—C. H. T.]

P. 223, ll. 11, f. The verse is omitted in the edition.

P. 223, ll. 24-27 ('Such . . . Nala'). This passage is apparently an Áryá stanza in the Sanskrit; at any rate, Nílamaṇi has one here, though its first line is irregular. It reads as follows:

> *Kariçikshá-kuçalatvaṃ súryapákasya ca karaṇa-sámarthyaṃ*
> *Atyadbhutaṃ ca dánaṃ Nalaṃ viná 'nyasya násty eva.*

[Professor Leumann's conjecture is supported by C.]

P. 226, ll. 20-32. This insipid invention is again discarded by Nílamaṇi. He ought, however, also to have omitted the preceding words ('one test of Nala is the delicious dish'). These give no sense now with him; it does not help a bit if he adds a note to explain *eká* ('one') by *mukhyá* ('chief'). Before *áha* ('she said') he inserts *tataḥ Davadanti kubjasamípaṃ gatvá*.

P. 227, l. 14. Read Candrayaçá as before.

P. 227, ll. 14-16. Also Nílamaṇi has this passage, *tathá ca Tápasapurasvámi Vasantaḥ Çriçekhara ákáritaḥ*. With him the last two names have no sense, as he has discarded before the respective passage (on p. 215) which would make clear what they mean.

P. 227, l. 17 ('One'), up to l. 24 ('place'). Rightly omitted by Nílamaṇi, because he left out before (pp. 210-212) the corresponding passage.

P. 228, l. 6, to p. 231, l. 28. The whole of this final fancy is dropped by Nílamaṇi as being purely Jainic. It is, however, interesting as a novelistic fabrication. For, the mention of Mammaṇa and of Dhanya's (*i.e.*, Mammaṇa's) bullock shows that the writer possessed an entirely vague notion of the story about Mammaṇa and his golden bullock related in the commentaries on 'Ávaçyaka-niry.,' ix., verse 49[b]. The story itself is absolutely different, but the slight connection becomes certain in this case from the fact that the name *Mammaṇa* occurs nowhere else. I have derived it elsewhere from the Christian notion of the μαμωνᾶς, his golden bullock being the same as the golden calf of the Jews. See Weber, 'Die Griechen in Indien,' 'Sitzungsberichte der Berliner Akad.' 1890, p. 919, note 2.

P. 228, l. 7, and p. 231, l. 21. Read Nishadha as before.

# INDEX OF NAMES.

C.

D.

L.

S.

T.

# GENERAL INDEX.

I.



J.



K.



L.



M.

BILLING AND SONS, PRINTERS, GUILDFORD.